THE LAW SOCIETY'S CODE OF CONDUCT [2004] AND RECOGNISED BODIES REGULATIONS [2004]

NOT YET IN FORCE

D0234794

(Student edition)

The Law Society

The Law Society

© The Law Society 2005, 2006

ISBN: 1-85328-528-5

This limited edition for students taking the Legal Practice Course
first published in 2005 by the Law Society
113 Chancery Lane, London WC2A 1PL
Reprinted 2006

NOT FOR SALE

Printed by TJ International, Padstow, Cornwall

IMPORTANT NOTE

The Law Society's Code of Conduct is NOT YET IN FORCE. It is currently being considered by the Department of Constitutional Affairs and the Legal Services Consultative Panel under Schedule 4 to the Courts and Legal Services Act 1990.

It is set out here on the basis that it should be coming into force before you begin practice as a solicitor.

You should also note, however, that it is possible that some provisions of the Code as it comes into force may be modified from those shown here.

The current requirements of professional conduct are contained in *The Guide to the Professional Conduct of Solicitors* (8th edition, 1999) as amended. These can be found on Guide Online at **www.lawsociety.org.uk**.

When the Code comes into force, the finalised version of it will also appear on the Law Society website.

August 2006

THE LAW SOCIETY'S CODE OF CONDUCT [2004] AND RECOGNISED BODIES REGULATIONS [2004]

Contents

The Law Society's Code of Conduct [2004]

Rules dated [the date of commencement] made by the Council of the Law Society under Part II of the Solicitors Act 1974 and section 9 of the Administration of Justice Act 1985 with the concurrence of the Master of the Rolls under that section and the approval of the Lord Chancellor under Schedule 4 to the Courts and Legal Services Act 1990, regulating the conduct of solicitors, Registered European Lawyers, Registered Foreign Lawyers and recognised bodies.

The guidance printed with these rules is not mandatory and does not form part of the Code of Conduct.

Rule 1 – Core duties

Introduction

A modern just society needs a legal profession which adopts high standards of integrity and professionalism. As a solicitor, registered foreign lawyer, registered European lawyer or recognised body you serve both clients and society. In serving society, you uphold the rule of law and the proper administration of justice. In serving clients, you work in partnership with the client making the client's business your first concern. The core duties contained in rule 1 set the standards which will meet the needs of both clients and society.

Rule 1 – core duties

As a solicitor, registered foreign lawyer (RFL), registered European lawyer (REL) or recognised body you must comply with the following core duties, subject to any overriding legal considerations. Notwithstanding rule 22 (waivers), the Council of the Law Society shall not have power to waive any of the provisions of this rule.

1.01
Integrity

You must act with integrity towards clients, the courts, lawyers and others.

1.02
Independence

You must not allow your independence to be compromised in the face of pressure from:

- clients;

- the courts; or

- any other source.

1.03
Best interests of clients

You must treat the interests of clients as paramount, provided they do not conflict with:

- your obligations in professional conduct; or

- the public interest in the administration of justice.

1.04 **Confidentiality**	You must keep all information about clients confidential.
1.05 **Conflict of interests**	You must not act where there is a conflict between:

- your interests and your client's interests; or

- the interests of two or more clients (except in strict accordance with rule 3).

1.06 **Competence**	You must act only when you are able to provide a competent service.
1.07 **Fairness**	In your professional dealings you must treat others fairly, reasonably and without unlawful discrimination.
1.08 **Client care**	You must maintain appropriate client care procedures. These must recognise a client's right to be given information on costs and other matters which is sufficiently:

- clear;

- timely; and

- frequent,

to enable clients to make informed decisions.

1.09 **Supervision and management**	You must operate appropriate supervision and management arrangements to meet your duties to clients.
1.10 **Profession**	You must not behave in a way which damages or is likely to damage the reputation or integrity of the profession.

Guidance to rule 1 – Core duties

1. A breach of rule 1, as with any rule, may constitute misconduct. The core duties, however, represent overarching principles, with the other rules providing greater detail addressed to specific situations – for example, how to preserve your independence and avoid a conflict of interests.

2. Some of the core duties have a direct link to specific rules. 1.08 dealing with client care links to rule 2 (client relations). The core duties dealing with conflict and your duty of confidentiality are dealt with in more detail in rules 3 and 4. Other core duties are more general in their effect, such as 1.01 (integrity) and 1.02 (independence), in that they underpin everything you do as a solicitor, REL or RFL. 1.07 (fairness) is general in its application but also has a specific link with 10.01 (not taking unfair advantage). Note 1 of the guidance to rule 10

(relations with third parties) gives specific detail on situations where you must not use your professional position to take unfair advantage of others.

3. Core duty 1.10 (profession) applies to your conduct both in your practice as a solicitor, REL or RFL and outside it, to the extent that:

    (a) as a solicitor, you are an officer of the Supreme Court and must behave as befits a member of the solicitors' profession;

    (b) as an REL, you are to be treated under the Establishment Directive Regulations as if you were an officer of the Supreme Court; you must behave as befits a member of your own profession and as would befit a member of the solicitors' profession; and

    (c) as an RFL, you have been registered under the Courts and Legal Services Act 1990 as a lawyer suitable to be a solicitor's partner, a director of a recognised body which is a company, or a member of a recognised body which is an LLP, and must behave as befits a member of your own profession and as would befit a member of the solicitors' profession.

A recognised body has been recognised under the Administration of Justice Act 1985 as a suitable body to provide the services of practising solicitors and other lawyers, and must conduct itself accordingly.

Rule 2 – Client relations

Introduction

Rule 2 is designed to help both you and your clients understand each other's expectations and responsibilities. In particular, the purpose of 2.02 (client care) and 2.03 (information about the cost) is to ensure that clients are given the information necessary to enable them to make appropriate decisions about if and how their matter should proceed. Under rule 5 (business management) a principal in a firm, a director of a recognised body which is a company and a member of a recognised body which is an LLP, must effect supervision and put in place management arrangements to provide for compliance with rule 2. The rule does not apply to your overseas practice but you must comply with 15.02.

Rule 2 – Client relations

2.01 Taking on clients

(1)   You are generally free to decide whether or not to take on a particular client. However, you must refuse to act or cease acting for a client in the following circumstances:

    (a)   when to act would involve you in a breach of the law or a breach of the rules of professional conduct;

    (b)   where you have insufficient resources or lack the competence to deal with the matter;

    (c)   where instructions are given by someone other than the client, or by only one client on behalf of others in a joint matter, you must not proceed without checking that all clients agree with the instructions given; or

    (d)   where you know or have reasonable grounds for believing that the instructions are affected by duress or undue influence, you must not act on those instructions until you have satisfied yourself that they represent the client's wishes.

(2)   You must not cease acting for a client except for good reason and on reasonable notice.

2.02 Client care

(1)   You must:

    (a)   identify clearly the client's objectives in relation to the work to be done for the client;

    (b)   give the client a clear explanation of the issues involved and the options available to the client;

    (c)   agree with the client the next steps to be taken; and

(d)   keep the client informed of progress, unless otherwise agreed.

(2)   You must, both at the outset and, as necessary, during the course of the matter:

(a)   agree an appropriate level of service;

(b)   explain your responsibilities;

(c)   explain the client's responsibilities;

(d)   ensure that the client is given, in writing, the name and status of the person dealing with the matter and the name of the person responsible for its overall supervision; and

(e)   explain any limitations or conditions resulting from your relationship with a third party (for example a funder, fee sharer or introducer) which affect the steps you can take on the client's behalf.

(3)   If you can demonstrate that it was inappropriate in the circumstances to meet some or all of these requirements, you will not breach 2.02.

2.03 Information about the cost

(1)   You must give your client the best information possible about the likely overall cost of a matter both at the outset and, when appropriate, as the matter progresses. In particular you must:

(a)   advise the client of the basis and terms of your charges;

(b)   advise the client if charging rates are to be increased;

(c)   advise the client of likely payments which you or your client may need to make to others;

(d)   discuss with the client how the client will pay, in particular:

(i)   whether the client may be eligible and should apply for public funding; and

(ii)   whether the client's own costs are covered by insurance or may be paid by someone else such as an employer or trade union;

(e)   advise the client that there are circumstances where you may be entitled to exercise a lien for unpaid costs;

(f)   advise the client of their potential liability for any other party's costs; and

(g)   discuss with the client whether their liability for another party's costs may be covered by existing insurance or whether specially purchased insurance may be obtained.

(2) Where you are acting for the client under a conditional fee agreement, (including a collective conditional fee agreement) in addition to complying with (1) above and (4) and (5) below, you must explain the following, both at the outset and, when appropriate, as the matter progresses:

    (a) the circumstances in which your client may be liable for your costs and whether you will seek payment of these from the client, if entitled to do so; and

    (b) if you intend to seek payment of any or all of your costs from your client, you must advise your client of their right to an assessment of those costs.

(3) Where you are acting for a publicly funded client, in addition to complying with (1) above and (4) and (5) below, you must explain the following at the outset:

    (a) the circumstances in which they may be liable for your costs;

    (b) the effect of the statutory charge;

    (c) the client's duty to pay any fixed or periodic contribution assessed and the consequence of failing to do so; and

    (d) that even if your client is successful, the other party may not be ordered to pay costs or may not be in a position to pay them.

(4) Any information about the cost must be clear and confirmed in writing.

(5) You must discuss with your client whether the potential outcomes of any legal case will justify the expense or risk involved including, if relevant, the risk of having to pay an opponent's costs.

(6) If you can demonstrate that it was inappropriate in the circumstances to meet some or all of the requirements in 2.03(1) and (4), you will not breach 2.03.

2.04 Contingency fees

(1) You must not enter into an arrangement to receive a contingency fee for work done in prosecuting or defending any contentious proceedings before a court of England and Wales, a British court martial or an arbitrator hearing a matter in England and Wales, except as permitted by statute or the common law.

(2) You must not enter into an arrangement to receive a contingency fee for work done in prosecuting or defending any contentious proceedings before a court of an overseas jurisdiction or an arbitrator hearing a matter overseas except to the extent that a lawyer of that jurisdiction would be permitted to do so.

2.05 Complaints handling

(1) If you are a principal in a firm you must ensure:

    (a) that the firm has a written complaints procedure and that complaints are handled promptly, fairly and effectively in accordance with it;

    (b)   that the client is told, in writing, at the outset:

        (i)   that, in the event of a problem, the client is entitled to complain; and

        (ii)   to whom the client should complain;

    (c)   that the client is given a copy of the complaints procedure on request; and

    (d)   that once a complaint has been made, the person complaining is told in writing:

        (i)   how the complaint will be handled; and

        (ii)   within what time-scales they will be given an initial and/or substantive response.

(2)   If you can demonstrate that it was inappropriate in the circumstances to meet some or all of these requirements, you will not breach 2.05.

(3)   You must not charge your client for the cost of investigating a complaint.

2.06 Commissions

If you are a principal in a firm you must ensure that your firm pays to your client commission received over £20 unless the client, having been told the amount, or if the precise amount is not known, an approximate amount or how the amount is to be calculated, has agreed that your firm may keep it.

2.07 Limitation of civil liability by contract

If you are a principal in a firm you must not exclude or attempt to exclude by contract all liability to your clients. However, you may limit civil liability, provided that such limitation is not below the minimum level of cover required by the Solicitors' Indemnity Insurance Rules for a policy of qualifying insurance, and the agreement is in writing.

Guidance to rule 2 – Client relations

General

1.   The requirements of rule 2 do not exhaust your obligations to clients. As your client's trusted adviser, you must act in the client's best interests (see 1.03) and you must not abuse or exploit the relationship by taking advantage of a client's age, inexperience, ill health, lack of education or business experience, or emotional or other vulnerability.

2.   You should note that a material breach of 2.02, 2.03 or 2.05 may provide evidence against a solicitor, an REL or a recognised body of inadequate professional services under section 37A of the Solicitors Act 1974. The powers of the Law Society on a finding of an inadequate professional service include disallowing all or part of the solicitor's or REL's costs and directing the solicitor

or REL to pay compensation to the client. Section 37A does not apply to you if you are an RFL. Solicitor and REL partners in a multi-national partnership (MNP) are subject to section 37A in respect of services provided by the MNP.

Taking on clients – 2.01

3. 2.01 identifies some situations where you must refuse to act for a client or, if already acting, must stop doing so.

4. Your right to decide not to accept instructions is subject to restrictions, including the following:

   (a) You must not refuse for a reason that would breach rule 6 (avoiding discrimination).

   (b) Rule 11 (litigation and advocacy), governing a solicitor or REL acting as an advocate, contains restrictions on when the solicitor or REL may refuse instructions.

   (c) See the Criminal Contract Regulations for restrictions on when you can refuse to act or cease acting for a publicly funded client in a criminal matter.

5. If you are an in-house solicitor or in-house REL you are already in a contractual relationship with your employer who is for the purpose of these rules, your client. You are not therefore necessarily as free as a solicitor or REL in a firm to refuse instructions, and will need to use your professional judgement in applying 2.01.

6. 2.01 sets out situations in which you must refuse instructions   or, where appropriate, cease acting. These might include the following:

   (a) *breach of the law or rules*

      (i) conflict of interests between you and your client or between two or more clients - see rule 3 (conflict of interests);

      (ii) where money laundering is suspected, your freedom to cease acting is curtailed (see the Proceeds of Crime Act 2002, the Money Laundering Regulations 2003, other relevant law and directives, and guidance issued by the Law Society on this subject); and

      (iii) where the client is a child or a patient (within the meaning of the Mental Health Act 1983), special circumstances apply. You cannot enter into a contract with such a person and, furthermore, if your client loses mental capacity after you have started to act, the law will automatically end the contractual relationship. However, it is important that the client, who is in a very vulnerable situation, is not left without legal representation. Consequently, you should notify an appropriate person (e.g. the Court of Protection), or you may look for someone legally entitled to provide you with instructions, such as an attorney under an enduring power of attorney, or take the appropriate steps for such a person to be appointed, such as a receiver or a litigation friend. This is a particularly complex legal issue and you should satisfy yourself as to the law before deciding on your course of action.

(b)   *insufficient resources*

Before taking on a new matter, you must consider whether your firm has the resources – including knowledge, qualifications, expertise, time, sufficient support staff and, where appropriate, access to external expertise such as agents and counsel – to provide the support required to represent the client properly. The obligation is a continuing one, and you must ensure that an appropriate or agreed level of service can be delivered even if circumstances change.

(c)   *duress or undue influence*

It is important to be satisfied that clients give their instructions freely. Some clients, such as the elderly, those with language or learning difficulties and those with disabilities are particularly vulnerable to pressure from others. If you suspect that a client's instructions are the result of undue influence you need to exercise your judgement as to whether you can proceed on the client's behalf. For example, if you suspect that a friend or relative who accompanies the client is exerting undue influence, you should arrange to see the client alone or if appropriate with an independent third party or interpreter. Where there is no actual evidence of undue influence but the client appears to want to act against their best interests, it may be sufficient simply to explain the consequences of the instructions the client has given and confirm that the client wishes to proceed. For evidential purposes, it would be sensible to get this confirmation in writing.

7.   As a matter of good practice you should not act for a client who has instructed another firm in the same matter unless the other firm agrees. If you are asked to provide a second opinion, you may do so but you should satisfy yourself that you have sufficient information to handle the matter properly.

Ceasing to act

8.   A client can end the retainer with you at any time and for any reason. You may only end the relationship with the client if there is a good reason and after giving reasonable notice. The retainer is a contractual relationship and subject to legal considerations. Examples of good reasons include where there is a breakdown in confidence between you and the client, and where you are unable to obtain proper instructions.

9.   If there is good reason to cease acting, you must give reasonable notice to the client. What amounts to reasonable notice will depend on the circumstances. For example, it would normally be unreasonable to stop acting for a client immediately before a court hearing where it is impossible for the client to find alternative representation. In such a case, if there is no alternative but to cease acting immediately, you should attend and explain the circumstances to the court – see rule 11 (litigation and advocacy). There may be circumstances where it is reasonable to give no notice.

10.   The relationship between you and your client can also be ended automatically by law, for example by the client's bankruptcy or mental incapacity (see note 5(a)(iii) above).

11.   When you cease acting for a client, you will need to consider what should be done with the paperwork. You must hand over the client's files promptly on request subject to your right to exercise a lien in respect of outstanding costs. You should try to ensure the client's position is not prejudiced, and should also bear in mind his or her rights under the Data Protection Act 1998 Undertakings to secure the costs should be used as an alternative to the exercise of a lien if possible. There may be circumstances where it is unreasonable to exercise a lien, for example, where the amount of the outstanding costs is small and the value or importance of the matter is very great. In any dispute over the ownership of documents you should refer to the law. Further advice about the law of lien or the ownership of documents can be found in *Cordery on Solicitors* or other reference books on the subject.

Client care – 2.02

12.   The purpose of 2.02 is to set out the type of information that must normally be given to a client. This information must be provided in a clear and readily accessible form.

13.   2.02 is flexible about the extent of the information to be given in each individual case. Over-complex or lengthy terms of business letters may not be helpful.

14.   The "level of service" to be provided should be agreed at the outset. For example, the client may want regular written reports. Alternatively, the client may want to provide initial instructions then to hear no more until an agreed point has been reached. This will affect the projected costs of the matter.

15.   When considering the options available to the client (2.02(1) (b)), if the matter relates to a dispute between your client and a third party, you should discuss whether mediation or some other alternative dispute resolution (ADR) procedure may be more appropriate than litigation, arbitration or other formal processes. There may be costs sanctions if a party refuses ADR.- see Halsey v Milton Keynes NHS Trust and Steel and Joy [2004]. More information may be obtained from the Law Society's Practice Advice Service.

16.   2.02(2)(e) requires you to explain limitations or conditions on your acting arising from your relationship with a third party. Where such a relationship involves sharing any client information with a third party, you must inform the client and obtain their consent. Failure to do so would be a breach of client confidentiality (see rule 4 – confidentiality and disclosure) and possibly also a breach of the Data Protection Act 1998. Some arrangements with third parties, such as introducers under rule 9 (referrals of business) or fee sharers under rule 8 (fee sharing), may constrain the way in which you handle clients' matters.

17.   The constraints that such arrangements impose may fall into one of the following categories:

    (a)   Constraints which are proper and do not require disclosure to the client. These normally relate to service standards such as dealing with client enquiries within a specified time, the use of specified computer software, telecommunications systems, a particular advertising medium, or particular training provision.

(b) Constraints which are proper but require disclosure to the client. Some third parties may have a legitimate interest in the progress of the client's matter and the way it is dealt with – for instance, third parties who fund a client's matter, and insurers. Constraints that they impose, e.g. that you will not issue proceedings without the authority of the funder are proper provided they do not operate against the client's best interests, but should be disclosed to the client.

(c) Constraints which are improper cannot be remedied by disclosing them to the client. These are constraints which impair your independence and ability to act in the client's best interests. You cannot accept an arrangement which involves such constraints. They might include, for instance, requirements that you do not disclose information to the client to which the client is entitled, or give advice to the client which you know is contrary to the client's best interests, or with which you disagree, or that you act towards the court in a deceitful manner or lie to a third party.

18. You must give the required information to the client as soon as possible after you have agreed to act. You must then keep the client up to date with the progress of the matter and any changes affecting the original agreement.

19. The status of the person dealing with your client must be made absolutely clear, for legal and ethical reasons. For example, a person who is not a solicitor must not be described as one, either expressly or by implication. All staff having contact with clients, including reception, switchboard and secretarial staff, should be advised accordingly.

20. All clients affected by a material alteration to the composition of the firm must be informed personally. Where the person having conduct of a matter leaves a firm, the client in question must be informed, preferably in advance, and told the name and status of the person who is to take over their matter.

21. 2.02(2)(d) refers to the person responsible for the overall supervision of a matter. Supervision requirements are dealt with in rule 5 (business management) and guidance about who can supervise matters may be found there.

22. There may be circumstances when it would be inappropriate to provide any or all of the information required by 2.02. It will be for you to justify why compliance was not appropriate in an individual matter. For example, where you are asked for 'one off' advice, or where you have a long-standing client who is familiar with your firm's terms of business and knows the status of the person dealing with the matter, this information may not need to be repeated. However, other aspects of 2.02 must be complied with and the client must be kept up to date and informed of changes.

23. If you are an in-house solicitor or in-house REL much of 2.02 will be inappropriate when you are acting for your employer. However, it may be necessary for you to comply with aspects of 2.02 when you are acting for someone other than your employer in accordance with rule 13 (in-house practice).

24. If you receive instructions from someone other than your client, you must still give the client the information required under 2.02. There are, however, exceptions to this. For example, where your client is represented by an attorney under a power of attorney or where a receiver has been appointed because the client has lost mental capacity, the information required by 2.02 should be given to the attorney or receiver.

25. In order to provide evidence of compliance with 2.02, you should consider giving the information in writing even though this is not a requirement.

26. Where you are, in effect, your firm's client – for example, as an executor administering a deceased's estate or a trustee of a trust – you should consider what information, if any, should be given to interested parties. There is no requirement, for example, that beneficiaries under a will or trust should be treated as though they were clients. It may, however, be good practice to provide some information – for example, about the type of work to be carried out and approximate time scales.

Information about the cost – 2.03

27. The purpose of 2.03 is to ensure that the client is given relevant costs information and that this is clearly expressed. Information about costs must be worded in a way that is appropriate for the client. All costs information must be given in writing and regularly updated.

28. 2.03 recognises that there may be circumstances where it would be inappropriate to provide any or all of the information required. It will be for you to justify why compliance was not appropriate in an individual matter. For example, your firm may regularly do repeat work for the client on agreed terms and the client might not need the costs information repeated. However, the client should be informed, for example, of any changes in a firm's charging rates.

29. If you are an in-house solicitor or REL, much of 2.03 will be inappropriate if you are acting for your employer.

30. This guidance does not deal with the form a bill can take, final and interim bills, when they can be delivered and when and how a firm can sue on a bill. All these matters are governed by complex legal provisions, and there are many publications that provide help to firms and clients. Advice on some aspects of costs is available from the Law Society's Practice Advice Service.

31. You will usually be free to negotiate the cost and the method of payment with your clients. It will not normally be necessary for the client to be separately advised on the cost agreement. Different cost options may have different implications for the client – for example, where the choice is between a conditional fee agreement and an application for public funding. In those circumstances clients should be made aware of the implications of each option.

32. The rule requires you to advise the client of the circumstances in which you may be entitled to exercise a lien for unpaid costs. For more information see note 11 above.

33. Clients may be referred to you at a stage when they have already signed a contract for a funding arrangement – see also rule 9 (referrals of business).

You should explain the implications of any such arrangement fully including the extent to which the charges associated with such an arrangement may be recovered from another party to the proceedings.

34. There may be some unusual arrangements, however, where it should be suggested that the client considers separate advice on what is being proposed – for example, where you are to receive shares in a new company instead of costs. See also rule 3 (conflict of interests) and 9.02(g) for details about your obligations to clients who have been referred to you.

35. 2.03 does not cover all the different charging arrangements possible or the law governing them. However, it does require that the chosen option is explained as fully as possible to the client.

36. It is often impossible to tell at the outset what the overall cost will be. 2.03 allows for this and requires that you provide the client with as much information as possible at the start and that you keep the client updated. If a precise figure cannot be given at the outset, you should explain the reason to the client and agree a ceiling figure or review dates.

37. Particular information will be of relevance at particular stages of a client's matter. You should, for example, ensure that clients understand the costs implications of any offers of settlement. Where offers of settlement are made, clients must be fully informed of the amount to be deducted in respect of costs and how this figure is calculated. You should advise clients of their rights to assessment of your costs in such circumstances.

38. When a potential client contacts you with a view to giving you instructions you should always, when asked, try to be helpful in providing information on the likely costs of their matter.

Work under a conditional fee agreement or for a publicly funded client

39. 2.03(2) and (3) sets out additional information which must be explained to the client when work is done under a conditional fee agreement or on a publicly funded basis. Conditional fee agreements are subject to statutory requirements and all agreements must conform to these.

Payments to others

40. You must explain at the outset to your client any likely payments they will have to make. These could include court fees, search fees, experts' fees and counsels' fees. Where possible, you should give details of the probable cost and if this is not possible you should agree with the client to review these expenses and the need for them nearer the time they are likely to be incurred.

Contingency fees - 2.04

41. A "contingency fee" is defined in rule 24 as any sum (whether fixed, or calculated either as a percentage of the proceeds or otherwise) payable only in the event of success.

42. If you enter into an arrangement for a lawful contingency fee with a client, what amounts to "success" should be agreed between you and your client prior to entering into the arrangement.

43. Under rule 24, "contentious proceedings" is to be construed in accordance with the definition of "contentious business" in section 87 of the Solicitors Act 1974.

44. Conditional fees are a form of contingency fees. In England and Wales a conditional fee agreement for certain types of litigation is permitted by statute. See section 58 of the Courts and Legal Services Act 1990 (as amended by section 27 of the Access to Justice Act 1999) and 2.03(2) above for more information.

45. It is acceptable to enter into a contingency fee arrangement for non-contentious matters (see section 87 of the Solicitors Act 1974 for the definition of "non-contentious business") but you should note that to be enforceable the arrangement must be contained in a non-contentious business agreement.

46. An otherwise contentious matter remains non-contentious up to the commencement of proceedings. Consequently, you may enter into a contingency fee arrangement for, for example, the receipt of commission for the successful collection of debts owed to a client, provided legal proceedings are not started.

Complaints handling – 2.05

47. The purpose of 2.05 is to encourage complaints to be properly and openly dealt with. There are huge benefits in terms of time, money and client satisfaction if complaints can be dealt with effectively at firm level.

48. The content of your firm's complaints handling procedure is a matter for the firm, but the procedure must be in writing, clear and unambiguous. If a complaint is made to the Law Society the firm will need to be able to demonstrate compliance. Everyone in the firm will need to know about this obligation to ensure that clients know who to contact if they have a problem, the information to give the client when a complaint is made, and the importance of recording the stages of the complaint and the final outcome.

49. Your firm's arrangements for dealing with complaints must be fair and effective. Any investigation must be handled within an agreed time-scale. Any arrangements must also comply with rule 6 (avoiding discrimination).

50. 2.05(3) prevents you charging your client for the cost of investigating a complaint. Dealing properly with complaints is an integral part of any professional business. The associated costs are part of the firm's overheads, and complainants must not be charged separately.

51. A material breach of 2.05 may provide evidence of an inadequate professional service under section 37A of the Solicitors Act 1974.

52. 2.05 allows for situations where it may be inappropriate to give all the information required.

Commissions – 2.06

53. 2.06 mirrors the legal position, preventing a solicitor making a secret profit from the solicitor-client relationship.

54.   A commission is any financial benefit you may receive as a result of placing business on your client's behalf. Examples include payments received on the purchase of stocks and shares, the purchase or renewal of an insurance policy, and the opening of a bank account.

55.   If the client consents to you keeping a commission, after being told the amount involved or given details of how it will be calculated, you are free to keep it. If the commission is materially in excess of your estimate you must tell the client and ask for consent to be confirmed. The client's consent need not be in writing but to avoid disputes it is wise to keep a written record.

56.   The commission earned may be deducted from any outstanding costs or agreed as payment instead of costs.

57.   Where a client has agreed to commission being retained it can be paid into office account as soon as it is received. Where the client has not consented the money must be paid into client account. For the definition of client account see the Solicitors' Accounts Rules 1998.

58.   For further information about dealing with commissions, see Solicitors Financial Services (Scope) Rules 2001.

Limitation of civil liability by contract – 2.07

59.   For the qualifying insurance cover currently required see the Solicitors' Indemnity Insurance Rules.

60.   You must bring any limitation clearly to the attention of the client, and the client must understand and accept it and the agreement must be in writing.

61.   2.07 is subject to the position in law. The points which follow should be noted. The Law Society is entitled to expect you to undertake your own research and/or take appropriate advice as to the general law in this area. Relying upon this guidance alone may not be sufficient to ensure compliance with the law.

   (a)   Liability for fraud or reckless disregard of professional obligations cannot be limited.

   (b)   Existing legal restraints cannot be overridden. In particular, the courts will not enforce in your favour an unfair agreement with your client.

   (c)   Under section 60(5) of the Solicitors Act 1974 and paragraph 24 of Schedule 2 to the Administration of Justice Act 1985, a provision in a contentious business agreement that a firm shall not be liable for negligence, or shall be relieved from any responsibility which would otherwise apply is void.

   (d)   By section 2(2) of the Unfair Contract Terms Act 1977, a contract term which seeks to exclude liability for negligence is of no effect except insofar as it satisfies the requirement of reasonableness set out in section 11. Section 11 specifies that the contract term must be fair and reasonable having regard to the circumstances which were or ought reasonably to have been known to or in the contemplation of, the parties when the contract was made. Schedule 2 sets out guidelines as to the factors to be taken into account in considering whether the contract term meets the test of reasonableness.

(e) Section 11(4) of the Unfair Contract Terms Act 1977 provides that where a contractual term seeks to restrict liability to a specified sum of money, the question of whether the requirement of reasonableness has been satisfied must also take into account the resources available to you for the purpose of meeting the liability, and the extent to which insurance is available.

(f) The Unfair Terms in Consumer Contracts Regulations 1999 have a comparable effect to the Unfair Contract Terms Act 1977 as to limitation or exclusion of liability, where your client is a consumer and the term in question has not been individually negotiated. Regulation 3(1) defines a consumer as any natural person who, in contracts covered by those Regulations, is acting for purposes which are outside their trade, business or profession. Regulation 5(2) states that a term shall always be regarded as not having been individually negotiated where it has been drafted in advance and the consumer has therefore not been able to influence the substance of the term. Regulation 5(1) provides that a term is unfair if, contrary to the requirements of good faith, it causes a significant imbalance in the parties rights and obligations. Schedule 2 to the Regulations contains an indicative, non-exhaustive list of contract terms which may be regarded as unfair. The test of fairness under these Regulations is not identical to the test of reasonableness under the Unfair Contract Terms Act 1977.

(g) When the retainer may be affected by foreign law, such matters may need to be considered according to the law applicable to the contract.

62. You should also note that if you want to limit your firm's liability to a figure above the minimum level for qualifying insurance but within your firm's top-up insurance cover, you will need to consider whether the top-up insurance will adequately cover a claim arising from the matter in question. For example:

(a) If your firm agrees with a client that its liability will not exceed £4 million, and the top-up insurance is calculated on an aggregate yearly basis, there is no guarantee that the amount of the top-up cover would be sufficient where there have been multiple claims already.

(b) Because insurance cover available to meet any particular claim is usually ascertained by reference to the year in which the claim itself is first made, or notice of circumstances which may give rise to a claim, is first brought to the attention of insurers, the top-up cover when the claim is brought(or notice of circumstances given) may not be the same as it was when the contract was made.

63. You will not breach 2.07 by agreeing with your client that liability will rest with your firm and not with any employee, director, member or shareowner who might otherwise be liable. However, any such agreement is subject to section 60(5) of the Solicitors Act 1974, the Unfair Contract Terms Act and the Unfair Terms in Consumer Contracts Regulations.

64. 2.07 does not apply in relation to your overseas practice. However, if you are a principal or a recognised body 15.02(3) prohibits you from seeking to limit your

civil liability below the minimum level of cover you would need in order to comply with 15.26 (professional indemnity).

65. You will not breach 2.07 by a term limiting or excluding any liability to persons who are not your client under the principle in *Hedley Byrne & Co Ltd v Heller & Partners Ltd [1964]*. However, any such term will be subject to section 60(5) of the Solicitors Act 1974, the Unfair Contract Terms Act and the Unfair Terms in Consumer Contracts Regulations, where appropriate.

Rule 3 - Conflict of interests

Introduction

Rule 3 sets out provisions for dealing with conflicts of interests. Conflicts between the duty of confidentiality and duty of disclosure owed by an individual or a firm to two or more clients are dealt with in rule 4.

3.01 to 3.03 deal with conflicts generally.

3.04 to 3.06 deal with conflicts in particular high risk situations – gifts from clients, public offices and appointments leading to conflict, and alternative dispute resolution (ADR).

3.07 to 3.22 deal with conflicts in conveyancing. Note the special meaning of "you" in 3.07 to 3.15 (acting for seller and buyer) and 3.16 to 3.22 (acting for lender and borrower). See also 18.03 which sets out additional requirements which apply to the provision of property selling services.

3.23 sets out that there is no power to waive 3.01 – 3.05.

3.07 to 3.22 do not apply to your overseas practice unless the land conveyed is situated in England and Wales.

Rule 3 – Conflict of interests

3.01 Duty not to act

(1) You must not act if there is a conflict of interests (except in the limited circumstances dealt with in 3.02).

(2) There is a conflict of interests if:

   (a) you owe, or your firm owes, separate duties to act in the best interests of two or more clients in relation to the same or related matters, and those duties conflict, or there is a significant risk that those duties may conflict; or

   (b) your duty to act in the best interests of any client in relation to a matter conflicts, or there is a significant risk that it may conflict, with your own interests in relation to that or a related matter.

(3) For the purpose of 3.01(2), a related matter will always include any other matter which involves the same asset or liability.

3.02 Exceptions to duty not to act

(1) You or your firm may act for two or more clients in relation to a matter in situations of conflict or possible conflict if:

   (a) the different clients have a substantially common interest in relation to that matter or a particular aspect of it; and (b)　　all the clients have given in writing their informed consent to you or your firm acting.

(2)　　Your firm may act for two or more clients in relation to a matter in situations of conflict or possible conflict if:

(a)　　the clients are competing for the same asset which, if attained by one client, will make that asset unattainable to the other client(s);

(b)　　there is no other conflict, or significant risk of conflict, between the interests of any of the clients in relation to that matter;

(c)　　the clients have confirmed in writing that they want your firm to act in the knowledge that your firm acts, or may act, for one or more other clients who are competing for the same asset; and

(d)　　unless the clients specifically agree, no individual acts for, or is responsible for the supervision of, more than one of those clients.

(3)　　When acting in accordance with 3.02(1) or (2) it must be reasonable in all the circumstances for you or your firm to act for all those clients.

(4)　　If you are relying on the exceptions in 3.02(1) or (2), you must:

(a)　　draw all the relevant issues to the attention of the clients before agreeing to act or, where already acting, when the conflict arises or as soon as is reasonably practicable, and in such a way that the clients concerned can understand the issues and the risks involved;

(b)　　have a reasonable belief that the clients understand the relevant issues; and

(c)　　be reasonably satisfied that those clients are of full capacity.

3.03 Conflict when already acting

If you act, or your firm acts, for more than one client in a matter and, during the course of the conduct of that matter, a conflict arises between the interests of two or more of those clients, you, or your firm, may only continue to act for one of the clients (or a group of clients between whom there is no conflict) provided that the duty of confidentiality to the other client(s) is not put at risk.

3.04 Accepting gifts from clients

Where a client proposes to make a lifetime gift or a gift on death to, or for the benefit of:

(a)　　you;

(b)　　any principal, owner or employee of your firm;

(c)　　a family member of any of the above,

and the gift is of a significant amount, either in itself or having regard to the size of the client's estate and the reasonable expectations of the prospective beneficiaries, you must advise the client to take independent advice about the gift, unless the client is a member of the beneficiary's family. If the client refuses, you must stop acting for the client in relation to the gift.

3.05 Public office or appointment leading to conflict

You must decline to act where you, a member of your family, or a principal, owner or employee of your firm holds some public office or appointment as a result of which:

(a)   a conflict of interests, or a significant risk of a conflict, arises;

(b)   the public might reasonably conclude that you, or your firm, had been able to make use of the office or appointment for the advantage of the client; or

(c)   your ability to advise the client properly and impartially is inhibited.

3.06 Alternative dispute resolution (ADR)

If you provide ADR services you must not:

(a)   advise or act for any party in respect of a dispute in which you or any person within your firm is acting, or has acted, as mediator;

(b)   provide ADR services in connection with a matter in which you or any person within your firm has acted for any party; or

(c)   provide ADR services where you or any person within your firm has acted for any of the parties in issues not relating to the mediation, unless that has been disclosed to the parties and they consent to your acting.

3.07 Acting for seller and buyer in conveyancing, property selling and mortgage related services

(1)   3.07 to 3.15 apply to the transfer of land for value, and the grant or assignment of a lease or some other interest in land for value. Both commercial and residential conveyancing transactions are covered. The terms "seller" and "buyer" include a lessor and lessee. "You" is defined in 23.01, but is to be construed in 3.07 to 3.15 as including an associated firm (see rule 24 (interpretation) for the meaning of "associated firm").

(2)   You must not act for more than one party in conveyancing, property selling or mortgage related services other than as permitted by, and in accordance with, 3.08 to 3.15. "Property selling" means negotiating the sale for the seller. "Mortgage related services" means advising on or arranging a mortgage, or providing mortgage related financial services, for a buyer. "Mortgage" includes a remortgage.

3.08 Conveyancing transactions not at arm's length

Subject to the prohibition in 10.06(3) and (4), you may act for seller and buyer when the transaction between the parties is not at arm's length, provided there is no conflict or significant risk of conflict.

3.09 Conveyancing transactions at arm's length

Subject to the prohibition in 10.06(3) and (4), you may act for seller and buyer if the conditions set out in 3.10 are satisfied and one of the following applies:

(a)   both parties are established clients;

(b)   the consideration is £10,000 or less and the transaction is not the grant of a lease; or

(c)   seller and buyer are represented by two separate offices in different localities.

3.10 Conditions for acting under 3.09

In order to act for seller and buyer under 3.09, the following conditions must be met:

(a)   the written consent of both parties must be obtained;

(b)   no conflict of interests must exist or arise;

(c)   the seller must not be selling or leasing as a builder or developer; and

(d)   when the seller and buyer are represented by two separate offices in different localities:

        (i)   different individuals (either solicitors or RELs qualified to do conveyancing under regulation 12 of the European Communities (Lawyer's Practice) Regulations 2000) who normally work at each office, conduct or supervise the transaction for seller and buyer; and

        (ii)   no office of the firm (or an associated firm) referred either client to the office conducting the transactions.

3.11 Property selling and mortgage related services

Subject to the prohibition in 10.06(3) and (4), you may act for seller and buyer if the conditions set out in 3.13 are satisfied and one of the following applies:

(a)   the only way in which you are acting for the buyer is in providing mortgage related services; or

(b)   the only way in which you are acting for the seller is in providing property selling services through a Solicitors' Estate Agency Limited (SEAL).

3.12 SEALS and participating firms

A SEAL means a recognised body which:

(a)   does not undertake conveyancing;

(b)   is owned jointly by at least four participating firms which are not associated firms and none of which has majority control;

(c)   is conducted from accommodation physically divided from, and clearly differentiated from that of any participating firm; and

(d)   a "participating firm" means a firm one or more of whose principals (or members if it is an LLP, or owners if it is a company) is part owner of the SEAL.

3.13 Conditions for acting under 3.11

In order to act for seller and buyer under 3.11, the following conditions must be met:

(a)   the written consent of both parties must be obtained;

(b)   no conflict of interests must exist or arise;

(c)   the seller must not be selling or leasing as a builder or developer;

(d)   different individuals must conduct the work for the seller and the work for the buyer and, if these individuals need supervision, they must be supervised by different solicitors or RELs who are qualified to do conveyancing under regulation 12 of the European Communities (Lawyer's Practice) Regulations 2000;

(e)   you must inform the seller in writing, before accepting instructions to deal with the property selling, of any services which might be offered to a buyer, whether through the same firm or any associated firm; and

(f)   you must explain to the buyer, before the buyer gives consent to the arrangement:

   (i)   the implications of a conflict of interests arising;

   (ii)   your financial interest in the sale going through; and

   (iii)   if you propose to provide mortgage related services to the buyer through a SEAL which is also acting for the seller, that you cannot advise the buyer on the merits of the purchase.

3.14 Special circumstances in property selling and conveyancing

If any of the circumstances set out in 3.09 apply (established clients; consideration of £10,000 or less; representation by two separate offices), you may sell the property, provide mortgage related services, and act for seller and buyer in the conveyancing, subject to the prohibition in 10.06(3) and (4) and compliance with the conditions set out in 3.10 and 3.13 as appropriate.

3.15 Conflict arising when acting for seller and buyer

If a conflict arises during the course of a transaction in which you are acting for more than one party, you may continue to act for one of the parties only if the duty of confidentiality to the other party is not at risk.

3.16 Acting for lender and borrower in conveyancing transactions

(1) 3.16 to 3.22 cover the grant of a mortgage of land and are intended to avoid conflicts of interests. "Mortgage" includes a remortgage. Both commercial and residential conveyancing transactions are covered. "You" is defined in 23.01, but is to be construed in 3.16 to 3.22 as including an associated firm (see rule 24 (interpretation) for the meaning of "associated firm").

(2) You must not act for both lender and borrower on the grant of a mortgage of land:

    (a) if a conflict of interests exists or arises;

    (b) on the grant of an individual mortgage of land at arm's length;

    (c) if, in the case of a standard mortgage of property to be used as the borrower's private residence only, the lender's mortgage instructions extend beyond the limitations contained in 3.19 and 3.21, or do not permit the use of the certificate of title required by 3.20; or

    (d) if, in the case of any other standard mortgage, the lender's mortgage instructions extend beyond the limitations contained in 3.19 and 3.21

3.17 Standard and individual mortgages

(1) A mortgage is a "standard mortgage" where:

    (a) it is provided in the normal course of the lender's activities;

    (b) a significant part of the lender's activities consists of lending; and

    (c) the mortgage is on standard terms.

An "individual mortgage" is any other mortgage.

(2) A mortgage will not be on standard terms if material terms in any of the documents relating to the mortgage transaction are negotiated between the lender's and borrower's lawyers or licensed conveyancers contemporaneously with effecting the mortgage. In commercial transactions, the element of negotiation will often relate to the facility letter or facility agreement rather than the mortgage deed itself.

(3) Provided there has been no contemporaneous negotiation of material terms between the parties' lawyers or licensed conveyancers, a mortgage will be on standard terms where the lender uses a prescribed form of mortgage deed. Minor variations, such as the usual clause limiting the liability of trustee mortgagors, are not regarded as material and do not alter the nature of these terms as standard.

(4) In addition to its normal standard terms, a lender may have a different set or sets of standard terms applicable to specialised types of borrower, such as registered social landlords. Provided these terms are applied by the lender to all equivalent specialist borrowers or have been agreed between the lender and

a specialist borrower as applicable to all transactions between them, they will constitute standard terms for the purposes of 3.16 to 3.22.

(5)   The lender and the borrower must be separately represented on the grant of an individual mortgage at arm's length (see 3.16(2)(b)).   3.16 to 3.22 are not then applicable.

(6)   You may act for both lender and borrower in a standard mortgage (see 3.16(2)(c) – (d)), provided:

(a)   there is no conflict of interests;

(b)   the mortgage instructions do not go beyond the limits set out in 3.19; and

(c)   in the case of a property to be used solely as the borrower's private residence, the approved certificate of title set out in the annex to rule 3 is used.

(7)   The limitations of 3.19 also apply to a standard mortgage where the lender and the borrower are separately represented (see 3.22(1) which includes certificates of title). However, 3.22(2) allows the borrower's lawyer or licensed conveyancer, in a transaction where the property is not to be used solely as the borrower's private residence, to give a certificate of title in any form recognised by the Law Society. You also remain free to give any other form of certificate which complies with this rule.

(8)   There may be cases where the lapse of time between the mortgage offer and completion (for example, when new properties are added) results in use of an earlier edition of a recognised certificate. That is acceptable.

3.18 Notification of certain circumstances to lender

(1)   If you wish to act for both lender and borrower on the grant of a standard mortgage of land, you must first inform the lender in writing of the circumstances if:

(a)   the prospective borrower is:

(i)   a principal in the firm (or a member if the firm is an LLP, or owner or director if the firm is a company), or a member of their immediate family;

(ii)   a principal in an associated firm (or a member if the firm is an LLP, or owner or director if the firm is a company), or a member of their immediate family; and/or

(iii)   the solicitor or REL conducting or supervising the transaction, or a member of their immediate family; or

(b)   you propose to act for seller, buyer and lender in the same transaction.

(2)   "Immediate family" means spouse, children, parents, brothers and sisters.

3.19 Types of instruction which may be accepted

If acting for both lender and borrower in a standard mortgage, you and the individual solicitor or REL conducting or supervising the transaction may only accept or act upon instructions from the lender which are limited to the following matters:

(a) (i) taking reasonable steps to check the identity of the borrower (and anyone else required to sign the mortgage deed or other document connected with the mortgage) by reference to a document or documents, such as a passport, precisely specified in writing by the lender;

    (ii) following the guidance given by the Law Society on property fraud and on money laundering;

    (iii) checking that the seller's conveyancers (if unknown to you) appear in a current legal directory or hold practising certificates issued by their professional body; and

    (iv) in the case of a lender with no branch office within reasonable proximity of the borrower, carrying out the money laundering checks precisely specified in writing by the lender;

(b) making appropriate searches relating to the property in public registers (for example, local searches, commons registration searches, mining searches), and reporting any results specified by the lender or which you consider may adversely affect the lender; or effecting search insurance;

(c) making enquiries on legal matters relating to the property reasonably specified by the lender, and reporting the replies;

(d) reporting the purchase price stated in the transfer and on how the borrower says that the purchase money (other than the mortgage advance) is to be provided; and reporting if you will not have control over the payment of all the purchase money (other than a deposit paid to an estate agent or a reservation fee paid to a builder or developer);

(e) reporting if the seller or the borrower (if the property is already owned by the borrower) has not owned or been the registered owner of the property for at least six months;

(f) if the lender does not arrange insurance, confirming receipt of satisfactory evidence that the buildings insurance is in place for at least the sum required by the lender and covers the risks specified by the lender; giving notice to the insurer of the lender's interest and requesting confirmation that the insurer will notify the lender if the policy is not renewed or is cancelled; and supplying particulars of the insurance and the last premium receipt to the lender;

(g) investigating title to the property and appurtenant rights; reporting any defects revealed, advising on the need for any consequential statutory declarations or indemnity insurance, and approving and effecting indemnity cover if required by the lender; and reporting if you are aware of any rights needed for the use or enjoyment of the property over other land;

(h) reporting on any financial charges (for example, improvement or repair grants or Housing Act discounts) secured on the property revealed by your searches and enquiries which will affect the property after completion of the mortgage;

(i) in the case of a leasehold property:

   (i) confirming that the lease contains the terms stipulated by the lender and does not include any terms specified by the lender as unacceptable;

   (ii) obtaining a suitable deed of variation or indemnity insurance if the terms of the lease are unsatisfactory;

   (iii) enquiring of the seller or the borrower (if the property is already owned by the borrower) as to any known breaches of covenant by the landlord or any superior landlord and reporting any such breaches to the lender;

   (iv) reporting if you become aware of the landlord's absence or insolvency;

   (v) making a company search and checking the last three years' published accounts of any management company with responsibilities under the lease;

   (vi) if the borrower is required to be a shareholder in the management company, obtaining the share certificate, a blank stock transfer form signed by the borrower and a copy of the memorandum and articles of association;

   (vii) obtaining any necessary consent to or prior approval of the assignment and mortgage;

   (viii) obtaining a clear receipt for the last payment of rent and service charge; and

   (ix) serving notice of the assignment and mortgage on the landlord;

(j) in the case of a commonhold unit:

   (i) confirming receipt of satisfactory evidence that common parts insurance is in place for at least the sum required by the lender and covers the risks specified by the lender;

   (ii) confirming that the commonhold community statement contains the terms specified by the lender and does not include any restrictions on occupation or use specified by the lender as unacceptable;

   (iii) enquiring of the seller (or the borrower if the property is already owned by the borrower) and the commonhold association as to any known breaches of the commonhold community statement by the commonhold association or any unit-holder, and reporting any such breaches to the lender;

(iv) making a company search to verify that the commonhold association is in existence and remains registered, and that there is no registered indication that it is to be wound up;

(v) obtaining the last three years' published accounts of the commonhold association and reporting any apparent problems with the association to the lender;

(vi) obtaining a commonhold unit information certificate; and

(vii) serving notice of the transfer and mortgage of the commonhold unit on the commonhold association;

(k) if the property is subject to a letting, checking that the type of letting and its terms comply with the lender's requirements;

(l) making appropriate pre-completion searches, including a bankruptcy search against the borrower, any other person in whom the legal estate is vested and any guarantor;

(m) receiving, releasing and transmitting the mortgage advance, including asking for any final inspection needed and dealing with any retentions and cashbacks;

(n) procuring execution of the mortgage deed and form of guarantee as appropriate by the persons whose identities have been checked in accordance with any requirements of the lender under (a) above as those of the borrower, any other person in whom the legal estate is vested and any guarantor; obtaining their signatures to the forms of undertaking required by the lender in relation to the use, occupation or physical state of the property; and complying with the lender's requirements if any document is to be executed under a power of attorney;

(o) asking the borrower for confirmation that the information about occupants given in the mortgage instructions or offer is correct; obtaining consents in the form required by the lender from existing or prospective occupiers of the property aged 17 or over specified by the lender, or of whom you are aware;

(p) advising the borrower on the terms of any document required by the lender to be signed by the borrower;

(q) advising any other person required to sign any document on the terms of that document or, if there is a conflict of interests between that person and the borrower or the lender, advising that person on the need for separate legal advice and arranging for them to see an independent conveyancer;

(r) obtaining the legal transfer of the property to the mortgagor;

(s) procuring the redemption of:

(i) existing mortgages on property the subject of any associated sale of which you are aware; and

(ii) any other mortgages secured against a property located in England or Wales made by an identified lender where an identified account number or numbers or a property address has been given by the lender;

(t) ensuring the redemption or postponement of existing mortgages on the property, and registering the mortgage with the priority required by the lender;

(u) making administrative arrangements in relation to any collateral security, such as an endowment policy, or in relation to any collateral warranty or guarantee relating to the physical condition of the property, such as NHBC documentation;

(v) registering the transfer and mortgage;

(w) giving legal advice on any matters reported on under 3.19, suggesting courses of action open to the lender, and complying with the lender's instructions on the action to be taken;

(x) disclosing any relationship specified by the lender between you and the borrower;

(y) storing safely the title deeds and documents pending registration and delivery to or as directed by the lender; and

(z) retaining the information contained in your conveyancing file for at least six years from the date of the mortgage.

3.20 Using the approved certificate of title

In addition, if acting for both lender and borrower in a standard mortgage of property to be used as the borrower's private residence only:

(a) you must use the certificate of title set out in the annex to rule 3 (below), or as substituted from time to time by the Council of the Law Society with the concurrence of the Master of the Rolls ("the approved certificate"); and

(b) unless the lender has certified that its mortgage instructions are subject to the limitations contained in 3.19 and 3.21, you must notify the lender on receipt of instructions that the approved certificate will be used, and that your duties to the lender are limited to the matters contained in the approved certificate.

3.21 Terms of rule to prevail

The terms of 3.16 to 3.22 will prevail in the event of any ambiguity in the lender's instructions, or discrepancy between the instructions and 3.19 or the approved certificate.

3.22 Anti-avoidance

(1)   Subject to (2) below, if acting only for the borrower in a standard mortgage of property you must not accept or act upon any requirements by way of undertaking, warranty, guarantee or otherwise of the lender, the lender's solicitor or other agent which extend beyond the limitations contained in 3.19.

(2)   Provided the property is not to be used solely as the borrower's private residence, (1) above does not prevent you from giving any form of certificate of title recognised from time to time by the Council of the Law Society (a "recognised certificate").   Additions or amendments which arise from the individual transaction may be made to the text of a recognised certificate but, to the extent to which they create an increased or additional obligation, must not extend beyond the limitations contained in 3.19.

3.23 Waivers

Notwithstanding rule 22, the Council of the Law Society shall not have power to waive any of the provisions of 3.01 - 3.05.

ANNEX

CERTIFICATE OF TITLE

Details box

TO: (Lender)
Lender's Reference or Account No:
The Borrower:
Property:
Title Number:
Mortgage Advance:
Price stated in transfer:
Completion Date:
Conveyancer's Name & Address:
Conveyancer's Reference:
Conveyancer's bank, sort code and account number:
Date of instructions:

WE THE CONVEYANCERS NAMED ABOVE CERTIFY as follows:

(1)   If so instructed, we have checked the identity of the Borrower (and anyone else required to sign the mortgage deed or other document connected with the mortgage) by reference to the document or documents precisely specified in writing by you.

(2)   Except as otherwise disclosed to you in writing:

(i)   we have investigated the title to the Property, we are not aware of any other financial charges secured on the Property which will affect the Property after completion of the mortgage and, upon completion of the mortgage, both you and the mortgagor (whose identity has been checked in accordance with paragraph (1) above) will have a good and marketable title to the Property and to appurtenant rights free from prior mortgages or charges and from onerous encumbrances which title will be registered with absolute title;

(ii) we have compared the extent of the Property shown on any plan provided by you against relevant plans in the title deeds and/or the description of the Property in any valuation which you have supplied to us, and in our opinion there are no material discrepancies;

(iii) the assumptions stated by the valuer about the title (its tenure, easements, boundaries and restrictions on use) in any valuation which you have supplied to us are correct;

(iv) if the Property is leasehold the terms of the lease accord with your instructions, including any requirements you have for covenants by the Landlord and/or a management company and/or by a deed of mutual covenant for the insurance, repair and maintenance of the structure, exterior and common parts of any building of which the Property forms part, and we have or will obtain on or before completion a clear receipt for the last payment of rent and service charge;

(v) if the property is a commonhold unit, the commonhold community statement contains the terms specified by you and does not include any restrictions on occupation or use specified by you as unacceptable, and we have or will obtain on or before completion a commonhold unit information certificate;

(vi) we have received satisfactory evidence that the buildings insurance is in place, or will be on completion, for the sum and in the terms required by you;

(vii) if the Property is to be purchased by the Borrower:

  (a) the contract for sale provides for vacant possession on completion;

  (b) the seller has owned or been the registered owner of the Property for not less than six months; and

  (c) we are not acting on behalf of the seller;

(viii) we are in possession of:

  (a) either a local search or local search insurance; and

  (b) such other searches or search insurance as are appropriate to the Property, the mortgagor and any guarantor, in each case in accordance with your instructions;

(ix) nothing has been revealed by our searches and enquiries which would prevent the Property being used by any occupant for residential purposes; and

(x) neither any principal nor any other solicitor or registered European lawyer in the firm giving this certificate nor any spouse, child, parent, brother or sister of such a person is interested in the Property (whether alone or jointly with any other) as mortgagor.

WE:

(a) undertake, prior to use of the mortgage advance, to obtain in the form required by you the execution of a mortgage and a guarantee as appropriate by the persons whose identities have been checked in accordance with paragraph (1) above as those of the Borrower, any other person in whom the legal estate is vested and any guarantor; and, if required by you:

   (i) to obtain their signatures to the forms of undertaking required by you in relation to the use, occupation or physical state of the Property;

   (ii) to ask the Borrower for confirmation that the information about occupants given in your mortgage instructions or offer is correct; and

   (iii) to obtain consents in the form required by you from any existing or prospective occupier(s) aged 17 or over of the Property specified by you or of whom we are aware;

(b) have made or will make such Bankruptcy, Land Registry or Land Charges Searches as may be necessary to justify certificate no. (2)(i) above;

(c) will within the period of protection afforded by the searches referred to in paragraph (b) above:

   (i) complete the mortgage;

   (ii) arrange for the issue of a stamp duty land tax certificate if appropriate;

   (iii) deliver to the Land Registry the documents necessary to register the mortgage in your favour and any relevant prior dealings; and

   (iv) effect any other registrations necessary to protect your interests as mortgagee;

(d) will despatch to you such deeds and documents relating to the Property as you require with a list of them in the form prescribed by you within ten working days of receipt by us of the title information document from the Land Registry;

(e) will not part with the mortgage advance (and will return it to you if required) if it shall come to our notice prior to completion that the Property will at completion be occupied in whole or in part otherwise than in accordance with your instructions;

(f) will not accept instructions, except with your consent in writing, to prepare any lease or tenancy agreement relating to the Property or any part of it prior to despatch of the Charge Certificate to you;

(g) will not use the mortgage advance until satisfied that, prior to or contemporaneously with the transfer of the Property to the mortgagor, there will be discharged:

(i)   any existing mortgage on property the subject of an associated sale of which we are aware; and

(ii)   any other mortgages made by a lender identified by you secured against a property located in England or Wales where you have given either an account number or numbers or a property address;

(h)   will notify you in writing if any matter comes to our attention before completion which would render the certificate given above untrue or inaccurate and, in those circumstances, will defer completion pending your authority to proceed and will return the mortgage advance to you if required; and

(i)   confirm that we have complied, or will comply, with your instructions in all other respects to the extent that they do not extend beyond the limitations contained in the Law Society's Code of Conduct, 3.19 (conflict of interests – types of instruction which may be accepted).

OUR duties to you are limited to the matters set out in this certificate and we accept no further liability or responsibility whatsoever. The payment by you to us (by whatever means) of the mortgage advance or any part of it constitutes acceptance of this limitation and any assignment to you by the Borrower of any rights of action against us to which the Borrower may be entitled shall take effect subject to this limitation.

Signature box

SIGNED on behalf of
THE CONVEYANCERS

....

NAME of Authorised Signatory...

QUALIFICATION
of Authorised Signatory   ....

DATE of Signature

....

Guidance to rule 3 – Conflict of interests

General

1.   3.01 to 3.05 mirror the rule 16D of the former Solicitors' Practice Rules 1990. That rule was added to the Practice Rules in 2005 and was the first time that conflicts of interests, other than in relation to conveyancing, had been dealt with as a subject in statutory rule form. The previous requirements set out in Chapter 15 of The Guide to the Professional Conduct of Solicitors (1999) were subject to significant change. The main differences are set out below.

Conflict is defined – 3.01

2.   Conflict is defined as a conflict between the duties to act in the best interests of two or more different clients, or between your interests and those of a client. The definition appears in 3.01(2). This will encompass all situations where

doing the best for one client in a matter will result in prejudice to another client in that matter or a related matter.

3.   The definition of conflict in 3.01(2) requires you to assess when two matters are "related". 3.01(3) makes it clear that if the two matters concern the same asset or liability, then they are "related". Accordingly, if you act for one client which is negotiating with publishers for the publication of a novel, an instruction from another client alleging that the novel is plagiarised and breaches copyright would be a related matter.

4.   However, there would need to be some reasonable degree of relationship for a conflict to arise. If you act for a company on a dispute with a garage about the cost of repairs to a company car, your firm would not be prevented from acting for a potential bidder for the company, even though the car is a minor asset of the company and would be included in the purchase. If you act for a client selling a business, you might conclude that your firm could also act for a prospective purchaser on the creation of an employee share scheme which would cover all the entities in the purchaser's group, this work perhaps requiring the future inclusion of the target within the scheme and consideration as to whether this raised any particular issues.

5.   In each case, you will need to make a judgement on the facts.   In making this judgement, you might want to consider the view of your existing client where you are professionally able to raise the issue with him or her. You should also take care to consider whether your firm holds any confidential information from your existing client which would be relevant to the new instructions and if so, to ensure that you comply with rule 4 (confidentiality and disclosure).

You or your firm are permitted to act with clients' consent in defined circumstances of conflict subject to suitable safeguards

6.   This reflects the fact that there may be circumstances in which, despite peripheral or potential conflict, the clients' best interests are served by you, or your firm, being able to act for two or more clients who are able to give informed consent. The circumstances in which you could act despite a conflict are set out in 3.02.

7.   Two different situations are defined. These are in 3.02(1) and 3.02(2):

(a)   (i)   3.02(1) deals with the situation where the clients have a "common interest", they all want to continue to instruct you and it would be disproportionate, for example, in terms of cost and general disruption to their matter, to require them to instruct separate solicitors.

        (ii)   For there to be a "common interest" there must be a clear common purpose and a strong consensus on how it is to be achieved. However, it will be for you to decide objectively on the facts in each case whether there is a "common interest" and it is appropriate to act. In making this decision, you should always consider whether the clients will be represented even-handedly with equal weight being given to the instructions from each.

        (iii)   The "common interest" might arise, for example, where you are acting for several members of a family in relation to their affairs or acting for various individuals in the setting up of a company. Any areas of conflict must be substantially less important to all the clients than their common purpose and may, for example, relate to slightly different views on how the common purpose is to be achieved. It will be your duty to keep the differences under review with the clients and to decide if the point has been reached when it would be untenable to continue to represent all of them in a fair and open manner or without any of them being prejudiced.

(iv) There exist some multi-party complex commercial transactions, where sophisticated users of legal services, who have a common purpose, may expect a firm to act for two or more parties, because this will facilitate efficient handling of the matter (taking into account amongst other things the desire to complete the transaction quickly, the availability of necessary experience/expertise and the overall costs). Indeed in many cases it may already be accepted business practice for firms to act in this manner. An example is acting for different tiers of lenders (for example senior lenders and mezzanine lenders) and/or different parties (for example arrangers/underwriters and bond/security trustees) in entering into a financing transaction where there is already an agreed or commonly understood structure with regard to the ranking of their respective claims, the content of their respective obligations and associated commercial issues.

(v) While accepted business practice can be considered as a factor in determining whether an appropriate common purpose exists, you and your firm should always exercise caution when proposing to act in accordance with 3.02 and should be mindful of the residual test of reasonableness referred to in 3.02(3).

(vi) In some situations it might be possible for you to consider whether the retainer could be limited to those areas where there is no conflict with the clients seeking separate advice on any areas of conflict. This could only be done where the conflict did not undermine the overriding common purpose (see below for further guidance on limiting retainers).

(vii) In some circumstances it might be possible that, while a conflict would prevent you from acting for another party on all aspects of a matter, a mandate limited to a specific issue where there is common purpose might be accepted. For example, you may be retained by the owner of a company to advise on its disposal. In that case you would not generally be able to advise another party on the purchase of the company. However, in the hope and anticipation of a successful sale a seller client which is a sophisticated user of legal services might agree that you should also accept a limited retainer to provide competition law advice to the prospective purchaser regarding the filings for competition law purposes that would be required in the event that the two businesses were combined.

(viii) When acting under this exception, especially in family situations, you need to consider the developing legal position. Courts are likely to make a presumption of undue influence where one of the parties who is considered vulnerable through age or other circumstances places trust and confidence in the other party. In any situation of doubt it may well be in the best interests of the clients that they are separately represented.

(b)   (i)   3.02(2) is intended to apply to specialised areas of legal services where the clients are sophisticated users of those services and conclude that rather than seek out new advisers they would rather use their usual advisers in the knowledge that those advisers might also act for competing interests. An "asset" is not necessarily physical, and can include a contract or a business opportunity. Examples where this exception might apply include:

    (A)   acting on insolvencies so that a firm can act for more than one creditor;

    (B)   acting for competing bidders, and/or for those involved with the funding of bidders, for a p business being sold by auction; and

    (C)   acting for competing tenderers submitting tenders to perform a contract.

   (ii)   The wording of 3.02(2) is sufficiently wide to permit other transactional work in the commercial field where clients can give consent. Solicitors and their firms should exercise considerable caution when proposing to act in accordance with 3.02(2) in categories of work where to do so is not already accepted business practice.

   (iii)   3.02(2) should not be applied to disputes over assets other than in the context of corporate restructurings and insolvencies.

8.   Reasonableness is an important rider to 3.02. There may be situations where, despite compliance with 3.02, it would still not be reasonable to act. The apparent unequal bargaining position of the parties, concerns about the mental stability of one of the parties, a family arrangement where an elderly parent is providing security for their son's or daughter's business loan, and the importance of one of the clients to the firm may all be situations where instructions to act for both or all parties should be declined.

9.   The criteria against which reasonableness will be judged is whether one client is at risk of prejudice because of the lack of separate representation. In relation to all situations where you are proposing to act for two or more clients under the provisions of 3.02, the onus will be on you to demonstrate why it was reasonable to act for all the clients at the time the instructions were accepted. Above all, you must be satisfied that unfettered advice can be given, without fear or favour, to the clients. You must also keep under review whether it remains reasonable to continue to act for them.

10. (a)   3.02(4) places obligations on you to discuss with the clients the implications of you, or your firm, continuing to act for all of them. You must be satisfied that the clients understand the issues and that their consent is independently and freely given. Extreme caution will be required where one of the clients is particularly vulnerable due to mental health, language or other problems affecting their understanding of the

issues, although where a litigation friend acts for a person who lacks capacity they will be able to consent on that person's behalf. Similarly, you must always be alert to situations where a client might be consenting under duress or undue influence and in those circumstances must insist on separate representation. For the avoidance of doubt, and for evidential purposes, you should always keep a written record of all discussions with the clients about the implications of your acting for them. You must always obtain all the clients' written consent on each occasion when acting under either of the exceptions.

(b)   Where seeking informed consent under 3.02(1)(b) you should identify by name the other clients you or your firm propose to act for, or be able to do so when their identities are known. Provided that you do this and comply with the requirements of 3.02(4), the obligation to obtain "informed" consent in 3.02(1)(b) will have been satisfied. Where consent is sought under 3.02(2), you need to comply with the requirements of 3.02(4) but you need not identify by name the other clients you or your firm propose to act for.

11.   The rule does not specifically deal with potential or future conflict, although it does make clear that a significant risk of conflict should prevent a solicitor from acting. You should always be cautious, therefore, about accepting instructions where the possibility of future conflict is evident. The risks should be explained to the clients about the problems and expense which the requirement for future separate representation could bring.

Limited/defined retainers

12.   There may be situations where, when acting for two or more clients, it is appropriate to continue to advise them but necessary to make clear that there are defined areas of conflict on which you cannot advise, and one or more of them may need separate advice. Your retainer with your clients will, when these situations arise, need to be limited to exclude those areas of work or advice. Care must always be taken, however, to ensure that the clients understand:

(a)   exactly what you are proposing to deal with on their behalf; and

(b)   those contested areas which are to be excluded from the retainer.

13.   A limited retainer would be unlikely to be appropriate in any situation where one of the clients was disadvantaged in some way as against the other. This might be because of an unequal bargaining position or because one had some form of disability. In any situation where you agree to act for two or more clients by limiting the retainer it is important that you keep all developments under review to ensure that it remains appropriate to continue to act.

Professional embarrassment

14.   There may be some circumstances in which you should refuse instructions when, although there is no actual conflict of interests as defined in rule 3, you might feel unable to do your best for a client because of some form of professional embarrassment. It may be, for example, that if you have acted for a client in the past and accept instructions to act against that client you may feel inhibited in doing your best for the new client because of the past

relationship with the former client. If so, the instructions from the new client should be refused as you would, otherwise, be in breach of core duties 1.02 (independence) and 1.03 (best interests of client).

15. There may also be situations where you and your firm are asked to act with consent, using an information barrier in accordance with rule 4 (confidentiality and disclosure), but the information you hold and which you cannot disclose to your client is of such a nature that it would cause severe embarrassment to your firm if, or when, it later came to light that your firm held such information. It may be, for example, that you are asked to act for a client on the acquisition of a business in circumstances where confidential information is held by your firm that the business has a serious problem with its accounts. Similarly, it may be that you are asked to prepare an employment contract for a company which is planning to recruit an individual who is known, confidentially, to be under investigation for fraud. In those circumstances you and your firm would be seriously embarrassed acting for a client who you knew was wasting legal fees on an outcome the client would not want to pursue if in possession of the knowledge held by your firm. It could be argued that you are not acting in the best interests of the client (see 1.03) or that you are damaging the reputation of the profession (see 1.10).

16. Where professional embarrassment is not a factor and the circumstances which would otherwise prevent you from acting in 4.03 (duty not to put confidentiality at risk by acting) do not arise, it will be a purely commercial decision as to whether you should act against the interests of another client or former client, provided there is no conflict as defined in 3.01 or 3.02.

In-house practice

17. If you are employed as an in-house lawyer your employer is your client. The nature of this relationship may cause problems because you do not have the same freedom as a firm would have to decline instructions. There may be occasions, for example, when you are asked to advise your employer in situations where conflict or potential conflict arises between your interests and the interests of your employer. These include:

   (a) where your personal interests as an employee may conflict with the interests of your employer who wants advice on a course of action which could be detrimental to you as an employee where, for example, a merger could lead to your redundancy;

   (b) where your employer asks you to do something which would place you in breach of your professional obligations, for example, to file a document with the court which you know contains false information; or

   (c) where your employer may act against your advice and, for example, engage in criminal activity which may require you to take action against your employer.

18. In relation to situations where your personal interests may conflict with a course of action proposed by your employer you need not necessarily be excluded from advising your employer. Your employer will usually be aware of exactly how you will be affected by its proposals, and if you are able to give objective advice on the legal issues where your expertise is required you would normally be free to do so. There may, however, be situations where you are so affected

by the advice you are asked to give that you feel your objectivity and independence are impaired and in those situations you would have to ask your employer to seek other advice, either internally or externally. What is important in these situations is that there is transparency about your interests. Beyond that, you will have to make a judgement about whether you feel you have the necessary objectivity to advise.

19. If your employer was unaware of your interests – and, therefore, the potential for conflict - the position would be different. If, for example, you had a large shareholding in another company and your employer's proposed action could adversely affect the value of those shares then you would either have to disclose your interest or explain that a conflict prevented you from advising on that issue.

20. In situations where you are asked to act contrary to your professional obligations then you should not compromise your position and you must refuse to carry out instructions which would have this result, even if ultimately this led to the loss of your job.

21. There may be situations where there is a positive legal obligation on you to take action against your employer where, for example, your employer is engaging in money laundering or where there are 'whistle blowing' obligations. Legal issues of this nature are beyond the remit of this guidance. They are situations where your relationship with your employer has reached the stage where you would need to consider the advisability of seeking legal advice on your own position.

22. Finally, as an in-house lawyer you are, under rule 13 (in-house practice), able to act for a limited number of other bodies and individuals. For example, if employed by a company, you may act for a holding, associated or subsidiary company of that company employer. If you do so you must ensure that you do not act in any situation where there would be a conflict between the interests of your employer and the other company for whom you are also acting (see 13.01 and 13.03). Similarly, if employed in local government you may act, for example, for local councillors in certain circumstances, provided you can comply with rule 3.

Co-defendants

23. The Criminal Defence Service Regulations require one solicitor to be appointed to act for all co-defendants in a legal aid case unless there is, or is likely to be, a conflict. The purpose of this is to ensure economy in the use of public funds by ensuring that a single solicitor represents co-defendants where it is proper to do so.. The professional conduct obligations which deal with conflicts of interest have always prevented a solicitor or firm acting for two or more clients where there is a conflict or significant risk of a conflict arising between the interests of two or more clients. A solicitor can act however, for co-defendants where conflict is not a factor. The difficulty often lies, however, in spotting potential conflict and deciding whether it is sufficiently real to refuse instructions.

24. Your starting point should always be your fundamental professional obligation to act in each client's best interests. Can you discharge this obligation to each client? This means firstly asking each client if they are aware of any actual or potential conflict between them and then, if they indicate that there is no such

conflict, asking yourself whether you feel there are any constraints on the advice you would want to give to one client, or on the action you would want to take on that client's behalf, which are likely to arise because you act for another co-defendant.

25. A conflict of interest arises wherever there is a constraint of that sort, for example where it is in the best interests of client A:

   (a)   to give evidence against client B;

   (b)   to make a statement incriminating client B;

   (c)   to implicate client B in a police interview;

   (d)   to provide prejudicial information regarding client B to an investigator;

   (e)   to cross examine client B in such a manner as to call into question his or her credibility;

   (f)   to rely upon confidential information given by client B without his or her consent; or

   (g)   to adopt tactics in the course of the retainer which potentially or actually harm client B.

26. If these obligations actually come into conflict when acting for two or more clients you will have to cease to act for one and often both. This can cause considerable disruption and expense, which is why the rules require that you should not accept instructions if there is a significant risk of this happening.

27. Many criminal clients will, of course, have retained you at the police station prior to a police interview and are thus not at that stage defendants. The obligations referred to above apply at this early stage, and you must be satisfied that accepting instructions on behalf of a client prior to a police interview does not place you in conflict with another client who is also to be interviewed. In order to assess whether you can act for both clients it is important that you do not interview the clients together and that you get instructions which are as full as possible from the first client before any substantive contact with the second client. However, never let the police deter you from seeing the second client because they think there is a conflict – that decision must be yours.

28. A further consideration when taking instructions at the police station, especially out of office hours when an immediate conflict check is not possible, is that the firm may already act for another defendant in that matter or information obtained at the police station may be relevant to another client on an unrelated matter. For example, the firm may be acting in divorce proceedings for a wife where violence is alleged and information that her husband has been charged with an offence involving violence would be relevant and may make it impossible to continue acting for the wife. This highlights the importance of carrying out a conflict check at the earliest opportunity.

29. When considering accepting instructions from more than one client in the same matter you need to assess not only whether there is a conflict at the outset, but whether events are likely to arise which will prevent you from continuing to act

for one or both at a later stage in the proceedings. In almost all cases there will be some possibility of differences in instructions between the clients but the rules do not prevent you acting unless the risk of conflict is significant. Assessing the risk is often not easy. It is also important that where you have accepted instructions from co-defendants you remain alert to the risk of conflict arising as the case progresses.

30. When considering whether there is an actual conflict there are obvious indicators such as whether the clients have differing accounts of the important relevant circumstances of the alleged crime or where one seems likely to change his or her plea. There are also less obvious indicators. These would include situations where there is some clear inequality between the co-defendants which might, for example, suggest that one client is acting under the influence of the other rather than on his or her own initiative. If you are acting for both this may make it difficult for you to raise and discuss these issues equally with them. In trying to help one, you might be undermining the other. If you believe you are going to be unable to do your best for one without worrying about whether this might prejudice the other you should only accept instructions from one.

31. The risk of future conflict can be an even more difficult issue to assess. It may be that you have two clients who are pleading not guilty and who are apparently in total agreement on the factual evidence. Should they both be found guilty, you need to consider at the outset whether you would be able to mitigate fully and freely on behalf of one client without in so doing harming the interests of the other. It may be that one has a long list of convictions and is considerably older than the other. If so, it may be that the younger client with a comparatively clean record was led astray or pressurised into committing the crime and would want you to emphasise this in mitigation. If there is a significant risk of this happening you should not accept instructions from both.

32. Even where care is taken when accepting instructions from more than one client in the same matter there will inevitably be situations where a conflict subsequently arises. This will commonly happen where one defendant changes his or her plea or evidence. A decision will then have to be taken as to whether it is proper to continue to represent one client or whether both will have to instruct new firms. In making this decision you need to consider whether in the changed circumstances your duty to disclose all relevant information to the retained client will place you in breach of your duty of confidentiality to the other client. In other words, you need to decide whether you hold confidential information about the departing client which is now relevant to the retained client. If you do have such information then you cannot act for either client.

33. Following the changes to the Regulations, some practitioners have reported pressure from some court clerks on solicitors to represent co-defendants even where there is a clear risk of conflict. Similar pressure has been applied by police at police stations prior to interviews. However, the professional rules of conduct preclude you acting for both clients in those circumstances, and the Regulations are not intended to put solicitors in a position where they are asked to act contrary to their professional responsibilities. If asked by the court for your reasons why you cannot act for both defendants, you must not give information which would breach your duty of confidentiality to your client/s. This will normally mean that you can say no more than that it would be unprofessional for you to continue to act.

34. For the avoidance of doubt, you cannot resolve a conflict by instructing another firm or counsel to undertake the advocacy on behalf of one client. Neither can you pass one of the clients to another member of your firm. The rules make it quite clear that your firm cannot act for clients whose interests conflict.

35. Any decision to act, or not to act, for co-defendants should be recorded with a brief note of the reasons.

Mediation

36. There is no objection to your acting as a conciliator and mediator between parties in a dispute. However, in so acting you should have regard to the appropriate codes of practice such as those issued by the Law Society from time to time. These codes provide detailed guidance on dealing with conflict when acting as mediators.

Local authority client

37. If tendering for local authority work, your firm will need to consider how frequently the range of work is likely to give rise to conflicts between existing clients and the local authority, for example, in housing and custody matters where the firm acts against the local authority.

Insolvency practice

38. If you are a licensed insolvency practitioner you must consider whether any relationship which you have, or your firm has, with clients or others might affect your independence and create a conflict preventing you accepting an appointment to administer an insolvent estate or bankruptcy. See also rule 17 (insolvency practice).

Your interests conflicting with the client's – 3.01(2)(b)

39. There are no circumstances where you can act for a client whose interests conflict with your own interests. The situations outlined in 3.02 where you can act for two or more clients whose interests conflict have no application in this situation. This is because of the fiduciary relationship which exists between you and your client which prevents you taking advantage of the client or acting where there is a conflict or potential conflict of interests between you and your client. Examples appear below.

40. In conduct there is a conflict of interests where you in your personal capacity sell to, or buy from, or lend to, or borrow from, your client. In all these cases you should insist the client takes independent legal advice. If the client refuses you must not proceed with the transaction.

41. You should never enter into any arrangement or understanding with a client or prospective client prior to the conclusion of a matter under which you acquire an interest in the publication rights with respect to that matter. This applies equally to non-contentious business.

42. Whilst you are entitled to take security for costs you should be aware of the risk of the court finding undue influence. Before you do take a charge over a client's property it is advisable, therefore, to suggest the client consider seeking independent legal advice. Such advice would not normally be

essential unless the terms of the proposed charge are particularly onerous or would give you some unusual benefit or profit. It is, however, important always to ensure that the client understands that a charge is being taken and the effect of such a charge.

43. You are not able to secure costs by a first legal charge over your client's property if this means that you are entering into a regulated mortgage contract as a lender. A regulated mortgage contract is an investment which is regulated by the Financial Services Authority. It arises where the lender provides credit to an individual or trustee, and it is secured by a first legal mortgage on land which is in the United Kingdom, and at least 40% of the land is, or is to be, used as a dwelling by the borrower or, where the borrower is a trustee, by a beneficiary of the trust or by a related person. You must be authorised by the FSA in order to secure your costs in this way. Detailed guidance on this is in the booklet "Financial Services and Solicitors" (September 2004) available from the Law Society's Professional Ethics department.

44. You must always disclose with complete frankness whenever you have, or might obtain, any personal interest or benefit in a transaction in which you are acting for the client. In such circumstances, you must insist that the client receives independent advice.

45. Independent advice means both legal advice and, where appropriate, competent advice from a member of another profession, e.g. a chartered surveyor.

46. Your interests referred to in this rule may be direct (for example, where you seek to sell to or buy property from the client or lend to, or borrow from, the client), or indirect (for example, where your business interests lead you to recommend the client to invest in a concern in which you are interested).

47. This rule applies, therefore, not only where you are personally interested in a transaction, but equally where another person working in your firm has an interest of which you are aware and it impairs your ability to give independent and impartial advice.

48. The interests envisaged by this rule are not restricted to those of a primarily economic nature only. For example, if you become involved in a sexual relationship with a client you must consider whether this may place your interests in conflict with those of the client or otherwise impair your ability to act in the best interests of the client.

49. If you are a director of a company for which you act, or own shares in the company, you must consider whether you are in a position of conflict when asked to advise the company upon steps it has taken or should take. It may sometimes be necessary to resign from the board or for another solicitor (including a solicitor from the same firm if appropriate) to advise the company in a particular matter where your own interests conflict, or are likely to conflict. If acting for a company in which you have a personal interest you should always ensure that your ability to give independent and impartial advice is not, for that reason, impaired.

50. If you hold a power of attorney for a client you must not use that power to gain a benefit which, if acting as a professional adviser to that client, you would not be prepared to allow to an independent third party. This applies regardless of

the legal position, for example, as to whether you could lend the donor's money to yourself.

51. You are free to negotiate your terms of business, including costs, with your clients. This includes negotiating conditional fees which are subject to statutory regulation. In all these negotiations you are not acting for the client. There may be situations, however, where the terms of business are particularly unusual and it would be prudent for you to suggest the client seeks independent advice. It would be advisable to do so if, for example, as part, or all, of your remuneration you are to receive shares in a company you are setting up on behalf of your client.

52. You need to consider whether the conditional fee agreement involves you in insurance mediation activities, (such as arranging and/or advising on after the event insurance contracts etc). Solicitors who carry on insurance mediation activities either need to be able to comply with the Solicitors' Financial Services (Scope) Rules 2001 or be authorised by the FSA. Detailed guidance is in the booklet "Financial Services and Solicitors" (September 2004) available from the Law Society's Professional Ethics department.

53. You must always be careful to ensure that any settlement achieved for a client, or any advice given in a non-contentious matter conducted on a contingency fee basis, is in the client's best interests and not made with a view to your obtaining your fee.

54. Where you discover an act or omission which would justify a claim against you, you must inform the client, and recommend they seek independent advice. You must also inform the client that independent advice should be sought in cases where the client makes a claim against you, or notifies an intention to do so. If the client refuses to seek independent advice, you should not continue to act unless you are satisfied that there is no conflict of interest. See 20.07 (dealing with claims).

Accepting gifts from clients – 3.04

55. 3.04 does not prevent you accepting a client's gift but does require the client to take independent advice where the gift is significant, or significant as compared with the client's likely estate and the reasonable expectations of prospective beneficiaries.

56. 3.04 allows you to prepare a will for a family member under which you receive a significant gift without requiring the client to seek independent advice on that gift. However, extreme caution should always be exercised in these circumstances as your ability to give independent, dispassionate advice could easily be undermined by your relationship with others within, and outside, the family. The risk of conflict, therefore, is very high. If you are to receive a significant gift from the estate you need also to consider the reasonable expectations of the other prospective beneficiaries, who are likely to be your relatives. If, having taken these reasonable expectations into account, it appears that you are to receive a benefit which is in any way disproportionately large you should always ensure that the client is separately advised on that gift. "Prospective beneficiaries" in the context of this rule means others who would be reasonably expected to benefit because of their relationship to the client and their reasonable expectations would be dependent on the closeness

of that relationship. An objective test would be applied in the event of a complaint.

57.   There are other factors which should be taken into account when preparing a will for a family member under which you benefit. It may also be far easier for a close family member to talk through their proposals for their will with someone who has no personal interest in its contents and who is unlikely to be offended by any suggestions they might wish to make. Finally, your relative's bequests are secure from allegations of undue influence if their will is drawn by someone totally independent and who does not take a benefit from it. "Family member" is not defined in 3.04 to allow a flexible approach to be taken. Co-habitants are not included in the exception to independent advice because their legal position is less secure than those related by blood, marriage or adoption.

58.   A "significant amount" for the purposes of 3.04 cannot be quantified because the particular circumstances of the proposed gift must be taken into account. In general, however, anything more than a token gift will be considered significant. If, therefore, anything more than a token amount is accepted without the client having separate advice (other than where you are acting for a family member as permitted by 3.04) you may be exposed to allegations of misconduct.

59.   When considering whether a gift is of a "significant amount" the date of preparation of the document is relevant when determining the size of the estate.

60.   If more than one gift is made to members of a firm, for example, £1,000 to each of the partners in the firm, they should be amalgamated for the purpose of establishing whether the gift is "significant".

61.   The implications of 3.04 need to be made clear to all members of your firm who take instructions from clients, whether solicitors or not. Supervision is important to ensure compliance.

62.   Where you are given money or property to distribute for the benefit of others, such as in a secret trust, this is not considered to be a "gift" for the purposes of 3.04. However, care should be taken to ensure that records are kept confirming the arrangement and to ensure that the transaction is not one which could contain a potential for money laundering.

Public office or appointment leading to conflict – 3.05

63.   Examples of the public offices and appointments which 3.05 covers are:

(a)   local councillor;

(b)   judicial appointments;

(c)   justices and justices clerks;

(d)   gaming board;

(e)   coroners;

(f)   police authority;

(g)   the Legal Services Commission's Regional Legal Services Committees; and

(h)   Criminal Injuries Compensation Board.

64.   Where you hold (or a member of your firm or family holds) any of these, or similar, offices or appointments it will be up to you in every case to consider:

(a)   whether any political or other interest which you may have in connection with the office or appointment may conflict with, or affect, your duty to act in the best interests of any of your clients (including your ability to advise impartially and independently);

(b)   whether any duties which arise from your office or appointment conflict with, or affect, your duty to act in the best interests of your clients;

(c)   whether the terms of appointment, or any statutory provisions, restrict your ability to act in any particular matter; and

(d)   whether there is likely to be a public perception that you, or your firm, have been able to obtain an unfair advantage for your client(s) as a result of the office or appointment.

65.   Where you are aware that a member of your firm or family has accepted an appointment it is important for you to consider whether there is likely to be a public perception of your firm gaining an unfair advantage for your client(s).

ADR and conflict – 3.06

66.   You may provide ADR services as part of your practice or through a separate business. For more information on separate businesses see rule 21(separate businesses).

67.   3.06 also applies when you provide ADR services through a separate business.

68.   "ADR" service means the service provided by you when acting as an independent neutral, for example, as mediator, conciliator or arbitrator.

69.   The Law Society recommends that those who offer ADR services comply with a code of practice such as the Law Society's Codes for Civil / Commercial Mediation and Family Mediation.

Acting for seller and buyer in conveyancing, property selling and mortgage related services

70.   3.07 to 3.15 set out the limited circumstances in which you may act for more than one party in conveyancing, property selling or mortgage related services. They apply to all types of conveyancing transaction, commercial and residential.

71.   The general rule is that separate representation is required because conveyancing is an area where the risk of a conflict arising between two parties is high and where any conflict may affect a conveyancing chain.

72. When judging whether or not a transaction is "at arm's length", you need to look at the relationship between the parties and the context of the transaction. A transaction may be regarded as not "at arm's length", even if it is at market value or is stated to be on arm's length terms. A transaction would not usually be at arm's length, for example, if the parties are:

    (a) related by blood, adoption or marriage, or living together;

    (b) the settlor of a trust and the trustees;

    (c) the trustees of a trust and its beneficiary or the beneficiary's relative;

    (d) personal representatives and a beneficiary;

    (e) the trustees of separate trusts for the same family;

    (f) a sole trader or partners and a limited company set up to enable the business to be incorporated;

    (g) associated companies (i.e. where one is a holding company and the other is its subsidiary within the meaning of the Companies Act 1985, or both are subsidiaries of the same holding company); or

    (h) a local authority and a related body within the meaning of 13.08(c).

73. 10.06(3) and (4) deal with the prohibition on acting for more than one prospective buyer, or for seller and buyer where there is more than one prospective buyer. These provisions recognise the inevitable conflict of interests which makes it impossible to act for more than one prospective buyer, or for the seller and one of several prospective buyers. If you were already acting for seller and buyer (for example, both are established clients), you would be unable to continue acting for both if another prospective buyer were introduced during the course of the transaction. There is a significant inherent conflict in these circumstances. It would be impossible, for example, to reconcile the interests of both clients if it were in the seller's best interests to exchange with the other prospective buyer.

74. The test of whether a person is an "established client" is an objective one – is it reasonable to regard the person as an established client? A seller or buyer who instructs you for the first time is not an established client. A former client is not necessarily the same as an established client. There needs to be a degree of permanence in the solicitor-client relationship as exemplified by some continuity of instruction over time and the likelihood of future instruction. An individual related by blood, adoption or marriage to an established client, or who is living with an established client, counts as an established client. A person also counts as an established client if selling or buying jointly with an established client.

75. The consideration will only count as £10,000 or less if the value of any property given in exchange or part exchange is taken into account.

76. A builder or developer who acquires a property in part exchange, and sells it on without development, is not selling "as a builder or developer" within the meaning of 3.10(c) and 3.13(c).

77.   If acting for seller and buyer under the provisions of 3.07 – 3.15, you would have to stop acting for at least one of the clients if a conflict were to arise during the course of the transaction. Clients should be made aware of the consequent disruption and additional expense involved in such circumstances, and of the advantages of separate representation, before giving their written consent.

78.   An RFL cannot undertake conveyancing. RELs may undertake conveyancing only if they are entitled to do so under regulation 12 of the European Communities (Lawyer's Practice) Regulations 2000.

79.   The effect of 3.11 is as follows:

    (a)   if providing mortgage related services to the buyer (either through your own firm or a SEAL - see 3.12 for the definition of a SEAL), you may also provide property selling services to the seller (either through your own firm or a SEAL) and do the seller's conveyancing;

    (b)   if providing property selling services to the seller through a SEAL (not your own firm), you may also provide mortgage related services to the buyer (either through your own firm or the SEAL) and do the buyer's conveyancing.

80.   A SEAL may act for the seller and provide mortgage related services to the buyer; one of the participating firms may do the seller's conveyancing, and another participating firm may do the buyer's conveyancing.

Acting for lender and borrower in conveyancing transactions

81.   There will be no breach of 3.16(2)(c)-(d) or 3.19 if the lender has certified that its mortgage instructions and documents sent pursuant to those instructions are subject to the limitations set out in 3.19 and 3.21, and certifies any subsequent instructions and documents in the same way. If there is no certification, when acting in a transaction involving the charge of property to be used solely as the borrower's private residence you must notify the lender that the approved certificate of title will be used and that your duties to the lender will be limited accordingly (see 3.20(b)). In other types of transaction, you should draw the lender's attention to the provisions of 3.19 and 3.21 and state that you cannot act on any instructions which extend beyond the matters contained in 3.19.

82.   As an alternative to printing the approved certificate for each transaction, it is acceptable for a lender to use a short form certificate of title which incorporates the approved certificate by reference. The form must include in the following order:

    (a)   the title "Certificate of Title";

    (b)   the contents of the details box in the order set out in the approved certificate (use of two columns is acceptable) but with details not required shaded out or stated not to be required; and

    (c)   the wording "We, the conveyancers named above, give the Certificate of Title set out in the annex to rule 3 of the Law Society's Code of Conduct as if the same were set out in full, subject to the limitations contained in it."

Administrative details, such as a request for cheque, may follow the Certificate of Title.

83. The approved certificate is only required for a transaction where the property is to be used solely as the borrower's private residence. The approved certificate need not, therefore, be used for investment properties such as blocks of flats, business premises such as shops (even if living accommodation is attached), or 'buy to let mortgages' on properties which are not intended for owner-occupation.

84. You must inform the lender of the circumstances, in accordance with 3.18, so that the lender can decide whether or not to instruct you.

85. A lender's instructions (see 3.19(x)) may require a wider disclosure of your circumstances than 3.18 requires; and you must assess whether the circumstances give rise to a conflict. For example, there will be a conflict between lender and borrower if you become involved in negotiations relating to the terms of the loan. A conflict might arise from the relationship you or your firm has with the borrower - for example, if you or your firm is the borrower's creditor or debtor or the borrower's business associate or co-habitant.

86. In relation to 3.22(2), the limitations contained in 3.19 will not apply to the insertion into a recognised certificate of any information required by that certificate. For example, where the recognised certificate requires details of the parties' repairing obligations under a lease of the property, you may provide a summary of the relevant terms of the lease despite the general limitation contained in 3.19(i). However, any additions or amendments to the text of a recognised certificate to suit a particular transaction must not, to the extent to which they create an increased or additional obligation, extend beyond the limitations contained in 3.19.

87. Many lenders require their lawyer or licensed conveyancer to check the *vires* of corporate borrowers and that the correct procedures have been followed to ensure the validity of the mortgage. 3.19(n) enables lenders to impose duties on their lawyer or licensed conveyancer in relation to the execution of the mortgage and guarantee. Within this context it is perfectly proper for a lender to require you to obtain such information as the circumstances may require in relation to the capacity of, or execution of documents by, the borrower, third party mortgagor or guarantor; for instance, by way of certified copy minutes or an opinion from a lawyer of the relevant jurisdiction as to the validity and enforceability of the security or guarantee given by a foreign registered company. There is no reason why you should not assist corporate clients by drafting minutes or board resolutions. You should not, however, certify the validity or passing of resolutions unless you were present at the meeting and have verified that it was convened and held strictly in accordance with all relevant requirements.

88. 3.19(u) allows you to accept instructions from a lender to carry out administrative arrangements in relation to any collateral security. This expression includes associated debentures, collateral warranties, second charges, rent assignments, charges over rent income and deeds of priority.

The administrative arrangements necessarily include the preparation and execution of the relevant documents and subsequent registration.

Rule 4 – Confidentiality and disclosure

Introduction

Rule 4 sets out provisions for dealing with the protection of clients' confidential information and the duty of disclosure owed to clients.

Rule 4 – Confidentiality and disclosure

4.01 Duty of confidentiality

You and your firm must keep the affairs of clients and <u>former</u> clients confidential except where disclosure is required or permitted by law or by your client (or former client).

4.02 Duty of disclosure

You must disclose to a client all information of which you are aware which is material to that client's matter regardless of the source of the information, subject to:

(a)   the duty of confidentiality in 4.01 above, which always overrides the duty to disclose; and

(b)   the following where the duty does not apply:

   (i)   where such disclosure is prohibited by law;

   (ii)   it is agreed expressly that no duty to disclose arises or a different standard of disclosure applies; or

   (iii)   where you reasonably believe that serious physical or mental injury will be caused to any person if the information is disclosed to a client.

4.03 Duty not to put confidentiality at risk by acting

If you hold, or your firm holds, confidential information in relation to a client or former client, you must not risk breaching confidentiality by acting, or continuing to act, for another client on a matter where:

(a)   that information might reasonably be expected to be material; and

(b)   that client has an interest adverse to the first-mentioned client or former client,

except where proper arrangements can be made to protect that information in accordance with 4.04 and 4.05.

4.04   Exception to duty not to put confidentiality at risk by acting – with clients' consent

(1)   You may act, or continue to act, in the circumstances otherwise prohibited by 4.03 with the informed consent of both clients but only if:

   (a)   the client for whom you act or are proposing to act knows that your firm, or a member of your firm, holds, or might hold, material information (in circumstances described in 4.03) in relation to their matter which you cannot disclose;

   (b)   you have a reasonable belief that both clients understand the relevant issues after these have been brought to their attention;

   (c)   both clients have agreed to the conditions under which you will be acting or continuing to act; and

   (d)   it is reasonable in all the circumstances to do so.

(2)   "Both clients" in the context of 4.04(1) means:

   (a)   an existing or former client for whom your firm, or a member of your firm, holds confidential information; and

   (b)   an existing or new client for whom you act or are proposing to act and to whom information held on behalf of the other client is material (in circumstances described in 4.03).

(3)   If you, or you and your firm, have been acting for two or more clients in compliance with rule 3 (conflict of interests) and can no longer fulfil its requirements you may continue to act for one client with the consent of the other client provided you comply with 4.04.

4.05   Exception to duty not to put confidentiality at risk by acting – without clients' consent

You may continue to act for a client on an existing matter, or on a matter related to an existing matter, in the circumstances otherwise prohibited by 4.03 without the consent of the client for whom your firm, or a member of your firm, holds, or might hold, confidential information which is material to your client (in circumstances described in 4.03) but only if:

   (a)   it is not possible to obtain informed consent under 4.04 from the client for whom your firm, or a member of your firm, holds, or might hold, material confidential information;

   (b)   your client has agreed to your acting in the knowledge that your firm, or a member of your firm, holds, or might hold, information material to their matter which you cannot disclose;

   (c)   any safeguards which comply with the standards required by law at the time they are implemented are put in place; and

(d)   it is reasonable in all the circumstances to do so.

4.06 Waivers

Notwithstanding rule 22 of these rules, the Council of the Law Society shall not have power to waive any of the provisions of this rule.

Guidance to rule 4 – Confidentiality and disclosure

Introduction

1.   This rule mirrors rule 16E of the former Solicitors' Practice Rules 1990. That rule was added to the Practice Rules in 2005 and was the first time that confidentiality, disclosure and information barriers had been dealt with as a subject in statutory form.

2.   Previously, conflicts between the duties of confidentiality and disclosure were dealt with as a conflict issue. This rule now draws together, and describes the interaction of, the obligations created by these duties. It also reinforces the common law duty whereby you and your firm must not put confidential information obtained from one client/former client at risk by acting adverse to the interests of that client/former client in a matter where the confidential information would be material. The rule also establishes that where a conflict between these duties arises the duty of confidentiality is paramount. The rule does recognise that confidential information can be protected by the use of information barriers with the consent of the client and, in very limited circumstances, without that consent.

3.   The rule should be read in conjunction with rule 3 (conflict of interests) as there are important cross-references contained in both the rules and the guidance.

The duty of confidentiality – 4.01 – general

4.   4.01 sets out your fundamental duty to keep all clients' affairs confidential. It is important to bear in mind the distinction between this duty and the concept of law known as legal professional privilege. The duty of confidentiality extends to all confidential information about a client's affairs, irrespective of the source of the information, subject to the limited exceptions described below. Legal professional privilege protects certain communications between you and your client from being disclosed, even in court. However, not all communications are protected from disclosure and you should, if necessary, refer to an appropriate authority on the law of evidence.

5.   The duty of confidentiality continues after the end of the retainer. After the client dies the right to confidentiality passes to the personal representatives, but note that an administrator's power dates only from the grant of the letters of administration.

6.   Information received in the context of a joint retainer must be available between the clients. They must, however, all consent to any confidential information being disclosed to a third party. Information communicated to you when acting for one of the clients in relation to a separate matter must not be disclosed to the other client(s) without the consent of that client.

7.   If you obtain information in relation to a prospective client you may still be bound by a duty of confidentiality, even if that prospective client does not subsequently instruct your firm. There may be circumstances, however, where you receive information where there is no real or genuine interest in instructing your firm and that information is unlikely to be confidential.

Insolvency

8.   If a client becomes insolvent you will need to consider to whom you owe a duty of confidentiality. To some extent this will depend on whether your client is a company or an individual and you will need to refer to the relevant statutory authority, such as the Insolvency Act 1986. Where a statutory power overrides confidentiality you should consider carefully to what extent it is overridden. It may, for example, require you to disclose only certain categories of information or documents. You should ensure than any disclosure you make is strictly limited to what is required by the law.

Specific instances where confidentiality is required

9.   (a)   You must not disclose the contents of a will, even after the death of the testator, other than to, or with the consent of, the executor(s), until probate has been obtained.

     (b)   You must not disclose the address of a client without the client's consent.

     (c)   Where a lender asks for a conveyancing file and you have kept a joint file for both borrower and lender clients, you cannot, without the consent of the borrower, send the whole file to the lender, unless the lender can show to your satisfaction that there is a prima facie case of fraud. If the client does not consent, you should send only those parts of the file which relate to work done for the lender.

     (d)   You cannot, without the consent of the relevant client (or, if applicable, its administrator or similar officeholder), sell book debts to a factoring company because of the confidential nature of your bill. If your firm grants, as security to a lender, a charge over your firm's book debts, you need to ensure that you protect clients' confidential information should the lender need to enforce the security. Further advice on this issue can be obtained from the Law Society's Professional Ethics department.

     (e)   You should only share office services with other businesses if confidentiality can be ensured.

     (f)   If you outsource services such as word processing, telephone call handling or photocopying you must be satisfied that the provider of those services is able to ensure the confidentiality of any information concerning your clients. This would normally require confidentiality undertakings from the provider and checks to ensure that the terms of the arrangements regarding confidentiality are being complied with. Whilst you might have implied consent to confidential information being passed to external service providers, it would be prudent to inform clients of any such services you propose to use in your terms of business or client care letters.

Disclosure of confidential information in exceptional circumstances

10. Despite your duty of confidentiality you may be required to disclose confidential information in certain circumstances. A number of statutes empower government and other bodies, for example the Inland Revenue, to require any person to disclose documents and/or information. In the absence of the client's specific consent, you should ask under which statutory power the information is sought, consider the relevant provisions and consider whether privileged information is protected from disclosure. You should only provide such information as you are strictly required by law to disclose.

11. There are reporting requirements in relation to money laundering which override the duty of confidentiality and these are set out in the Proceeds of Crime Act 2002, the terrorism legislation and the Money Laundering Regulations 2003. These often require difficult judgements to be made as to whether or not a situation has arisen which would require you to report information to the relevant authorities. You should, however, always be mindful of the importance of your duty of confidentiality to your client. If you are uncertain as to whether you should report confidential information you should consider seeking legal advice or contact the Law Society's Professional Ethics department for advice.

12. The Freedom of Information Act 2000 applies to the majority of public bodies and to local authorities. This act establishes a right to know the content of records held by certain public bodies subject to certain exemptions such as legal professional privilege. The legal professional privilege exemption is conditional and can only be relied upon where the public interest in maintaining the exemption outweighs the public interest in disclosing the information. In some cases, disclosure of matters which are on legal files may be required by law under the Act. The Information Commissioner's website provides Awareness Guidance upon this area of the Act.

13. You may reveal confidential information to the extent that you believe necessary to prevent the client or a third party committing a criminal act that you reasonably believe is likely to result in serious bodily harm.

14. There may be exceptional circumstances involving children where you should consider revealing confidential information to an appropriate authority. This may be where the child is the client and the child reveals information which indicates continuing sexual or other physical abuse but refuses to allow disclosure of such information. Similarly, there may be situations where an adult discloses abuse either by himself or herself or by another adult against a child but refuses to allow any disclosure. You must consider whether the threat to the child's life or health, both mental and physical, is sufficiently serious to justify a breach of the duty of confidentiality.

15. In proceedings under the Children Act 1989 you are under a duty to reveal experts' reports commissioned for the purposes of proceedings, as these reports are not privileged. The position in relation to voluntary disclosure of other documents or solicitor/client communications is uncertain. Under 11.01, an advocate is under a duty not to mislead the court. Therefore, if you are an advocate, and have certain knowledge which you realise is adverse to the client's case, you may be extremely limited in what you can state in the client's

favour. In this situation, you should seek the client's agreement for full voluntary disclosure, for three reasons:

(a) the matters the client wants to hide will probably emerge anyway;

(b) you will be able to do a better job for the client if all the relevant information is presented to the court; and

(c) if the information is not voluntarily disclosed, you may be severely criticised by the court.

If the client refuses to give you authority to disclose the relevant information, you are entitled to refuse to continue to act for the client if to do so will place you in breach of your obligations to the court.

16. You should reveal matters which are otherwise subject to the duty to preserve confidentiality where a court orders that such matters are to be disclosed or where a warrant permits a police officer or other authority to seize confidential documents. If you believe that the documents are subject to legal privilege or that for some other reason the order or warrant ought not to have been made or issued, you should normally, without unlawfully obstructing its execution, discuss with the client the possibility of making an application to have the order or warrant set aside. Advice may be obtained from the Law Society's Professional Ethics department.

17. Occasionally you may be asked by the police or a third party to give information or to show them documents which you have obtained when acting for a client. Unless the client is prepared to waive confidentiality, or where you have strong prima facie evidence that you have been used by the client to perpetrate a fraud or other crime and the duty of confidence does not arise, you should insist upon receiving a witness summons or subpoena so that, where appropriate, privilege may be claimed and the court asked to decide the issue. If the request is made by the police under the Police and Criminal Evidence Act 1984 you should, where appropriate, leave the question of privilege to the court to decide on the particular circumstances. Advice may be obtained from the Law Society's Professional Ethics department.

18. Certain communications from a client are not confidential if they are a matter of public record. For example, the fact that you have been instructed by a named client in connection with contentious business for which that client's name is on the public record is not confidential, but the type of business involved will usually be confidential.

19. You may reveal confidential information concerning a client to the extent that it is reasonably necessary to establish a defence to a criminal charge or civil claim by your client against you, or where your conduct is under investigation by the Law Society, or under consideration by the Solicitors Disciplinary Tribunal.

20. In the case of a publicly funded client, you may be under a duty to report to the Legal Services Commission information concerning the client which is confidential and privileged.

Duty to disclose information to a client – 4.02

21.   You have a duty to disclose all information material to your client's matter. Your duty is limited to information of which you are aware (and does not extend to information of which others in your firm may be aware) but is not limited to information obtained while acting on the client's matter. You will not be liable, therefore, for failing to disclose material information held by others within your firm of which you were unaware. There are, however, some circumstances where you should not disclose material information because it is not in the best interests of your client to do so or because disclosure is prohibited by law. These include situations where:

   (a)   disclosure may be harmful to the client because of the client's physical or mental condition;

   (b)   the provisions in the money laundering legislation effectively prohibit you from passing information to clients;

   (c)   it is obvious that privileged documents have been mistakenly disclosed to you; or

   (d)   you come into possession of information relating to state security or intelligence matters to which the Official Secrets Act 1989 applies.

22.   4.02 also prevents you from disclosing information where this would breach your firm's duty of confidentiality to another client. The duty of confidentiality will always override the duty of disclosure.

23.   You cannot, however, excuse a failure to disclose material information because to do so would breach a separate duty of confidentiality. Unless the retainer with the client to which the information cannot be disclosed can be varied so that the inability to disclose is not a breach of duty (see paragraph 26 below), you should refuse the instructions or, if already acting, immediately cease to act for that client. Any delay in ceasing to act is likely to increase the risk that you are liable for breach of duty.

24.   You should not seek to pass the client to a colleague (who would not be bound by the same duty because he or she is personally unaware of the material information) unless the client agrees to this, knowing the reason for the transfer and, if you have already started to act for the client, agreeing that you are released from your duty to disclose up to the time when you personally cease to act for the client on that matter. Further, you should consider carefully whether, even if these conditions are satisfied, it is appropriate for any members of your firm to act. A firm which holds information which it cannot convey to a client but which, if known to that client, might affect the instructions to the firm in a material way will usually be in an invidious position and quite possibly unable to act in the best interests of the client - see rule 3 (conflict of interests). See also guidance note 15 to rule 3.

25.   The rule does not define "information which is material to that client's matter" but it must be information which is relevant to the specific retainer with the client and not just information which might be of general interest to the client. The information must also be more than of inconsequential interest to the

client. It must, therefore, be information which might reasonably be expected to affect the client's decision making with regard to its matter in a way which is significant having regard to the matter as a whole.

26. The duty outlined above reflects and builds on the fiduciary duty which exists at common law. As 4.02(b)(ii) makes clear, however, you or your firm can expressly agree a different degree of duty. For example, a client might wish to instruct you because it knows that you act for other entities which operate in the same market and because it knows that you, therefore, understand the market. The client would not be surprised that you hold material market intelligence of a confidential nature from such other clients, and would not expect you to divulge it. The client might, therefore, agree that the usual duty to disclose would not apply.

Duties of confidentiality and disclosure conflicting – 4.03

27. 4.03 sets out the duty not to put confidentiality at risk by acting for a client where to do so might put at risk the confidential information held by your firm for another client (or former client). The rule makes clear that the relevant circumstances of risk arise where:

    (a) the confidential information "might reasonably be expected to be material" to the client for whom you wish to act; and

    (b) the work for the client for whom you wish to act would be adverse to the interests of the client or former client to whom the duty of confidentiality is owed.

    The effect of (b) is that you can act if the confidential information your firm holds is not reasonably expected to be material to your new client or is reasonably expected to be material to your new client but the interests of the clients are not adverse. The confidential information would, however, have to be protected and you and your firm would be answerable in law and conduct if it leaked.

28. The rule does not define adverse interest, but the intention is to mirror what is considered adverse for these purposes at common law (see Bolkiah v KPMG H.L. [1999] 2 WLR p.215 and subsequent cases). Essentially, adversity arises where one party is, or is likely to become, the opposing party on a matter, whether in negotiations or some form of dispute resolution. For example, if your firm acted for a client in a criminal case in which the client was convicted of assault and the client's wife, unaware of the conviction, then wished you to represent her in divorce proceedings you would have to refuse the instructions. The confidential information held about the husband would be material to her case and, if so, her interests would be adverse to his.

29. In contrast, action which seeks to improve the new client's commercial position as against others generally within a particular sector would not be "adverse" to the interests of another client which is one such competitor. This should be the case even if there might be some risk that such a market competitor might seek to challenge the activities of the client before, for example, the competition authorities.

30. There may, however, be some circumstances where you are permitted to act under 4.03 but where other considerations will prevent you from doing so. It

might be that you personally have confidential information from another client/former client which would be material to the new instruction but, since the instruction would not be adverse to the other client/former client, 4.03 does not bite. In this situation, the duty of confidentiality conflicts with your personal duty to disclose, and you should therefore not act, unless the new client has expressly agreed a lesser duty of disclosure (4.02(b)(ii)).

31. You may act, or continue to act, despite the prohibition in 4.03 if the confidential information can be protected through the use of appropriate safeguards in the circumstances set out in 4.04 and 4.05, and as more fully explained in the following guidance notes.

Acting with appropriate safeguards (information barriers) – 4.04 and 4.05

32. 4.03 sets the basic standard that you should not normally act on a matter where material confidential information is held elsewhere in the firm and where the matter would be adverse to the interests of the client/former client to which the duty of confidentiality is owed.   To act in these circumstances might increase the risk that the confidential information could be put at risk. The firm can act if the confidential information is not material to the instructions. For guidance on the meaning of "material" see paragraph 25 above.

33. 4.04 and 4.05 set out two situations where you can act even when material confidential information is held by another member of the firm. Both recognise for the first time that it can be acceptable to use information barriers. The first situation is where the party to whom the duty of confidentiality is owed consents. The second situation is where you are already acting and consent has not been given or cannot be sought.

34. Where the client consents as envisaged by 4.04 there is scope for more flexibility in the arrangements for the information barrier as the safeguards can be discussed with, and agreed by, the client. It is important, nonetheless, that the safeguards are effective to avoid a real risk of disclosure. A firm will be liable if confidential information does leak in breach of that agreement.

35. 4.04 requires "informed consent" and one of the difficulties with seeking such consent of the client is that it is often not possible to disclose sufficient information about the identity and business of the other client without risk of breaching that other client's confidentiality. You will have to decide in each case whether you are able to provide sufficient information for the client to be able to give "informed consent". Every situation will be different but generally it will be only sophisticated clients, for example, a corporate body with in-house legal advisers or other appropriate expertise, who will have the expertise and ability to weigh up the issues and the risks of giving consent on the basis of the information they have been given. If there is a risk of prejudicing the position of either client then consent should not be sought and you and your firm should not act. It would be inappropriate to seek consent through standard terms of engagement. It may, however, be possible to give sufficient information to obtain informed consent even if the identity of the other client(s) and the nature of their particular interest(s) are not disclosed.

36. Where the client does not consent or does not know about the arrangements, an extremely high standard in relation to the protection of confidential information must be satisfied. In this situation, as has been demonstrated in recent case law, the client can have the firm removed from acting with all the

attendant disruption for the other client, if there is shown to be a real risk of confidential information being leaked.

37. Where your firm holds material confidential information you may not without consent take on new instructions adverse to the interests of the client or former client to whom the duty of confidentiality is owed (4.04). However, where you are already acting and discover that your firm has - or comes to possess - such information, you may continue to act on that matter, or a related matter, in circumstances where the party to whom the duty of confidentiality is owed refuses consent or cannot be asked (4.05). This may be because it cannot be contacted or because making the request would itself breach confidentiality. You should always seek consent when you can reasonably do so.

38. Where under 4.04 your firm has erected an information barrier without the consent of the party to whom the duty of confidentiality is owed, the firm should try to inform that party as soon as circumstances permit, and outline the steps which have been taken to ensure confidentiality is preserved. If some material points (such as the name of the client to whose matter the confidential information might be relevant, or the nature of that matter) still cannot be divulged for reasons of confidentiality and it is reasonably supposed that that party would be more concerned at news of your retention than if fuller details could be given, it might be appropriate to continue to wait before informing that party. There may be circumstances, however, where it is impossible to inform that party.

39. Where two or more firms amalgamate, or one firm takes over another, the new firm needs to ensure that this does not result in any breach of confidentiality. If the firm holds confidential information, which is material to a matter being handled for another client, the firm must be able to ensure that the confidential information is protected by ceasing to act for both clients, or ceasing to act for the client to whom the information is relevant, or by setting up adequate safeguards in accordance with either 4.04 or 4.05.

40. Confidential information may also be put at risk when partners or staff leave one firm and join another. This might happen where, for example, an individual joins a firm which is acting against one of the individual's former clients. An individual joining a new firm could not act personally for a client of the new firm where to do so would put at risk confidential information which the he or she personally possesses about a client of the previous firm. In addition, the individual and the firm which the individual is joining must ensure that adequate safeguards are put in place in accordance with 4.04 or 4.05 to ensure that confidential information held by that individual is safeguarded.

Safeguards for information barriers

41. Rigid safeguards for information barriers have not been enshrined in the rules. Where 4.04 applies (i.e. consent has been given), it is for the firm to agree the appropriate safeguards, but it would normally be necessary to satisfy guidance note 44 (a) to (f) below. Some of (g) to (n) may also be applicable. Where 4.05 applies, the firm must satisfy the requirements of common law and at least most, if not all, of note 44 (a) to (n) might be essential.

42. If, at any stage after an information barrier has been established, it becomes impossible to comply with any of the terms, the firm may have to cease to act. The possibility of this happening should always be discussed when instructions

are accepted so that the client is aware of this risk, or addressed with reasonable prominence in standard terms of engagement.

43.   Firms will always need to consider whether it is appropriate in any case for an information barrier to be used, and also whether the size or structure of a firm means that it could not in any circumstances be appropriate. It is unlikely that, for example, safeguards could ever be considered adequate where:

(a)   a firm has only one principal and no other qualified staff;

(b)   the solicitor possessing, or likely to possess, the confidential information is supervised by a solicitor who acts for, or supervises another solicitor in the firm who acts for a client to whom the information is or may be relevant; or

(c)   the physical structure or layout of the firm is such that confidentiality would be difficult to preserve having regard to other safeguards which are in place.

44.   The following (a) to (f) would normally be appropriate to demonstrate the adequacy of an information barrier when you are proposing to act in circumstances set out in 4.04. It might also be appropriate to agree some or all of (a) to (f) where you are acting with consent in accordance with 4.05:

(a)   that the client who or which might be interested in the confidential information acknowledges in writing that the information held by the firm will not be given to them;

(b)   that all members of the firm who hold the relevant confidential information ("the restricted group") are identified and have no involvement with or for the other client;

(c)   that no member of the restricted group is managed or supervised in relation to that matter by someone from outside the restricted group;

(d)   that all members of the restricted group confirm at the start of the engagement that they understand that they possess or might come to possess information which is confidential, and that they must not discuss it with any other member of the firm unless that person is, or becomes a member of the restricted group, and that this obligation shall be regarded by everyone as an on-going one;

(e)   that each member of the restricted group confirms when the barrier is established that they have not done anything which would amount to a breach of the information barrier; and

(f)   that only members of the restricted group have access to documents containing the confidential information.

The following arrangements may also be appropriate, and might in particular be necessary where acting in circumstances set out in 4.05:

(g)   that the restricted group is physically separated from those acting for the other client, for example, by being in a separate building, on a separate floor or in a segregated part of the offices, and that some form of "access restriction" be put in place to ensure physical segregation;

(h)   that confidential information on computer systems is protected by use of separate computer networks or through use of password protection or similar means;

(i)   that the firm issues a statement that it will treat any breach, even an inadvertent one, of the information barrier as a serious disciplinary offence;

(j)   that each member of the restricted group gives a written statement at the start of the engagement that they understand the terms of the information barrier and will comply with them;

(k)   that the firm undertakes that it will do nothing which would or might prevent or hinder any member of the restricted group from complying with the information barrier;

(l)   that the firm identifies a specific partner or other appropriate person within the restricted group with overall responsibility for the information barrier;

(m)   that the firm provides formal and regular training for members of the firm on duties of confidentiality and responsibility under information barriers or will ensure that such training is provided prior to the work being undertaken; and

(n)   that the firm implements a system for the opening of post, receipt of faxes and distribution of email which will ensure that confidential information is not disclosed to anyone outside the restricted group.

"Member", in the context of this guidance note, applies to principals and all staff members including secretaries, but does not apply to any staff member (not having any involvement on behalf of any relevant client) whose duties include the maintenance of computer systems or conflict/compliance procedures and who is subject to a general obligation of confidentiality in relation to all information to which he or she may have access in the course of his or her duties.

This guidance should not be read as a representation that compliance with (a) to (n) above will necessarily be considered sufficient at common law.

45.   Where a firm proposes to erect an information barrier (whether under 4.04 or 4.05) it must first inform the client for whom it acts - or wishes to act - on the matter to which the confidential information might be material. The firm should not act - or continue to act - without that client's consent, with that client understanding that the firm holds information which might be material and which will not be communicated to it; see 4.04(1)(a) and 4.05(b). Although the rule does not require consent to be in writing, it is recommended that this be obtained for evidential purposes to protect both your client's position and your own position.

Rule 5 – Business management in England and Wales

Introduction

1. Rule 5 deals with the supervision and management of a firm or in-house practice, the maintenance of competence, and the internal business arrangements essential to the proper delivery of services to clients. "Supervision" and "management" refer, respectively, to the professional overseeing of staff and clients' matters; and to the overall direction and development of the firm or in-house practice and its day-to-day administration. The rule does not apply to your overseas practice but you must comply with 15.05.

2. Rule 5 relates to two core duties:

    (a) 1.09 – supervision and management: "You must operate appropriate supervision and management arrangements to meet your duties to clients"; and

    (b) 1.06 – competence: "You must act only when you are able to provide a competent service."

3. Broadly, the rule aims to set out:

    (a) responsibility for the overall supervision and management framework of your firm or in-house practice;

    (b) the minimum requirements to be met in order to be "qualified to supervise";

    (c) the minimum standards applying to supervision of clients' matters; and

    (d) the minimum requirements in relation to those business arrangements considered to be essential to good practice and integral to compliance with supervision and other duties to clients.

Rule 5 – Business management in England and Wales

5.01 Supervision and management responsibilities

(1) If you are a principal in a firm, a director of a recognised body which is a company, or a member of a recognised body which is an LLP, you must make arrangements for the effective management of the firm as whole, and in particular provide for:

    (a) compliance with the duties of a principal, in law and conduct, to exercise appropriate supervision over all staff, and ensure adequate supervision and direction of clients' matters;

    (b) compliance with the Money Laundering Regulations, where applicable;

    (c) compliance with Law Society regulatory obligations;

(d)   the identification of conflicts of interests;

(e)   compliance with the requirements of rule 2 on client care, costs information and complaints handling;

(f)   control of undertakings;

(g)   the safekeeping of documents and assets entrusted to the firm;

(h)   compliance with rule 6 on avoiding discrimination;

(i)   the training of individuals working in the firm to maintain a level of competence appropriate to their work and level of responsibility;

(j)   financial control of budgets, expenditure and cashflow;

(k)   the continuation of the practice of the firm in the event of temporary absences and emergencies, with the minimum interruption to clients' business; and

(l)   the management of risk.

(2)   If you are a solicitor or REL employed as the head of an in-house legal department, you must effect supervision and management arrangements within your department to provide for:

(a)   adequate supervision and direction of those assisting in your in-house practice;

(b)   control of undertakings; and

(c)   identification of conflicts of interests.

5.02 Persons who must be "qualified to supervise"

(1)   The following persons must be "qualified to supervise":

(a)   a sole principal;

(b)   one of the partners of a partnership;

(c)   one of the members of a recognised body which is an LLP;

(d)   one of the directors of a recognised body which is a company;

(e)   one of the solicitors or RELs employed by a law centre; or

(f)   one in-house solicitor or in-house REL in any department where solicitors and/or RELs, as part of that employment:

(i)   do publicly funded work; or

(ii)   exercise or supervise the exercise of any right of audience or right to conduct litigation when advising or acting for members of the public.

(2)   To be "qualified to supervise" under this paragraph a person:

    (a)   must have completed the training specified from time to time by the Law Society for this purpose; and

    (b)   must have been entitled to practise as a lawyer for at least 36 months within the last ten years; and must be able to demonstrate this if asked by the Law Society.

5.03 Supervision of work for clients and members of the public

(1)   If you are a principal in a firm, you must ensure that your firm has in place a system for supervising clients' matters.

(2)   If you are an in-house solicitor or in-house REL and you are required to be "qualified to supervise" under 5.02(1)(e) or (f), you must ensure that your law centre or in-house legal department has in place a system for supervising work undertaken for members of the public.

(3)   The system for supervision under 5.03(1) and (2) must include appropriate and effective procedures under which the quality of work undertaken for clients and members of the public is checked with reasonable regularity by suitably experienced and competent persons within the firm, law centre or in-house legal department.

Guidance to rule 5 – Business management in England and Wales

Geographical scope of the rule

1.   Rule 5 applies only to practice from an office in England and Wales; but if you are a solicitor practising from an office outside England and Wales or an REL practising from an office in Scotland or Northern Ireland, you will need to comply with 15.05 in relation to that practice.

Guidance on 5.01 generally

2.   The term "arrangements" is used broadly in 5.01 to encompass all systems, procedures, processes and methods of organisation put in place to achieve the required outcome. There is no requirement that these take a particular form; the method of delivery is a matter for the firm. Evidence that appropriate arrangements are actually in place and are operating will be required to demonstrate compliance. It is anticipated that most well run firms will already be complying.

3.   Factors to be taken into account in determining the appropriateness of a set of arrangements will include the size and complexity of the firm; the number, experience and qualifications of staff; and the nature of the work undertaken. Arrangements are unlikely to be considered appropriate unless they include a mechanism for periodic review of their effectiveness.

4.　The overarching responsibility for the management of the firm in the broadest sense – including, for example, practice development and business efficiency – rests with the principals, members of a recognised body which is an LLP and directors of a recognised body which is a company.

5.　Firms will be expected to be able to produce evidence of a systematic and effective approach to management, and this may include the implementation by the firm of one or more of the following:

(a)　guidance issued from time to time by the Law Society on the supervision and execution of particular types of work, including guidance on solicitors' responsibilities for the supervision of clerks exercising rights of audience under section 27(2)(e) of the Courts and Legal Services Act 1990;

(b)　the firm's own properly documented standards and procedures;

(c)　practice management standards promoted from time to time by the Law Society;

(d)　accounting standards and procedures promoted from time to time by the Law Society;

(e)　external quality standards such as BS EN ISO 9000, Investors in People, or quality standards required by the Legal Services Commission in connection with undertaking publicly funded work, or the LEXCEL standard; and

(f)　in the case of an in-house solicitor or in-house REL employed by a law centre, charitable or similar non-commercial advice service, management standards or procedures laid down by its management committee, the Law Centres Federation or equivalent 'umbrella' organisation.

6.　The day-to-day management of a firm can be delegated to an employee who is suitably experienced and competent, and a fit and proper person to perform the role. Firms must be able to demonstrate this if required.

7.　Sections 41 – 44 of the Solicitors Act 1974 impose restrictions on the employment or remuneration of certain persons by a solicitor or REL.

(a)　Under section 41, permission must be obtained from the Law Society by a solicitor or REL if he or she wishes to employ or remunerate any struck-off or suspended solicitor or REL. You can check with the Law Society whether a solicitor has been struck off or suspended.

(b)　Under section 43, the Solicitors Disciplinary Tribunal can order that a former employee of a solicitor or REL may not be employed in future by any solicitor or REL without permission from the Law Society. You can check with the Law Society whether such an order exists.

Compliance with duties in law and conduct etc – 5.01(1)(a)

8.　Principals are responsible in law and in conduct for their firms, including exercising proper control over their staff. For example, certain work may only be done by unqualified staff under the supervision and/or at the direction of persons who are allowed by law to do that work themselves. (See sections

22(2A) and 23(3) of the Solicitors Act 1974, section 9(4) of the Administration of Justice Act 1985, and section 84(2) of the Immigration and Asylum Act 1999.) Principals must therefore ensure that arrangements are in place to satisfy these statutory requirements, and this would mean that neither conveyancing nor probate work could be supervised by:

(a) an RFL partner in an MNP; or

(b) an REL who is not qualified to do the work under regulation 12 or 13 of the European Communities (Lawyer's Practice) Regulations 2000.

9. In conduct, principals are responsible for the acts and omissions of all staff, admitted and unadmitted alike. The duty to supervise staff covers not only employees but also independent contractors engaged to carry out work on behalf of the firm, e.g. consultants, locums, and outdoor clerks. You cannot avoid responsibility for work carried out by the firm by leaving it entirely to staff, however well qualified.

10. Responsibility for the overall supervision framework rests with principals, members of a recognised body which is an LLP, and directors of a recognised body which is a company. This includes, for example, matching staff expertise with relevant work so that work is supervised by the most appropriate individuals. More detailed requirements for the day to day supervision of work for clients and members of the public are set out in 5.03.

11. Operationally, supervision can be delegated within an established framework of reporting and accountability. However, careful consideration should be given to the issues set out below.

12. If a firm has more than one office, its principals, directors or members must be able to demonstrate the adequacy of their arrangements throughout the firm. This includes supervision and management of staff not working from a conventional office – for example, homeworkers, teleworkers, those visiting clients, attending court, at a police station, at a consulting room open only for a few hours a week, or staffing a stand at an exhibition.

13. As a general guide, the lower the ratio of principals to offices and staff, the greater will be the onus on principals to demonstrate the adequacy of their supervision arrangements. For example, the more staff a sole principal employs, the higher the degree of personal involvement the sole principal may be expected to take in the supervision process, especially if those staff are inexperienced and/or unqualified.

Money laundering – 5.01(1)(b)

14. See the Money Laundering Regulations 2003 (and any subsequent regulations), and any guidance on compliance issued by the Law Society, including guidance on firms' internal anti-money laundering systems.

Compliance with Law Society regulatory obligations – 5.01(1)(c)

15. The purpose of 5.01(1)(c) is to foster collective responsibility for the governance of the firm by requiring you to establish arrangements which provide for compliance with key regulatory obligations. These include arrangements to ensure that:

    (a) every solicitor in the firm holds a practising certificate, and that the practising certificate is renewed promptly when required;

    (b) every lawyer in the firm who is required to be registered in the UK under the Establishment Directive and is not registered with another UK regulatory body for lawyers, is registered as an REL and that registration is renewed promptly when required;

    (c) every lawyer in the firm who is required under these rules to be an RFL (as a partner, member or director of the firm) is registered as an RFL and that the registration is renewed promptly when required;

    (d) if the firm is a body corporate (or owns a body corporate which is required under these rules to be a recognised body), the body corporate has obtained recognition as a recognised body, its recognition is renewed promptly every three years when required, and it complies with the requirements of rule 14 (incorporated practice);

    (e) the firm complies with the Solicitors' Indemnity Insurance Rules;

    (f) an accountant's report is delivered in accordance with the Solicitors' Accounts Rules; and

    (g) the firm notifies the Law Society of any change in the place or places of business of the solicitors, RELs and RFLs in the firm (a solicitor has a legal obligation to do this, under section 84 of the Solicitors Act 1974).

16. Some of these obligations mirror personal obligations of each solicitor, REL, RFL or recognised body (such as to renew a practising certificate or renew registration). The fact that 5.01(1)(c) is aimed at principals, members and directors will not relieve an individual solicitor, REL, RFL, or recognised body, of responsibility in this regard. The precise nature of the arrangements required are for the firm to decide. See 20.01.

17. If you are a partner in a partnership, a member of a recognised body which is an LLP, or a director of a recognised body which is a company, you are personally responsible for complying with the rules relating to solicitors' accounts and the delivery of an annual accountant's report. You will be liable to disciplinary action if there is a failure to comply with those rules, even if you have delegated book-keeping to someone else in the firm. The nature of the disciplinary action will depend on the seriousness of the breach and the extent to which you knew or should have known of the breach.

18. If you are an in-house solicitor or in-house REL and you receive or hold clients' money you must comply with the Solicitors' Accounts Rules and must submit an accountant's report.

Identification of conflicts – 5.01(1)(d)

19.   Firms must adopt a systematic approach to identifying and avoiding conflicts of interests, dealing with conflicts between the duties of confidentiality and disclosure, and maintaining client confidentiality. See also the guidance to rule 3 (conflict of interests) and to rule 4 (confidentiality and disclosure) for assistance in identifying the sort of issues your arrangements will need to address.

Compliance with the requirements of rule 2 on client care, costs information and complaints handling – 5.01(1)(e)

20.   This provision is designed to ensure that compliance with 2.02, 2.03 and 2.05 is addressed at the level of the firm's systems and procedures. If you have appropriate arrangements for compliance but a member of staff fails to follow established procedures in a one-off case, you will nevertheless have satisfied 5.01(1)(e). However, a serious breach or repeated 'minor' breaches of 2.02, 2.03 or 2.05 might indicate a failure to put in place effective arrangements, as required under 5.01(1)(e).

Control of undertakings – 5.01(1)(f)

21.   See 10.05 and the guidance to it for assistance in identifying the sort of issues your arrangements will need to address.

Safekeeping of documents and assets – 5.01(1)(g)

22.   The terms "documents" and "assets" should be interpreted in a non-technical way to include, for example, client money, wills, deeds, investments and other property entrusted to the firm by clients and others.

23.   The detail of the firm's arrangements will be a matter for you to decide in all the circumstances if you are a principal (or if your firm is a recognised body, if you are a company director or LLP member). However, as a minimum requirement you must be able to identify to whom documents and assets belong, and in connection with which matter.

Avoiding discrimination – 5.01(1)(h)

24.   For guidance on avoiding discrimination, see the guidance to rule 6 (avoiding discrimination).

The training of individuals working in the firm to maintain a level of competence appropriate to their work and level of responsibility – 5.01(1)(i)

25.   "Competence" is the ability to perform a task or role to a required standard by the application of essential knowledge, skill and understanding. The purpose of 5.01(1)(i) is to ensure that the competence of everyone in the firm involved in the provision of legal services is addressed systematically, at management level. Consequently, 5.01(1)(i) focuses on effecting arrangements to "provide for" competence levels to be maintained, and leaves it to the firm to determine the best method of doing this. It is anticipated that most firms will already have such arrangements in place.

26.   The nature of the arrangements will vary significantly depending on the work and level of responsibility of each individual. However, if a breach of 5.01(1)(i) is alleged, evidence may be required to demonstrate that issues of competence are addressed in the firm's procedures in relation to for example, recruitment, ongoing work assessment, and training.

27.   Training is an integral element of maintaining competence. 5.01(1)(i) assumes that arrangements will include provision for training, but does not lay down any specific requirements. Training can be of any kind relevant to the work or responsibilities of the individual, and can be delivered by any appropriate method. For example, it could include on-the-job learning, mentoring schemes, in-house training, individual study, etc. It need not be accredited under the compulsory continuing professional development scheme (CPD) or involve attendance at courses.

28.   5.01(1)(i) does not relieve an individual of the duty to decline to act when unable to provide a competent service, or allow an individual to escape obligations under the CPD scheme.

29.   5.01(1)(i) is limited to effecting suitable arrangements. Therefore, an isolated case of incompetence would not normally indicate a breach. However, if you do not address issues of competence systematically, at management level, in your firm's arrangements for recruitment, ongoing work assessment and training, you would breach 5.01(1)(i).

30.   It should be noted that training for the purpose of becoming "qualified to supervise" under 5.02 must be of a kind specified by the Law Society from time to time (see note 44).

Financial control of budgets, expenditure and cashflow – 5.01(1)(j)

31.   Clients' money is more likely to be at risk in a firm whose principals do not exercise adequate oversight of the firms' own financial arrangements. The purpose of 5.01(1)(j) is to ensure this is addressed in the overall management framework — not to prescribe particular financial systems or to prevent principals from delegating day-to-day financial operations to suitable staff. It may also help firms to ensure that they are looking forward when undertaking their financial management, so that they will know they will be able to cover their commitments and plan their resources properly. It should be noted, however, that some accounting and management information systems do not assist in this regard, as they tend to deal only with historic information.

Continuation of the practice of the firm in the event of temporary absences and emergencies etc – 5.01(1)(k)

32.   There is a continuing duty to ensure that the practice of your firm will be carried on with the minimum interruption to clients' business even if you are absent. Your supervision and management arrangements must therefore provide for the running of the firm during any period of absence (for example, holiday or sick leave), particularly if you are a sole principal, sole director or sole member. The arrangements must ensure that any duties to clients and others can be fully met.

33.   If you are away for a month or more, and you are the only person in the firm "qualified to supervise" under 5.02, the arrangements for complying with

5.01(1)(k) will normally need to include the provision of another person qualified to supervise.

34. Rule 23 of the Solicitors' Accounts Rules 1998 requires that a withdrawal from a client account cannot be made without a specific authority. This rule cannot be complied with if a principal, director or member leaves blank cheques for completion by staff at a later date, as signing a blank cheque is not giving a specific authority.

35. If you have not made adequate arrangements in advance to meet unforeseen circumstances, difficulties may arise in the conduct of clients' affairs and in the administration of your own business. For example, an accountant's report must be submitted, a practising certificate must be applied for, and indemnity cover must be obtained notwithstanding your absence. Consequently, if you are a sole principal or the sole member of a recognised body which is an LLP, or sole director of a recognised body which is a company, you should have an arrangement with another solicitor or REL (sufficiently experienced and entitled to practise) to supervise your firm until you return. You should notify your bank of these arrangements in advance, so that the solicitor or REL covering your absence can operate your client and office accounts.

36. If you are a sole principal and your absence lasts beyond the period covered by your practising certificate, you may be able to obtain permission, through the Law Society, for another solicitor to complete the application for a practising certificate. Your name can only remain on your professional stationery as principal if you continue to hold a practising certificate.

37. If you are a sole principal and you are struck off or suspended, any solicitor or REL with whom you have an arrangement to look after your firm in your absence will be left with full responsibility for the firm, as principal (but see the guidance to rule 12 for restrictions on the work an REL can do or supervise). They must inform clients of the firm, your bank, insurers, and the Law Society. Note that this will not apply if you are the sole director and owner of a recognised body because the recognised body would have become liable to revocation of its recognition – see rule 14 and the guidance to it.

38. If you are a sole principal and you decide to stop practising, you must inform clients of the fact so that they may instruct another firm. Failure to inform clients could amount not only to negligence but also to misconduct. If you are considering retirement, guidance can be obtained from the Law Society's Professional Ethics department .

Management of risk – 5.01(1)(l)

39. Firms should have arrangements in place for assessing the risks attaching to each area of their operation. The rule is aimed at ensuring risk is addressed in the firm's overall management framework. If a particular risk materialises which had not been foreseen in the firm's systems, this would not necessarily constitute a breach of 5.01(1)(l). Risk management arrangements are unlikely to be considered adequate unless they include periodic reviews of the firm's risk profile.

40. Ideally the scope of the arrangements should not be confined to risks arising from professional negligence, but should extend to client-related and business–related risks of all sorts. A non-exhaustive list might include

complaints (including a complaints log); client-related credit risks and exposure; claims under legislation relating to such matters as data protection; IT failures and abuses; and damage to offices.

In-house practice – 5.01(2)

41.   As the head of an in-house legal department you do not have to institute all the arrangements required under 5.01(1). However, you must under 5.01(2) institute arrangements to ensure that:

(a)   work done for members of the public is adequately supervised, and if unqualified staff within the department undertake work reserved to solicitors, they are supervised by a person qualified to do that work, and the work is done in the name of that qualified person;

(b)   undertakings given by members of the department, whether or not they are solicitors or RELs, are given appropriately and can be fulfilled (you will be primarily responsible in conduct for fulfilling such undertakings); and

(c)   conflicts of interests are identified.

Qualified to supervise – 5.02

42.   The purpose of 5.02 is to protect the public by ensuring that there is at least one person responsible for running the firm (or law centre or in-house legal practice falling within 5.02(1)(e) or (f)) who has the right kind of experience. The responsibilities involved relate to the management of the firm rather than the supervision of particular work, so the person "qualified to supervise" under 5.02 does not have to be personally entitled by law to supervise all work undertaken by the firm. However, an important part of that person's responsibilities would be to ensure that unqualified persons did not undertake reserved work except under the supervision of a suitably qualified person - see note 8 above.

43.   Waivers may be granted in individual cases. An applicant must satisfy the Council of the Law Society that his or her circumstances are sufficiently exceptional to justify a departure from the requirements of 5.02, bearing in mind its purpose. Applications should be made to the Waivers Executive in the Law Society's Professional Ethics department.

44.   The training presently specified by the Law Society is attendance at or participation in any course(s) or programme(s) of learning on management skills, for a minimum of 12 hours. The courses or programmes do not have to be accredited with CPD hours in order to satisfy the requirement. It is not normally necessary to check with the Law Society before undertaking a course or programme unless the course is unusual and outside the mainstream of management training. Advice may be sought from the Law Society's Professional Ethics department.

Supervision of work for clients and members of the public – 5.03

45.   5.03 is mainly aimed at principals in firms. However, it also applies to you if you are an in-house solicitor or in-house REL who acts for members of the

public and fulfils the role of the person "qualified to supervise" under 5.02(1)(e) or (f).

46. A suitably experienced and competent person must undertake the supervision required by 5.03. This person need not hold a particular qualification or have been in legal practice for a particular time; but in certain circumstances (for example, where a sole principal has more than one office) these may be relevant factors in determining compliance with 5.03.

47. In supervising staff you would need to have sufficient legal knowledge and experience to be able to identify problems with the quality or conduct of the work; but you might not need to be an expert in the area of work you are supervising. The training and experience of the member of staff you are supervising will be relevant.

48. 5.03 requires that work for clients and members of the public is supervised wherever staff happen to be working, including at home or from 'virtual' offices.

49. Supervision is an inherently internal function. The phrase "within the firm, law centre or in-house legal department" is included to ensure that supervision is not delegated outside your control but undertaken by someone who is genuinely part of the practice.

50. If a complaint is made, you will have to demonstrate that the work-checking procedures are "appropriate", "effective", and undertaken with "reasonable regularity". Relevant factors will include the size and complexity of the firm, law centre or in-house department; the nature of the work; the experience of the individuals undertaking the work, and their level of responsibility.

51. 5.03 does not apply to the business development and practice management work of principals, directors or members.

52. Supervising "work for clients and members of the public" embraces all aspects of the work, including the handling of client money and compliance with rule 2 (client relations).

53. For guidance on the supervision of immigration work, see The Law Society's Gazette, 99/40, 17 October 2002.

Rule 6 – Avoiding discrimination

Introduction

Rule 6 is designed to help you to avoid incidents of discrimination within your firm or in-house practice and to assist you in maximising your firm's potential by operating a policy of equality and diversity. The rule does not apply to your overseas practice but you must comply with 1.07 (fairness).

Rule 6 – Avoiding discrimination

6.01 Duty not to discriminate

(1) You must comply with all anti-discrimination legislation from time to time in force.

(2) You must, at all times, in your professional dealings with staff, partners, barristers, other lawyers, clients or third parties:

    (a) not discriminate against any person, directly or indirectly, nor victimise or harass them on the grounds of their:

        (i) sex (including their marital status);

        (ii) race or racial group;

        (iii) ethnic or national origins;

        (iv) colour;

        (v) nationality;

        (vi) religion or belief; or

        (vii) sexual orientation; or

    (b) not discriminate against any person on grounds of disability except where, in relation to legislation, there is a specific exception or limitation preventing such discrimination from being unlawful.

6.02 Burden of proof

Where there has been a finding by an employment tribunal, or a county court or (in Scotland) Sheriff Court or other relevant court or tribunal that you have committed, or are to be treated as having committed, an unlawful act of discrimination (including victimisation or harassment) then, where you are a party to the action in question, that finding shall be treated as prima facie evidence of the fact that you have committed an act of discrimination (including victimisation or harassment) in breach of this rule.

6.03 Equality and diversity policy

(1)   If you are a principal in a firm, you must adopt and implement an appropriate policy for avoiding discrimination and promoting equality and diversity within your firm.

(2)   To be appropriate the policy adopted must include, as a minimum, all of the provisions which appear in the Law Society model policy and any additional provisions should not conflict with those provisions.

(3)   If you have not adopted and implemented your own policy dealing with avoiding discrimination and promoting equality and diversity you will in any event be bound by the provisions of the Law Society model policy in effect at that time.

6.04 In-house practice

If you have management responsibilities in in-house practice you must use all reasonable endeavours to secure the operation of a policy for dealing with the avoidance of discrimination and the promotion of equality and diversity within your department.

6.05 Applicable anti-discrimination legislation

"Anti-discrimination legislation" means such legislation as is in force at the relevant time, including any amendments, and includes:

(a)   the Equal Pay Act 1970;

(b)   the Sex Discrimination Act 1975;

(c)   the Race Relations Act 1976;

(d)   the Disability Discrimination Act 1995;

(e)   the Employment Rights Act 1996;

(f)   the Employment Equality (Sexual Orientation) Regulations 2003;

(g)   the Employment Equality (Religion or Belief) Regulations 2003; and

(h)   any further anti-discrimination legislation as may from time to time be enacted and brought into force in England and Wales.

6.06 Waivers

Notwithstanding rule 22 of these rules, the Council of the Law Society shall not have power to waive any of the provisions of this rule.

Guidance to rule 6 – Avoiding discrimination

General

Duty not to discriminate – 6.01

1. You and your staff should treat all persons with equal dignity, respect and fairness and with the same attention, courtesy and consideration.

The scope of the rule

2. This rule places two distinct requirements upon you:

    (a) to comply with all current anti-discrimination legislation (6.01(1)); and

    (b) not to discriminate in your professional dealings with the persons or groups listed, and in the circumstances set out, in this rule (6.01(2)).

    You should note that these two requirements are not identical and in many circumstances the scope of the latter is wider than that of the former.

3. The legislation which you must comply with is set out in 6.05 and specifically includes such future anti-discrimination legislation as may be enacted during the currency of this rule. You should familiarise yourself with the requirements of these provisions and operate your practice in accordance with them.

4. This rule, as with previous rules, goes beyond the scope of the legislation in a number of key areas. In particular, it extends the ambit of prohibited discrimination beyond employment and vocational and requires that you refrain from discrimination in all your professional dealings with partners, staff, clients and other third parties. In addition the rule covers discrimination in relation to training about sexual orientation and religion or belief. For example, whilst it may not be unlawful for you to discriminate against a client or third party on grounds of sexual orientation or religion and belief, it will be regarded as professional misconduct for you to do so.

5. The following points should be noted in relation to this rule:

    (a) It does not currently apply to discrimination on the ground of age. An amendment incorporating age will, however, be considered as soon as the government produces clear guidance on the legal provisions which will apply to this.

    (b) It does not address, but you should nevertheless be aware of, discrimination-related employment issues such as those which relate to fixed-term and part-time workers, the requirements of flexible working, and provisions relating to participation in or abstention from trade union activities.

    (c) Although the rule does not address issues set out in the Human Rights Act 1998 you should be aware of these, especially if you are working in the public sector.

(d)   The terms "employer" and "employment" which are used in this guidance and in the model policy which follows are used in their normal everyday sense and not as defined in rule 24 (interpretation).

What is discrimination?

6.   Discrimination occurs when, on one of the prohibited grounds, one person is treated less favourably than another would be treated in the same or similar circumstances and that treatment cannot be justified. The grounds upon which a person must not be discriminated against are sex (including their marital status); race or racial group; ethnic or national origins; colour; nationality; religion or belief; sexual orientation; or disability.

7.   For the purposes of interpreting the provisions of this rule, sex discrimination includes discrimination against a person who is about to undergo, is undergoing or has undergone gender reassignment. You should also note the provisions of the Equal Pay Act 1970.

8.   Discrimination can take a variety of forms including direct discrimination, indirect discrimination, harassment and victimisation. These terms are clarified below.

9.   For the purposes of this rule:

(a)   **Direct discrimination** occurs where one person treats another less favourably:

(i)   by reason of their sex (including their marital status and reasons relating to gender reassignment); race or racial group; ethnic or national origins; colour; nationality; religion or belief; or sexual orientation; or

(ii)   unjustifiably, by reason of their disability.

To treat a person less favourably for other reasons, for example because they have not performed adequately, will not generally be regarded as discrimination which amounts to professional misconduct unless it is given as a reason in order to conceal the fact that the true reason is one of the matters referred to above.

(b)   **Indirect discrimination** occurs where a provision, criterion or practice (or requirement or condition) which is applied to everyone, has the effect of placing at a disadvantage a particular person or group of people by reason of sex (including their marital status and reasons relating to gender reassignment); race or racial group; ethnic or national origins; colour; nationality; religion or belief; or sexual orientation; and it cannot be shown that to apply that provision, criterion or practice in that way is a proportionate means for achieving a legitimate aim.   Note that the provisions relating to indirect discrimination are not applicable to discrimination on the grounds of disability.

Indirect discrimination can occur whether or not the person applying the provision, criterion or practice intended to discriminate against the person or group of people affected.

(c) **Harassment** occurs when one person subjects another to threatening, abusive or insulting behaviour, words or actions which violate the other person's dignity or create a humiliating, intimidating or hostile environment. Harassment may involve physical acts or verbal and non-verbal communications and gestures. The intention of the person responsible for the harassment is not relevant – it is the effect which the harassment has upon the victim.

(d) **Victimisation** occurs when a person is treated less favourably than others are or would be treated in the same or similar circumstances because they have asserted a right, or assisted another to assert a right, not to be discriminated against on one of the grounds of sex (including their marital status and reasons relating to gender reassignment), race or racial group; ethnic or national origins; colour; nationality; religion or belief; sexual orientation; or disability; or have given evidence in a tribunal or court relating to the assertion of such a right.

(e) Failure to make reasonable adjustment applies to discrimination on the grounds of disability. You are under a duty to take such steps (adjustments) as are reasonable in all the circumstances so as to ensure that employment arrangements, arrangements for clients and the premises from which your business is undertaken and the service provided, does not put a disabled person at a disadvantage compared with a non-disabled person, without justification.

Permitted exceptions

10. There are a limited number of situations in which it is permitted to discriminate where otherwise it would amount to a breach of the legislation. In some of the legislation these situations are variously called (depending upon the legislation) Genuine Occupational Qualifications (GOQs) and Genuine Occupational Requirements (GORs). These terms do not apply, however, to the Disability Discrimination Act 1995 where a different concept – that of whether an act or omission is justifiable – applies.

11. Under section 7 of the Sex Discrimination Act 1975 (as amended) a job can be restricted to one sex provided that the sex of the worker is a genuine occupational qualification – i.e. where the essential nature of the job, or the duties which attach to it, require a person of a particular sex. A GOQ is interpreted in narrow terms and includes jobs where the work involves privacy, decency, personal welfare or educational services and the burden of proof is upon the employer to show that the GOQ applies to the job in question. An employer can refuse to employ someone who is planning to undergo, undergoing or has undergone a gender reassignment if being a man or a woman is a GOQ and the refusal is reasonable in the circumstances.

12. Sections 4A and 5 of the Race Relations Act 1976 (as amended) contain the provisions for a GOR and GOQ respectively. Section 4A provides that in relation to discrimination based on race or ethnic or national origins, any job may be restricted to those of a particular racial group, ethnic or national origin provided that their origin is a genuine occupational requirement for the job. For example, the holder of the job provides persons of that racial group with personal services promoting their welfare, and those services can most effectively be provided by a person of that racial group. It must be shown that the benefits of employing a particular person outweigh the disadvantages and

the duty to prove this is upon the employer. Section 5 deals with the situation where being of a particular racial group is important for purposes of authenticity in a dramatic performance, a visual image or for work in a restaurant or similar establishment where being of a particular racial group lends authenticity.

13. Regulation 7 of the Employment Equality (Sexual Orientation) Regulations 2003 allows for an employer to discriminate against someone of a particular sexual orientation where their orientation is "a genuine and determining occupational requirement" and "it is proportionate to apply that requirement in the particular case". This will be interpreted very narrowly, for example in circumstances where it is necessary to comply with the doctrines of a particular religion, and it is unlikely that this will apply to a solicitors' practice except in unusual circumstances where, for example, it is a genuine requirement of the job that a person work in a country where being a homosexual or lesbian is against the law.

14. Similarly, regulation 7 of the Employment Equality (Religion or Belief) Regulations 2003 provides for a genuine occupational requirement exemption where "being of a particular religion or belief is a genuine and determining occupational requirement" and is proportionate to the requirement of the case. Again it will be interpreted in a narrow way and will generally only apply where the employer has an ethos based on religion or belief and the nature of the employment warrants it being applied. As with sexual orientation, it is very unlikely that this exemption will be held to apply to the work of a solicitors' practice.

15. With regard to disability, the exceptions which apply are in a different form from those to be found in other areas of the law. Discrimination is permitted if an employer or service provider can show that the less favourable treatment or the failure to make reasonable provision is justified in all of the circumstances. The Disability Discrimination Act 1995 (as amended) sets out what will be regarded as reasonable.

Dealing with clients and third parties

16. You are generally free to decide whether to accept instructions from any particular client. However, any refusal to act must not be based upon any of the grounds in 6.01(2). You should also note 11.04 which limits the circumstances where you can refuse to act as an advocate and 2.01 which deals with taking on clients.

17. You should instruct barristers on the basis of their skill, experience and ability and should not instruct, or avoid instructing, them on any of the grounds in 6.01(2), nor should you request or encourage barristers' clerks to do so.

18. Whilst you should normally comply with a client's request to instruct a named barrister (subject to your duty to discuss the suitability of that barrister for a particular type of work), where a client's instructions as to the choice of barrister are based on any of the grounds in 6.01(2), you should encourage the client to modify their instructions and in the event that they refuse to do so, you should cease to act.

19. In relation to the instruction of a barrister, in addition to the requirements of this rule, you are subject to the provisions of section 26A(3) of the Race Relations Act 1976, section 35A(3) of the Sex Discrimination Act 1975, section 7A(3) of

the Disability Discrimination Act 1995, section 12(4) of the Employment Equality (Religion or Belief) Regulations 2003 and section 12(4) of the Employment Equality (Sexual Orientation) Regulations 2003 (provisions regarding discrimination against a barrister in relation to the giving, withholding or acceptance of instructions).

20. If you maintain lists or databases of contractors, agents and other third parties who are regarded as suitable to be instructed by others within the firm, you should ensure that those lists or databases are compiled on the basis only of the ability of those persons to undertake work of a particular type and ensure that those lists do not contain any discriminatory bias based on any of the grounds in 6.01(2).

Partners and partnerships

21. In relation to a position as partner in a firm, you should not discriminate against partners or potential partners and in this regard you are subject to the provisions of section 10 of the Race Relations Act 1976, section 11 of the Sex Discrimination Act 1975 as amended by section 1(3) of the Sex Discrimination Act 1986, sections 6A, 6B and 6C of the Disability Discrimination Act 1995, section 14 of the Employment Equality (Religion or Belief) Regulations 2003 and section 14 of the Employment Equality (Sexual Orientation) Regulations 2003 (provisions regarding discrimination in relation to a position as partner).

22. In addition, you should also comply with the various provisions which prohibit discrimination after the end of a relationship and which apply to both staff and partners. This means, for example, that you should exercise care when giving a reference for someone so as to ensure that you do not permit that reference to be in any way discriminatory or to appear to have been influenced by issues of a discriminatory nature.

Burden of proof – 6.02

23. Findings of unlawful discrimination by an employment tribunal have not previously been regarded as binding on either the Law Society or the Solicitors Disciplinary Tribunal, although they have been admissible in evidence. The provisions of 6.02 amend this position and place the burden of proof upon you in those cases where there has been such a finding. Whilst the Law Society must still determine whether an allegation or finding of discrimination against you amounts to professional misconduct, the starting point will be that such misconduct has taken place and it is for you to show why, despite the finding, there has not been misconduct.

Equality and diversity policy – 6.03

24. In order to encourage you to abide by the provisions of this rule and to assist you in ensuring that your partners and staff do so too, it is a requirement that your firm has an appropriate written policy for promoting equality, avoiding acts of discrimination and for dealing with any instances of discrimination which might arise. The minimum requirements of that policy are set out in the Law Society's Model Anti-Discrimination Policy. You should be aware that:

(a) the circumstances which apply to your firm may require more comprehensive provisions than are set out in the model policy;

    (b)   elements of the model policy may not be relevant to you and your firm; and

    (c)   the precise terms of the model policy may change from time to time and you must ensure that you and your firm comply with the Model Policy which is the most recent.

25.   Adoption of the model policy will not only help ensure compliance with legislation and this rule, but will assist your firm from a business and social perspective. From the business point of view:

    (a)   your firm will have access to a wider pool of talent, assisting it in recruiting in the best interests of the organisation;

    (b)   a diverse workforce will lead to the better provision of services to an increasingly diverse client base;

    (c)   if your firm is seeking publicly funded or public sector work, or work from large corporate clients, it will find itself better placed to satisfy tendering requirements;

    (d)   your firm will enjoy better employee relations whilst at the same time avoiding the costs and adverse publicity which can accompany claims of discrimination; and

    (e)   your firm will benefit from a better image generally, enabling it more easily to attract potential employees and clients.

From the social perspective, any profession which purports to assist others in accessing and asserting their rights must itself embrace values of fairness and equality, thus promoting a better image of the profession as a whole.

26.   Your firm may produce its own policy and need not adopt, verbatim, the Law Society's model policy. However, if it does so then that policy must cover, as a minimum, all of those matters referred to in the model policy and should contain provisions designed to ensure compliance with this rule. To the extent that the provisions of the model policy are not dealt with in your firm's own policy then the relevant provisions of the Law Society's model policy shall apply.

27.   If your firm neither formally adopts the Law Society's model policy nor produces its own policy it will still be subject and bound by the provisions of the model policy to the same extent as if it had formally adopted it and its acts and omissions will be dealt with accordingly.

28.   Whilst your firm will be expected to implement, monitor (where appropriate) and review the operation of its anti-discrimination policy, the extent to which it will be expected to do so will be proportionate, and will be dependant upon factors such as the size of your firm. Thus, whilst a sole principal would be expected to implement and apply an anti-discrimination policy, the duty to monitor and review will necessarily be less complex than for a firm with many partners and other staff.

In-house practice – 6.04

29.   If you are practising in-house then it is likely that you will not have the same opportunity to formulate, adopt and implement measures for avoiding discrimination and promoting equality and diversity, as your counterparts in firms. You should, however, have an opportunity to influence those measures which are implemented, especially within your own department.

30.   This rule requires that if you are practising in-house you must use your best endeavours to operate measures for avoiding discrimination and promoting equality and diversity within your own department wherever possible, without placing upon you the burden of professional misconduct where you are genuinely unable to do so.

31.   In the event of there being an allegation of misconduct based upon discrimination on any of the grounds listed in 6.01(2), then if you have management responsibility you will be required to show good reason why you were unable to secure the operation of an appropriate policy.

Applicable anti-discrimination legislation – 6.05

32.   6.01(1) requires you to observe the provisions of anti-discrimination legislation. 6.05 sets out what that legislation is.

33.   The Equal Pay Act 1970 (as amended) provides that women and men must be paid the same wage when their work is the same or broadly similar or of equal value. It also covers other terms of employment including working hours, holidays, sick pay and pensions.

34.   The Sex Discrimination Act 1975 (as amended) (SDA) makes it unlawful to discriminate in employment (including recruitment, training and promotion), education, housing, and the provision of goods or services (and in advertisements for these) on the grounds of a person's sex or, in employment related matters, on account of their marital status.

35.   Additionally, the SDA now makes it unlawful to discriminate against someone who is about to undergo, is undergoing or has undergone a gender reassignment. The Sex Discrimination (Gender Reassignment) Regulations 1999 define gender reassignment as "a process which is undertaken under medical supervision for the purpose of reassigning a person's sex by changing physiological or other characteristics of sex, and includes any part of such a process".

36.   The Race Relations Act 1976 makes it unlawful to discriminate on the grounds of a person's race, racial group, colour, nationality, ethnic or national origin.

37.   The Disability Discrimination Act 1995 makes it unlawful to discriminate against people with disabilities (other than in certain limited circumstances) or to fail to make reasonable adjustment to accommodate the needs of such a person in the work environment, housing and the delivery of goods, facilities and services.

38.   The Employment Rights Act 1996 part VIII, deals with maternity rights including adoption leave, parental leave, dependant's leave and flexible working.

39. The Employment Equality (Sexual Orientation) Regulations 2003 make it unlawful to discriminate in the work environment against anyone on the grounds of their sexual orientation.

40. The Employment Equality (Religion or Belief) Regulations 2003 make it unlawful to discriminate in the work environment against anyone on the grounds of their religious or other philosophical belief.

Law Society's Model anti-discrimination Policy

(policy issued under 6.03 of this rule)

A.   The firm's commitment

(1)   General commitment

This firm is committed to eliminating discrimination and promoting equality and diversity in its own policies, practices and procedures and in those areas in which it has influence.

This applies to the firm's professional dealings with staff and [partners]/[members]/[directors], other solicitors, barristers, clients and third parties.

The firm intends to treat everyone equally and with the same attention, courtesy and respect regardless of their sex (including their marital status), race or racial group, colour, ethnic or national origins, nationality, religion or belief, or sexual orientation or disability.

(2)   Regulation and legislation

In developing and implementing its anti-discrimination policy, the firm is committed to complying with rule 6 (avoiding discrimination) of the Law Society's Code of Conduct and with all current and any future anti-discrimination legislation and associated codes of practice including, but not limited to, the:

Legislation

(a)   Equal Pay Act 1970;

(b)   Sex Discrimination Act 1975;

(c)   Race Relations Act 1976;

(d)   Disability Discrimination Act 1995;

(e)   Employment Rights Act 1996;

(f)   Employment Equality (Sexual Orientation) Regulations 2003; and

(g)   Employment Equality (Religion or Belief) Regulations 2003; and

Codes of practice

(h)   Commission for Racial Equality code of practice for the elimination of racial discrimination and the promotion of equality of opportunity in employment (1983);

(i)   Equal Opportunities Commission code of practice on sex discrimination; equal opportunities policies, procedures and practices in employment (1985);

(j)   Equal Opportunities Commission code of practice on equal pay (2003);

(k)   Disability Discrimination Act 1995 codes of practice in relation to rights of access to facilities, services and premises in employment; and

(l)   European Community code of practice on the protection of the dignity of men and women at work.

B.   Forms of discrimination

The following are the kinds of discrimination which are against the firm's policy:

(a)   **Direct discrimination** occurs when, on one of the prohibited grounds, one person is treated less favourably than another would be treated in the same or similar circumstances and that treatment cannot be justified. The grounds upon which a person must not be discriminated against are sex (including their marital status); race or racial group; ethnic or national origins; colour; nationality; religion or belief; sexual orientation; or disability.

(b)   **Indirect discrimination**, where a requirement or condition, which cannot be justified, is applied equally to all groups but has a disproportionately adverse effect on one particular group.

(c)   **Harassment**, where a person behaves or acts in a way which violates another person's dignity, creates a humiliating, intimidating or hostile environment or causes distress.   This will include physical, verbal and non-verbal acts.

(d)   **Victimisation**, where someone is treated less favourably than others because they have taken action against the firm under one of the relevant Acts.

C.   Employment and training

(1)   General statement

As an employer, the firm will treat all employees and job applicants equally and fairly and not discriminate unjustifiably against them.   This will, for example, include arrangements for recruitment and selection, terms and conditions of employment, access to training opportunities, access to promotion and transfers, grievance and disciplinary processes, demotions, selection for redundancies, dress code, references, bonus schemes, work allocation and any other employment related activities.

(2) Recruitment and selection

This firm recognises the benefits of having a diverse workforce and will take steps to ensure that:

(a)   it endeavours to recruit from the widest pool of candidates possible;

(b)   employment opportunities are open and accessible to all;

(c)   where appropriate, positive action measures are taken to attract applications from all sections of society and especially from those groups which are under-represented in the workforce;

(d)   selection criteria and processes do not discriminate unjustifiably by treating one person less favourably than another in the same or similar circumstances and that treatment cannot be justified. The grounds upon which a person must not be discriminated against are sex (including their marital status); race or racial group; ethnic or national origins; colour; nationality; religion or belief; sexual orientation; or disability.

(e)   wherever necessary, lawful exemptions (genuine occupational requirements or genuine occupational qualifications) will be used to recruit suitable staff to meet the special needs of particular groups; and

(f)   all recruitment agencies acting for the firm are aware of its requirement not to discriminate and act accordingly.

(3) Targets

The firm will use its best endeavours to comply with Law Society policies and targets for the employment of ethnic minorities, as are produced from time to time.

(4) Conditions of service

The firm will treat all employees equally and create a working environment which is free from discrimination, victimisation and harassment and which respects, where appropriate, the diverse backgrounds and beliefs of employees.

Terms and conditions of service for employees will comply with anti-discrimination legislation. The provision of benefits such as working hours, maternity and other leave arrangements, performance appraisal systems, dress code, bonus schemes and any other conditions of employment will not discriminate against any employee on the grounds of sex (including their marital status); race or racial group; ethnic or national origins; colour; nationality; religion or belief; or sexual orientation.

Where necessary and possible, the firm will endeavour to provide appropriate facilities and conditions of service which take into account the specific needs of employees which arise from their racial or cultural background; gender; responsibilities as carers; disability; religion or belief; or sexual orientation.

(5)   *Promotion and career development*

Promotion within the firm (including to [partnership]/[membership]/ [directorship]) will be made without reference to discrimination when, on one of the prohibited grounds, one person is treated less favourably than another would be treated in the same or similar circumstances and that treatment cannot be justified. The grounds upon which a person must not be discriminated against are sex (including their marital status); race or racial group; ethnic or national origins; colour; nationality; religion or belief; sexual orientation; or disability.

The selection criteria and processes for promotion will be kept under review to ensure that there is no unjustifiably discriminatory impact on any particular group.

Whilst positive action measures may be taken to encourage under-represented groups to apply for promotion opportunities, recruitment and promotion to all positions will be based solely on merit.

All employees will have equal access to training and other career development opportunities appropriate to their experience and abilities. However, the firm will take appropriate positive action measures (as permitted by the legislation) to provide special training and support for groups which are under-represented in the workforce and encourage them to take up training and career development opportunities.

D.   **[Partners]/[Members]/[Directors]**

Arrangements and procedures for selecting [partners]/[members]/[directors], their terms and conditions of [partnership]/[membership]/[directorship], access to benefits, facilities or services and termination arrangements will be reviewed and amended where necessary to prevent discrimination on the prohibited grounds, one person is treated less favourably than another would be treated in the same or similar circumstances and that treatment cannot be justified. The grounds upon which a person must not be discriminated against are sex (including their marital status); race or racial group; ethnic or national origins; colour; nationality; religion or belief; sexual orientation; or disability.

Maternity rights available to [partners]/[members]/[directors] shall be no less favourable that those required by legislation for employees.

E.   **Barristers and third parties**

(1)   **Barristers**

Barristers should be instructed on the basis of their skills, experience and ability. The firm will not, on the grounds of sex (including their marital status); race or racial group; ethnic or national origins; colour; nationality; religion or belief; sexual orientation; or disability, give instructions to or withhold instructions from a barrister, and will not request barristers' clerks to do so.

Clients' requests for a named barrister should be complied with, subject to the firm's duty to discuss with the client the suitability of the barrister and to advise appropriately.

The firm will discuss with the client any request by the client that only a barrister who is not disabled or who is of a particular gender; marital status; race; racial group; colour; ethnic or national origin; nationality; religion or belief; or sexual orientation be instructed. In the absence of a valid reason for this request, which must be within the exemptions permitted by the anti-discrimination legislation, the firm will endeavour to persuade the client to modify their instructions in so far as they are given on discriminatory grounds. Should the client refuse to modify such instructions, the firm will cease to act.

(2)   Suppliers

All lists of approved suppliers and databases of contractors, agents and other third parties who, or which, are regarded as suitable to be instructed by those within the firm have been compiled only on the basis of the ability of those persons or organisations to undertake work of a particular type and contain no discriminatory bias based upon sex (including their marital status); race or racial group; ethnic or national origins; colour; nationality; religion or belief; sexual orientation; or disability.

F.   Clients

The firm is generally free to decide whether to accept instructions from any particular client, but any refusal to act will not be based upon sex (including their marital status); race or racial group; ethnic or national origins; colour; nationality; religion or belief; sexual orientation; or disability.

The firm will take steps to meet the different needs of particular clients arising from its obligations under the anti-discrimination legislation (such as the Disability Discrimination Act 1995) and The Law Society's Code of Conduct [2004].

In addition, where necessary and where it is permitted by legislation (for example, provisions relating to positive action or exemptions) the firm will seek to provide services which meet the specific needs and requests arising from clients' racial or cultural background; gender; responsibilities as carers; disability; religion or belief; sexual orientation or other relevant factors.

G.   Promoting equality and diversity

This firm is committed to promoting equality and diversity in the firm as well as in those areas in which it has influence.

Employees and [partners]/[members]/[directors] will be informed of this anti-discrimination policy and will be provided with equality and diversity training appropriate to their needs and responsibilities.

All those who act on the firm's behalf will be informed of this anti-discrimination policy and will be expected to pay due regard to it when conducting business on the firm's behalf.

In all its dealings, including those with suppliers, contractors and recruitment agencies, the firm will seek to promote the principles of equality and diversity.

The firm will make every effort to reflect its commitment to equality and diversity in its marketing and communication activities.

H.   Implementing the policy

(1)   Responsibility

Ultimate responsibility for implementing the policy rests with the [principal]/[partners]/[members]/[directors] of the firm. The firm will appoint a senior person within it to be responsible for the operation of the policy.

All employees and [partners]/[members]/[directors] of the firm are expected to pay due regard to the provisions of its anti-discrimination policy and are responsible for ensuring compliance with it when undertaking their jobs or representing the firm.

Acts of discrimination, victimisation or harassment on grounds of sex (including marital status); race or racial group; ethnic or national origins; colour; nationality; religion or belief; sexual orientation; or unreasonably on the grounds of disability by employees or [partners]/[members]/[directors] of the firm will result in disciplinary action. Failure to comply with this policy will be treated in a similar fashion.

Acts of discrimination, victimisation or harassment on grounds of sex (including marital status); race or racial group; ethnic or national origins; colour; nationality; religion or belief; sexual orientation; or unreasonably on the grounds of disability by those acting on behalf of the firm will lead to appropriate action including termination of services where appropriate.

(2)   Complaints of discrimination

The firm will treat seriously, and will take action where appropriate concerning, all complaints of discrimination, victimisation or harassment on the grounds of sex (including marital status); race or racial group; ethnic or national origins; colour; nationality; religion or belief; sexual orientation; or unreasonably on the grounds of disability made by employees, [partners]/ [members]/[directors], clients, barristers or other third parties.

All complaints will be investigated in accordance with the firm's grievance or complaints procedure and the complainant will be informed of the outcome.

(3)   Monitoring and review

The policy will be monitored and reviewed in a manner proportionate to the size and nature of the firm on a regular basis (and in any event at least annually) to measure its progress and judge its effectiveness. In particular, the firm will, as appropriate, monitor and record:

    (a)   the gender and racial composition of the workforce and [partners] / [members] / [directors] as well as the number of disabled staff, [partners]/[members]/[directors] at different levels of the organisation;

    (b)   the race, gender and disability of all applicants, short-listed applicants and successful applicants for jobs and training contracts;

(c)   the race, gender and disability of all applicants for promotion (including to partnership, to membership of a recognised body which is an LLP or director of a recognised body which is a company) and training opportunities and details of whether they were successful;

(d)   where it is possible to do so, and where doing so will not cause offence or discomfort to those whom it is intended to protect, the sexual orientation and religion or belief of all [partners] / [members] / [directors] and staff, so as to ensure that they are not being discriminated against in terms of the opportunities or benefits available to them. Firms should, however, be aware that [partners] / [members] / [directors] and staff may not choose to disclose their sexual orientation or religion or belief and that care should be taken to avoid inadvertent discrimination in such cases;

(e)   the number and outcome of complaints of discrimination made by staff, [partners] / [members] / [directors], barristers, clients and other third parties; and

(f)   the disciplinary action (if any) taken against employees by race, gender and disability.

This information will be used to review the progress and impact of the anti-discrimination policy. Any changes required will be made and implemented.

Rule 7 – Publicity

Introduction

You are generally free to publicise your practice as a solicitor, REL or RFL, subject to the requirements of this rule. The rule as it applies to your overseas practice is modified by 15.07.

Rule 7 – Publicity

7.01 Misleading or inaccurate publicity

Publicity must not be misleading or inaccurate.

7.02 Clarity as to charges

Any publicity relating to your charges must be clearly expressed. In relation to practice from an office in England and Wales it must be clear whether disbursements and VAT are included.

7.03 Unsolicited visits or telephone calls

(1)   You must not publicise your practice by making unsolicited visits or telephone calls to a member of the public.

(2)   "Member of the public" does not include:

(a)   a current or former client;

(b)   another lawyer;

(c)   an existing or potential professional or business connection; or

(d)   a commercial organisation or public body.

7.04 International aspects of publicity

Publicity intended for a jurisdiction outside England and Wales must comply with:

(a)   the provisions of rule 7 (and 15.07, if applicable); and

(b)   the rules in force in that jurisdiction concerning lawyers' publicity.

Publicity intended for a jurisdiction where it is permitted will not breach 7.04 through being incidentally received in a jurisdiction where it is not permitted.

7.05 Responsibility for publicity

You must not authorise any other person to conduct publicity for your practice in a way which would be contrary to rule 7 (and 15.07, if applicable).

7.06 Application

(1) Rule 7 applies to any publicity you or your firm conduct or authorise in relation to:

    (a)   your practice;

    (b)   any other business or activity carried on by you or your firm; or

    (c)   any other business or activity carried on by others.

(2) 7.01 to 7.05 apply to all forms of publicity including the name or description of your firm, stationery, advertisements, brochures, websites, directory entries, media appearances, promotional press releases, and direct approaches to potential clients and other persons, and whether conducted in person, in writing, or in electronic form.

7.07 Letterhead

(1) The letterhead of a firm must bear the words "regulated by the Law Society".

(2)   (a)   The letterhead of:

        (i)   a sole principal must include the name of the sole principal;

        (ii)   a partnership of 20 or fewer persons must include a list of the partners; and

        (iii)   a recognised body which is a company with a sole director must include the name of the director, identified as director.

    (b)   The letterhead of:

        (i)   a partnership of more than 20 persons must include either a list of the partners;

        (ii)   a recognised body which is an LLP must include either a list of the members, identified as members; and

        (iii)   a recognised body which is a company with more than one director must include either a list of the directors, identified as directors,

    or a statement that the list is open to inspection at the office.

    (c)   (i)   On the letterhead of a recognised body which is an unlimited company; or

        (ii)   in the list of partners referred to in 7.07(2)(a) or (b) if a partnership has an unlimited company as a member; or

        (iii)   in the list of members referred to in 7.07(2)(b) if an LLP has an unlimited company as a member, it must be stated, either as part of the unlimited company's name or otherwise, that the unlimited company is a body corporate.

(3)   In a firm, if the partners (or directors in the case of a company, or members in the case of an LLP) comprise both solicitors and foreign lawyers, the list referred to in 7.07(2)(a) or (b) must:

  (a)   identify any solicitor as a solicitor;

  (b)   in the case of any lawyer or notary of an Establishment Directive state other than the UK:

    (i)   identify the jurisdiction(s) – local or national as appropriate – under whose professional title the lawyer or notary is practising;

    (ii)   give the professional title(s), expressed in an official language of the Establishment Directive state(s) concerned; and

    (iii) if the lawyer is an REL, refer to that lawyer's registration with the Law Society; and

  (c)   indicate the professional qualification(s) as a lawyer and the country or jurisdiction of qualification of any RFL not included in (b) above.

(4)   Whenever an REL is named on the letterhead used by any firm or in-house practice, there must be compliance with 7.07(3)(b).

(5)   In 7.07 "letterhead" includes a fax heading.

Guidance to rule 7 – Publicity

Geographical scope of the rule

1.   (a)   Rule 7 applies to publicity in connection with practice from any office, whether in England and Wales or overseas – but the provisions are amended by 15.07 for publicity in connection with overseas practice.

  (b)   Rule 7 does not apply to the website, e-mails, text messages or similar electronic communications of any practice you conduct from an office in an EU state other than the UK (see 15.07(a)).

  (c)   7.07 (letterhead) does not apply to a solicitor's practice conducted from an office outside England and Wales or to an REL's practice conducted from an office in Scotland or Northern Ireland. However, you must comply with 15.07(b).

General

2.   In the delivery of professional services, there is an imbalance of knowledge between clients and the public on the one hand, and the service provider on the other. Rule 7 addresses this in a number of ways – for example, by ensuring that clients and the public have appropriate information about you, your firm, and the way you are regulated; and by prohibiting misleading publicity and inappropriate approaches for business.

Local law society involvement in dealing with minor breaches

3.   In the case of breaches of the rule which are not serious, the Law Society encourages local law societies to bring the breaches to the attention of the practitioners concerned. Serious or persistent cases should be reported to the Law Society.

Statutory requirements and voluntary codes

4.   You must comply with the general law on advertising, including:

(a)   any regulations made under the Consumer Credit Act 1974, concerning the content of advertisements;

(b)   sections 20 and 21 of the Consumer Protection Act 1987, regarding misleading price indications;

(c)   the Business Names Act 1985, concerning lists of partners and an address for service on stationery etc.;

(d)   chapter 1 of Part XI of the Companies Act 1985, regarding the appearance of the company name and other particulars on stationery etc.;

(e)   the Consumer Credit (Advertisements) Regulations 1989, in relation to advertisements to arrange mortgages;

(f)   the Control of Misleading Advertisements (Amendment) Regulations 2000, in relation to comparative advertising;

(g)   the Data Protection Act 1998;

(h)   E-Commerce Directive 2000/31/EC and the Electronic Commerce (EC Directive) Regulations 2002 (S.I.2002 no. 2013); and

(i)   the Privacy and Electronic Communications (EC Directive) Regulations 2003.

5.   You should also have regard to the British Code of Advertising, Sales Promotion and Direct Marketing. The main principle of the Code is that media advertisements be legal, decent, honest and truthful. For further information see http://www.asa.org.uk/index.asp.

6.   A breach of a statutory provision or the Code may also entail a breach of rule 7 or another rule of conduct, but would not necessarily do so. For example, an advert adjudged by the Advertising Standards Authority to be untruthful under the Code might also, in the context of a complaint, be found by the Law Society to breach 7.01 (which requires that publicity is not misleading or inaccurate).

Responsibility for publicity – 7.05

7.   Where you become aware of breaches of rule 7 in publicity conducted on your behalf, you should take reasonable steps to have the publicity changed or withdrawn.

Clarity as to charges – 7.02

8. Publicity relating to charges must not be misleading or inaccurate, and must be clearly expressed. The following examples on commissions from third parties, fees for conveyancing services, discounts and 'free' services will assist in complying.

Commissions from third parties

9. Particular care should be taken when quoting fees which are intended to be net fees, i.e. fees which are reduced by the availability of commission (such as that on an endowment policy). Any fee quoted in these circumstances should be the gross fee.

Fees for conveyancing services

10. The following are examples of publicity on conveyancing services which would breach 7.01 and/or 7.02:

     (a) publicity which includes an estimated fee pitched at an unrealistically low level;

     (b) publicity which refers to an estimated or fixed fee plus disbursements, if expenses which are in the nature of overheads (such as normal postage and telephone calls) are then charged as disbursements – unless the publicity explicitly states that such charges will be made; and

     (c) publicity which includes an estimated or fixed fee for conveyancing services, if you then make an additional charge for work on a related mortgage loan or repayment, including work done for a lender – unless the publicity makes it clear that any such additional charge may be payable (e.g. by the use of a phrase like "excluding VAT, disbursements, mortgage related charges and fees for work done for a lender").

Discounts and 'free' services

11. Offers of discounts could be misleading if there are no clear rates of charges included. Similarly, if you publicise a service or services as being 'free', this should genuinely be the case and should not be conditional upon some other factor (e.g. receiving further instructions or some other benefit).

Name of firm

12. It would be misleading for a name or description to include the word "solicitor(s)", if none of the principals or directors (or members in the case of an LLP) is a solicitor.

13. It would be misleading for a sole principal to use "and partners" or "and associates" in a firm name unless the firm did formerly have more than one principal.

E-commerce, e-mail and websites

14.   The Electronic Commerce (EC Directive) Regulations 2002 implementing the E-Commerce Directive 2000/31/EC came into force on 21 August 2002. The Directive covers cross-border e-commerce within the EU, including e-mails and websites. It will affect any firm with a website, because a website can be accessed from other member states.

15.   The Regulations require you to give certain information to persons visiting your firm's website or receiving e-mails from the firm (other than certain activities outside the scope of the Directive, e.g. litigation). The information you will need to give includes:

   (a)   details of the professional body with which you are registered;

   (b)   your professional title and the member state where it was granted; and

   (c)   a reference to the professional rules applicable to you in the member state where you are established and the means to access them.

16.   If you are "established" in the UK, the professional body will be the Law Society and the applicable rules will be the Law Society's rules. For the rules, you may wish to provide a link to http://www.guide-online.lawsociety.org.uk. If you are "established" in another member state, the professional body will be the bar or law society with which you are registered under the Establishment Directive, and the applicable rules will be their rules.

17.   Any promotional material is publicity. E-mails sent to individuals, companies or organisations with the intention of promoting your practice are advertisements and therefore publicity. Any promotional material in a business e-mail – such as the name and description of the firm – will also be publicity. In these cases 7.01 – 7.06 will apply.

18.   However, 7.07 applies only to "letterheads". E-mails do not normally have a letterhead, so 7.07 will not normally apply to an e-mail. If, however, you send an e-mail which has a letterhead, or attaches a document with a letterhead, 7.07 will apply.

19.   7.07 reflects some of the provisions of the Business Names Act 1985 and Chapter 1 of Part XI of the Companies Act 1985, which applies to "business letters". It is for the courts to determine whether or to what extent these Acts may apply to e-mails. However, the Law Society's guess is that e-mails will only be "business letters" when they are formally set out as such and not when they are used as an alternative to a telephone call, telegram or telex. In the meantime it would be prudent for you to ensure that third parties with whom you deal by e-mail are given your practising address at an early stage, together with the details which would normally appear on the firm's letterhead.

Unsolicited e-mails

20.   7.03 prohibits unsolicited visits or telephone calls to members of the public. E-mails do not fall within this prohibition. However, you should check the terms of your agreement with your internet service provider as to the use of

unsolicited mail, and in some jurisdictions the law prohibits unsolicited mail. See also note 30 below on data protection.

Websites

21. Websites are publicity and should comply with 7.01 – 7.06. See also notes 24 and 26 below.

22. If your website or e-mails are to include any financial promotion as defined in the Financial Services and Markets Act 2000, your firm will need to be authorised by the Financial Services Authority. See also notes 28 and 29 below.

International aspects of publicity – 7.04

23. The implementation of the E-Commerce Directive means that there are two different regimes governing international e-publicity:

   (a) cross border e-publicity within the EU; and

   (b) other cross-border e-publicity, i.e. the e-publicity of solicitors who are established outside the EU, wherever it is accessed or received; and the e-publicity of solicitors or RELs who are established in the EU, if it is accessed or received outside the EU.

24. Cross-border e-publicity within the EU is governed by the E-Commerce Directive and national implementing legislation. Other cross-border e-publicity is not. However, as a website can be accessed from anywhere, your website will have to comply with the E-Commerce Directive and the relevant implementing legislation if you are established anywhere within the EU.

25. 7.04 provides that publicity intended for a jurisdiction outside England and Wales must comply with rule 7 (or, in the case of overseas practice, 15.07) and with the rules in force in that jurisdiction concerning lawyers' publicity. Publicity intended for a jurisdiction where it is permitted will not breach this provision through being incidentally received in a jurisdiction where it is not permitted.

26. Websites can, of course, be accessed world-wide. The relevant factor is the jurisdiction or jurisdictions at which a website is targeted. For example, a website aimed at Australia must comply with rule 7 (if the solicitor's office is in England and Wales) or 15.07 (if the office is elsewhere), and any other restrictions in force in Australia concerning lawyers' publicity.

Mailshots

27. Unsolicited mailshots may be sent and may be targeted. However, you should note the data protection considerations discussed in note 30 below.

Financial promotions

28. Under section 21 of the Financial Services and Markets Act 2000 an unsolicited communication which invites or induces a person to enter into an investment activity is a financial promotion, and cannot be made by an unauthorised person.

29.   If you intend to make any form of unsolicited contact allowed under 7.03, where it relates to an investment activity you must consider carefully whether you are authorised to carry out the activity, and also consider whether your contact constitutes a financial promotion and whether you are authorised to make such an approach. Breach of the Act is a criminal offence.

Data protection

30.   7.03(2)(a) permits unsolicited visits or telephone calls to a current or former client. Before contacting clients or former clients in order to publicise your firm you should consider the requirements of the Data Protection Act 1998. It is advisable to give all clients the opportunity to refuse to receive direct marketing correspondence or contact – for example, in a terms of business letter. This applies to unsolicited mailshots to current or former clients as well as unsolicited visits and telephone calls.   Under the Privacy and Electronic Communications (EC Directive) Regulations 2003, prior opt-in consent is needed for direct marketing by e-mail.

Naming non-partners

31.   If non-partners are named on a partnership's letterhead, their status should be made clear. A printed line is not sufficient in itself to distinguish partners from non-partners in a list. A similar standard applies to a recognised body's letterhead.

Salaried partners

32.   A solicitor, REL or RFL who is held out on the letterhead of an unincorporated firm as a partner – even if separately designated as "salaried" or "associate" partner – is treated by the Law Society as a full partner, and therefore must comply with the Accounts Rules and the Indemnity Insurance Rules.

"Partners" in an LLP

33.   In the context of an LLP, it is appropriate to refer to members of the LLP as "partners", provided the firm complies with the provisions of the Companies Act 1985, the Business Names Act 1985 and 7.07(2) as regards the items that must appear on the firm's notepaper.

34.   Some firms may also wish to designate some non-members of the LLP as "partners". This is potentially misleading, so if a firm wishes to go down this path care must be taken to ensure that:

   (a)   no person is designated as a "partner" unless he or she:

      (i)   is a member of the LLP, or a consultant or employee of the LLP with equivalent standing to a member; and

      (ii)   would be entitled under the Law Society's rules to become a member of the LLP;

   (b)   appropriate explanatory wording (see 35 below) appears on:

      (i)   the firm's notepaper, faxes, e-mails, brochures and websites; and

      (ii)   any bill on which the word "partner" appears;

(c)   care is taken to distinguish between a member of the LLP and a person who is not a member but who is referred to as a "partner":

      (i)   in any agreement, terms of business letter or client care letter in which the word "partner" appears;

      (ii)   when addressing any client or third party who is not in receipt of a letter, fax or e-mail; and

      (iii)   in any formal context such as an affidavit, a statement to a court, or a communication with the Legal Services Commission.

35.   Appropriate explanatory wording for a firm's notepaper, faxes, e-mails, brochures, websites or bills would be to the effect that:

> *"We use the word 'partner' to refer to a member of the LLP, or an employee or consultant with equivalent standing and qualifications."*

If a firm wishes to refer to a list of "partners" as well as the statutory list of members, it is suggested that this might be done by way of some such wording as:

> *"A list of the members of the LLP is displayed at the above address, together with a list of those non-members who are designated as partners."*

36.   Note that an LLP which does not intend to designate any non-members as "partners" can ignore notes 34 and 35 above.

RELs

37.   7.07(3) and (4) set out the requirements to be followed when an REL is named on a letterhead, including a letterhead used by a firm or in-house practice. The following example illustrates how to comply:

"Paul van den Hoek, Advocaat (Brussels), registered with the Law Society of England and Wales".

Naming staff

38.   You may name staff on your letterhead. However, it would be misleading (and could involve a criminal offence) to use the word "solicitor" to refer to an individual who is not a solicitor of the Supreme Court of England and Wales.

39.   A lawyer whose professional title is "solicitor" in another jurisdiction but who is not a solicitor of England and Wales can only be referred to in publicity as "solicitor" if the word is suitably qualified, for example by the name of that lawyer's jurisdiction of qualification.

Naming clients

40.   The fact that you have acted for a client and details of the client's transactions are subject to the duty of confidentiality – see rule 4 (confidentiality and

disclosure) – and you will therefore normally need the client's consent before disclosing such information in any publicity.

Fee-earner leaving a firm

41.	It is not in itself misconduct for you to write to clients of a firm after leaving that firm, inviting their instructions.	However, this cannot absolve you from any legal obligations arising out of your former contract of employment or partnership agreement.

Rule 8 – Fee sharing

Introduction

Rule 8 restricts the persons and businesses with whom or with which you can share your professional fees. Broadly, you may not share fees with a non-lawyer unless the fee sharing is with an employee or, in the case of overseas practice, a partner, or in the strictly defined circumstances set out in this rule. Its purpose is to protect your independence and professional judgement in these situations for the ultimate public benefit.

Rule 8 – Fee sharing

8.01 Fee sharing with lawyers and colleagues

Except as permitted under 8.02 below you may only share or agree to share your professional fees with the following persons:

(a) practising members of legal professions covered by the Establishment Directive (other than a member of the English Bar practising in England and Wales);

(b) practising members of other legal professions (other than a person who is struck off or suspended from the register of foreign lawyers);

(c) bodies corporate wholly owned and directed by lawyers within (a) and (b) above for the purpose of practising law;

(d) your partner as permitted by rule 12 (framework of practice), your retired partner or predecessor, or the dependants or personal representatives of your deceased partner or predecessor;

(e) in the case of a recognised body, a retired director, member or shareowner, or the dependants or personal representatives of a deceased director, member or shareowner;

(f) your genuine employee (this does not allow you to disguise as "employment" what is in fact a partnership which rule 12 prohibits);

(g) a body corporate through which you practise as permitted by rule 12;

(h) your employer, if you are employed by a firm permitted under rule 12, or if you are practising in-house and acting in accordance with rule 13 (in-house practice) or 15.13 (in-house practice overseas);

(i) a law centre or advice service operated by a charitable or similar non-commercial organisation if you are working as a volunteer and receive fees or costs from public funds or recovered from a third party; or

(j) an estate agent who is your sub-agent for the sale of a property.

8.02 Fee sharing with other non-lawyers

(1)   Except in relation to cross-border practice, you may share your professional fees with another person or business ("the fee sharer") if:

    (a)   the purpose of the fee sharing arrangement is solely to facilitate the introduction of capital and/or the provision of services to your firm;

    (b)   neither the fee sharing agreement nor the extent of the fees shared permits any fee sharer to influence or constrain your professional judgement in relation to the advice which you give to any client;

    (c)   the operation of the agreement does not result in a partnership prohibited by rule 12;

    (d)   if requested by the Law Society to do so, you supply details of all agreements which you have made with fee sharers and the percentage of your firm's annual gross fees which has been paid to each fee sharer; and

    (e)   your fee sharing agreement does not involve a breach of rule 9 (referrals of business) or 15.09 (overseas practice – referrals of business).

(2)   "Fee sharer" means a person or business who or which shares your fees in reliance on (1) above and the expression includes any person or business connected to or associated with the fee sharer.

Guidance to rule 8 – Fee sharing

What is fee sharing?

1.   Fee sharing is not defined in rule 8. It can have a variety of forms and includes relationships where you make a payment within a firm or to a third party by reference to a percentage of the fees charged to a client in respect of a particular case, or a percentage of your gross or net fees, or your profits.

Fee sharing with lawyers and colleagues

2.   Sharing your fees within a firm, or with other lawyers, or in the other circumstances listed in 8.01, does not represent a serious risk to your independence and is therefore permitted.

3.   Note that, subject to certain restrictions, you may practise outside England and Wales in partnership with non-lawyers – see rule 12 (framework of practice). If you do, 8.01 allows you to share fees with your non-lawyer partners.

Fee sharing with other non-lawyers

4.   You may share your fees with third party non-lawyers in the strictly defined circumstances set out in 8.02. The aim of 8.02 is to give practitioners greater freedom of choice as to the methods available to fund their firms or to pay for services provided to their firms, subject to safeguards designed to protect the public interest. 8.02 allows you to enter into agreements with third party non-

lawyers which provide that, in return for the third party making available capital and/or a service to you, you make payment to the third party by reference to a percentage of your fees.

5.   You must take account of the requirements of rule 1 (core duties), specifically of the requirements of independence, integrity, and your duty to act in the best interests of the client. This means that although a fee sharer may properly require you to, for example, observe certain service delivery standards, it would be improper for the fee sharer to interfere with your professional judgement in relation to the advice given to clients.

6.   If the fee sharing relationship involves referrals between you and the fee sharer, you must also comply with rule 9 or 15.09 (referrals of business).

7.   You must also comply with rule 12 (framework of practice), which states that solicitors may practise in England and Wales in partnerships only with certain other lawyers, and with non-lawyers outside England and Wales only within strictly defined limits. Although fee sharing is an indicator of partnership, it is not the defining feature. Solicitors who do share fees in accordance with 8.02 should take care that they do not, even inadvertently, enter into an unauthorised partnership with the fee sharer.

8.   You must comply with rule 3 (conflict of interests) to ensure that there is no conflict between the interests of the client and your own interests by virtue of your agreement with the fee sharer. Should a fee sharer become your client, you should be particularly conscious of the need to ensure that conflicts of interests do not arise, and that the wish to avoid offending the fee sharer does not colour the actions taken and advice given in respect of other clients.

9.   8.02 allows you to share fees with a non-lawyer third party, but only in return for the fee sharer providing capital and/or services to your firm. The rule does not permit the fee sharer to provide services to your client as part of the fee sharing agreement.

10.   Examples of the kind of arrangements which 8.02 permits include:

        (a)   A bank may provide a loan to your firm in return for a sum, in whole or part, calculated as a percentage of the gross fees of your firm. The fact that some clients of your firm are also customers of the bank would not, of itself, prevent the bank from sharing your fees.

        (b)   A supplier of information and communications technology may provide computer hardware, software, back-up and training to your firm in return for a share of the firm's gross fees.

        (c)   You may pay a supplier of an interactive web based will-writing package on the basis of a percentage of the fee for each will.

11.   Although 8.02 does not specify any cap or limit on the amount of fees which you may share with third parties, you must ensure that the extent of the fees shared does not put at risk your duties to act independently and in the clients' best interests – see rule 1 (core duties). Firms should carry out an assessment of any risk to these core duties that could be created by any fee sharing arrangement, and take action to limit or manage that risk. In assessing whether a firm may have been in breach of these duties, particularly where the

percentage of all fees shared is higher than 15% of gross fees, the Law Society may ask for evidence of this risk assessment.

12. If you have a fee sharing relationship with a third party non-lawyer in accordance with 8.02, you may need to disclose the existence and nature of the fee sharing relationship to any client whose affairs are significantly and directly connected to it. Service delivery standards agreed with a fee sharer need not normally be disclosed. See also 2.02(2)(e) and notes 16 to 18 of the guidance to rule 2 (client relations).

13. There would, for example, be no obligation to disclose to clients that the firm has a fee sharing relationship with a bank which has supplied a loan to the firm, even to those clients who obtain banking services from that same bank.

14. 8.02 states that you must, if asked to do so, make available to the Law Society details of any fee sharing agreement. This may, for example, include the percentage of gross fees which has been passed to the fee sharer(s) pursuant to an agreement made under 8.02.

15. The Law Society will respect the commercial sensitivity of any information supplied to it.

16. In European cross-border activities, you are bound by rule 16 (European cross-border practice), which reflects the CCBE Code in prohibiting fee sharing with non-lawyer fee sharers. The following therefore remain prohibited by rule 16:

    (a) solicitors (wherever practising) sharing fees with a non-lawyer fee sharer situated in an EU state other than the UK, or in Iceland, Liechtenstein, Norway or Switzerland; and

    (b) solicitors practising in an EU state other than the UK, or in Iceland, Liechtenstein, Norway or Switzerland, sharing fees with a non-lawyer fee sharer (wherever situated) unless that non-lawyer is the solicitor's partner in an overseas partnership permitted under rule 12 (framework of practice).

    Further information can be found in rule 16 (European and cross-border practice) and guidance notes 5 and 6 to that rule.

Rule 9 – Referrals of business

Introduction

Rule 9 applies when you receive referrals of business from, or make referrals to, third parties. Its purpose is to protect your independence. Additional provisions apply when you have a financial arrangement with an introducer. The rule does not apply to your overseas practice but you must comply with 15.09.

Rule 9 – Referrals of business

9.01 General

(1)   When making or receiving referrals of clients to or from third parties you must do nothing which would compromise your independence or your ability to act and advise in the best interests of your clients.

(2)   You must draw the attention of potential introducers to this rule and to the relevant provisions of rule 7 (publicity).

(3)   This rule does not apply to referrals between lawyers.

9.02 Financial arrangements with introducers

The following additional requirements apply when you enter into a financial arrangement with an introducer:

    (a)   The agreement must be in writing and be available for inspection by the Law Society.

    (b)   The introducer must undertake, as part of the agreement, to comply with the provisions of this rule.

    (c)   You must be satisfied that clients referred by the introducer have not been acquired as a result of marketing or publicity or other activities which, if done by a person regulated by the Law Society, would be in breach of any of these rules.

    (d)   The agreement must not include any provision which would:

        (i)   compromise, infringe or impair any of the duties set out in these rules; or

        (ii)   allow the introducer to influence or constrain your professional judgement in relation to the advice given to the client.

    (e)   The agreement must provide that before making a referral the introducer must give the client all relevant information concerning the referral, in particular:

        (i)   the fact that the introducer has a financial arrangement with you; and

        (ii)   the amount of any payment to the introducer which is calculated by reference to that referral; or

        (iii)   where the introducer is paying you to provide services to the introducer's customers:

            (A)   the amount the introducer is paying you to provide those services; and

            (B)   the amount the client is required to pay the introducer.

(f)   If you have reason to believe that the introducer is breaching any of the terms of the agreement required by this rule, you must take all reasonable steps to ensure that the breach is remedied. If the introducer continues to breach it you must terminate the agreement.

(g)   Before accepting instructions to act for a client referred under 9.02 you must, in addition to the requirements contained in 2.02 to 2.04 of these rules, give the client, in writing, all relevant information concerning the referral, in particular:

        (i)   the fact that you have a financial arrangement with the introducer;

        (ii)   the amount of any payment to the introducer which is calculated by reference to that referral; or

        (iii)   where the introducer is paying you to provide services to the introducer's customers:

            (A)   the amount the introducer is paying you to provide those services; and

            (B)   the amount the client is required to pay the introducer;

        (iv)   a statement that any advice you give will be independent and that the client is free to raise questions on all aspects of the transaction; and

        (v)   confirmation that information disclosed to you by the client will not be disclosed to the introducer unless the client consents; but that where you are also acting for the introducer in the same matter and a conflict of interests arises, you might be obliged to cease acting.

(h)   You must not enter into a financial arrangement with an introducer for the referral of clients in respect of criminal proceedings or any matter in which you will act for the client with the benefit of public funding.

(i)   For the purpose of this rule:

        (i)   "financial arrangement" includes:

            (A)   any payment to a third party in respect of referrals; and

(B) any agreement to be paid by a third party introducer to provide services to the third party's customers; and

(ii) "payment" includes any other consideration but does not include normal hospitality, proper disbursements or normal business expenses.

9.03 Referrals to third parties

(1) If you recommend that a client use a particular firm, agency or business, you must do so in good faith, judging what is in the client's best interests.

(2) You must not enter into any agreement or association which would restrict your freedom to recommend any particular firm, agency or business.

(3) [Paragraph (2) does not apply to arrangements in connection with any of the following types of investments:

(a) regulated mortgage contracts;

(b) general insurance contracts; or

(c) pure protection contracts.

(4) The terms "regulated mortgage contracts", "general insurance contracts" and "pure protection contracts" in (3) above have the meanings given in 19.01(4).

(5)]If a client is likely to need an endowment policy, or similar life insurance with an investment element, you must refer them only to an independent intermediary authorised to give investment advice.

Guidance to rule 9 – Referrals of business

General

1. You must not allow the requirements of an introducer, nor your wish to avoid offending an introducer, to affect the advice you give to your clients. Neither must you become so reliant on an introducer as a source of work that this affects the advice you give to your client. It is therefore recommended that your firm conducts regular reviews of your referral arrangements to ensure that this is not happening. Factors you should consider in reviewing your arrangements are:

(a) whether you have complied with the provisions of rule 9;

(b) whether you have given referred clients independent advice, which has not been affected by the interests of the introducer; and

(c) the amount and proportion of your firm's income arising as a result of each referral arrangement.

2. You should always retain control of the work you do for clients. No arrangement with an introducer should affect your duty to communicate directly

with the client to obtain or confirm instructions, in the process of providing advice and at all appropriate stages of the transaction.

Financial arrangements with introducers

3.   Rule 9 permits you to pay for referrals, and to be paid by an introducer to provide services to the introducer's customers, subject to conditions. These conditions apply whenever you make a payment, or give other consideration, to a third party who refers clients to you, unless you can show that the payment is wholly unconnected with the referral of any client to you. The conditions also apply regardless of how the payment (or other consideration) is described. For example, the conditions would apply to the payment of administrative or marketing fees, payments described as 'disbursements' which are not proper disbursements, and panel membership fees. Equally, you will not be able to avoid the requirements of the rule by, for example, making the payment to an intermediary who, in turn, has an arrangement with the introducer. When investigating complaints the Law Society will consider the substance of any relationship rather than the mere form.

4.   "Other consideration" might include, for example, the provision of services and secondment of staff to the introducer, or an agreement to purchase services or products from the introducer (where such a purchase is a condition of referrals being made).

Disclosure – by you

5.   Where a payment is made to an introducer in relation to each client referred by the introducer, either as a fixed amount or as a proportion of the fee charged to the client, the amount of the payment must be disclosed to each client. Where a payment to an introducer is more general in nature (for example, it may be a fixed, annual or monthly fee), clients referred by the introducer should be informed that you are making a payment and of the nature of the financial arrangement (or other consideration given). If the client asks for more information about the overall amount of payments made, you should supply such information as you are able. In any case where it is reasonably possible for you to calculate how much of the payment to an introducer relates to a particular client, you must disclose the amount.

6.   Where you are being paid by an introducer to provide services to the introducer's customers, both you and the introducer are required to disclose both the amount the introducer is paying you to provide services to the client and the amount the introducer is charging the client for your services. This will enable the client to ascertain whether, and if so how much, the introducer is charging for making the referral and to make an informed decision whether to accept the referral on that basis.

7.   You may need to disclose to the client other information, apart from the payment, concerning the nature of the referral agreement. (See 2.02(2)(e)).

8.   The requirement that you should make disclosure "immediately upon receiving the referral" will normally mean that you should write to the client as soon as you are asked to act for the client, rather than waiting until the first interview with the client. If time does not permit this, disclosure should be made at the beginning of the interview and confirmed in writing.

Disclosure – by the introducer

9. 9.02(e) requires the introducer to provide the client with all information concerning the referral. It will therefore be necessary for you to agree the nature of this information with the introducer. See guidance note 5 above on disclosure of payments. It is recommended that you ask referred clients on a regular basis what information the introducer has provided about the referral arrangement. You should keep written records of checks made with clients for evidential purposes.

Publicity

10. 9.02(c) requires you to be satisfied that the introducer has not acquired the client as a consequence of marketing, publicity or other activities which, if done by a person regulated by the Law Society, would have been in breach of these rules (particularly rule 7 (publicity)). Three requirements of rule 7 are particularly important for you to bear in mind in the context of payments for referrals:

   (a)   the general ban on misleading or inaccurate publicity;

   (b)   the prohibition of unsolicited visits and telephone calls to a "member of the public" (cold calling); and

   (c)   the requirement that you must not authorise a third party to publicise your firm in a way which would be contrary to rule 7.

Duty to monitor/terminate referral agreements

11. You will be expected to have made suitable enquiries about the way in which an introducer publicises your firm. If you become aware of possible breaches of rule 9 or rule 7 (publicity), you must bring these to the attention of introducers, and if necessary must terminate a referral agreement.

Improper constraints

12. 9.02(d)(ii) aims to prevent the introducer from influencing or constraining your professional judgement in respect of advice given to clients. For example, the choice of an expert or the decision to instruct counsel are integral to your role in advising the client. See also note 15 of the guidance to rule 2 (client relations) regarding arrangements with introducers which may constrain your professional judgement.

Excepted work

13. 9.02(h) prohibits you having a financial arrangement with an introducer in respect of criminal proceedings, or in any matter in which you will act for the client with the benefit of public funding. You would, however, not be prohibited from continuing to act for a referred client if there was a subsequent unanticipated need to obtain public funding or to represent the client in criminal proceedings. In this situation you should retain evidence as to how those circumstances had arisen.

"Normal hospitality"

14. What amounts to "normal hospitality" (see 9.02(i)(ii)) will depend on the circumstances in every case. For example, corporate entertainment, dinners or lunches are acceptable and would not amount to payment for a referral, provided these are proportionate to the relationship with a business contact/introducer.

"Normal business expenses"

15. "Normal business expenses" (see 9.02(i)(ii)) are payments for services provided to your firm which are totally unrelated to the referral of any client. So, for example, you would not be prevented from accepting referrals from the company with which you place your firm's indemnity or buildings insurance, or from the accountant who prepares your annual report or tax return.

Referral to third parties

16. Any referral to a third party will be subject to rule 1 (core duties) and 9.01, as well as 9.03. You must therefore do nothing in respect of such referrals which would compromise your independence or your ability to act or advise in the best interests of your clients. Any agreement you enter into in respect of regulated mortgage contracts, general insurance contracts or pure protection contracts will need to provide that referrals will only be made where this is in the best interests of the particular client and the contract is suitable for the needs of that client.

17. Rule 19 (financial services) deals with referrals in relation to financial services.

18. 2.05 applies in relation to commission received for the introduction of clients.

European cross-border practice

19. Rule 16 (European cross-border practice) prohibits you from making payments for referrals to non-lawyers when undertaking cross-border activities (see 16.06) and guidance notes 8 and 9 to rule 16.

Rule 10 – Relations with third parties

Introduction

Rule 10 draws together a variety of obligations linked by the need to deal with third parties in a proper manner. The rule as it applies to your overseas practice is modified by 15.10.

Rule 10 – Relations with third parties

10.01 Not taking unfair advantage

You must not use your position to take unfair advantage of anyone either for your own benefit or for another person's benefit.

10.02 Agreeing costs with another party

When negotiating the payment of your client's costs by another firm's client or a third party, you must give sufficient time and information for the amount of your costs to be agreed or assessed.

10.03 Administering oaths

You can administer oaths or affirmations or take declarations if you are a solicitor or an REL. You must not do so where you or your firm is acting for any party in the matter.

10.04 Contacting other party to a matter

You must not communicate with any other party who to your knowledge has retained a lawyer or licensed conveyancer to act in a matter, except:

    (a)   to request the name and address of the other party's lawyer or licensed conveyancer;

    (b)   where it would be reasonable to conclude that the other party's lawyer or licensed conveyancer has refused or failed for no adequate reason either to pass on messages to their client or to reply to correspondence, and has been warned of your intention to contact their client direct;

    (c)   with that lawyer or licensed conveyancer's consent; or

    (d)   in exceptional circumstances.

10.05 Undertakings

(1)   You must fulfil an undertaking which is given in circumstances where:

    (a)   you give the undertaking in the course of practice;

    (b)   you are a principal in a firm, and any person within the firm gives the undertaking in the course of practice;

(c)   you give the undertaking outside the course of practice, but as a solicitor; or

(d)   you are an REL based at an office in England and Wales, and you give the undertaking within the UK, as a lawyer of an Establishment Directive state, but outside your practice as an REL.

(2)   You must fulfil an undertaking within a reasonable time.

(3)   If you give an undertaking which is dependent upon the happening of a future event, you must notify the recipient immediately if it becomes clear that the event will not occur.

(4)   When you give an undertaking to pay another's costs, the undertaking will be discharged if the matter does not proceed unless there is an express agreement that the costs are payable in any event.

10.06 Dealing with more than one prospective buyer in a conveyancing transaction

(1)   Each time a seller of land, other than in a sale by auction or tender, either:

(a)   instructs you to deal with more than one prospective buyer; or

(b)   to your knowledge:

(i)   deals directly with another prospective buyer (or their conveyancer); or

(ii)   instructs another conveyancer to deal with another prospective buyer;

you must, with the client's consent, immediately inform the conveyancer of each prospective buyer, or the prospective buyer if acting in person.

(2)   If the seller refuses to agree to such disclosure, you must immediately stop acting in the matter.

(3)   You must not act for both the seller and any of the prospective buyers.

(4)   You must not act for more than one of the prospective buyers.

10.07 Fees of lawyers of other jurisdictions

(1)   If in the course of practice you instruct a lawyer of another jurisdiction you must, as a matter of professional conduct, pay the lawyer's proper fees unless the lawyer is practising as a solicitor or barrister of England and Wales; or

(a)   you have expressly disclaimed that responsibility at the outset, or at a later date you have expressly disclaimed responsibility for any fees incurred after that date;

(b)   the lawyer is an REL or is registered with the Bar of England and Wales under the Establishment Directive; or

(c)   the lawyer is an RFL based in England and Wales and practising in a firm.

(2)   If in the course of practice you instruct a business carrying on the practice of a lawyer of another jurisdiction you must, as a matter of professional conduct, pay the proper fees for the work that lawyer does, unless:

    (a)   you have expressly disclaimed that responsibility at the outset, or at a later date you have expressly disclaimed responsibility for any fees incurred after that date; or

    (b)   the business is a firm.

Guidance to rule 10 – Relations with third parties

Not taking unfair advantage – 10.01

1.   10.01 does not only apply to your actions which arise out of acting for a client. For example, if you are personally involved in a road accident and use your position as a solicitor unfairly to harass or intimidate the other motorist, you would breach 10.01. If, on the other hand, you intimidated the other motorist without making reference to your position as a solicitor, you would not breach 10.01. However, you should have regard to 1.10 (profession) in respect of your general behaviour outside practice.

2.   Particular care should be taken when you are dealing with a person who does not have legal representation. You need to find a balance between fulfilling your obligations to your client and not taking unfair advantage of another person. To an extent, therefore, 10.01 limits your duty to act in the best interests of your client. For example, your duty may be limited where an unrepresented opponent provides badly drawn documentation. In the circumstances you should suggest the opponent finds legal representation. If the opponent does not do so, you need to ensure that a balance is maintained between doing your best for the client and not taking unfair advantage of the opponent's lack of legal knowledge and drafting skills.

3.   You should take care, when dealing with an unrepresented third party, that any help given does not inadvertently create a contractual relationship with that party. For further information see *Cordery on Solicitors*. You should also be careful, when dealing with unqualified persons, that you are not involved in possible breaches of the Solicitors Act 1974, in terms of the prohibitions relating to reserved work. For further details about reserved work see 20.02 (requirements of practice) and the guidance to that rule.

4.   There may be situations where it is inappropriate for you to use the title 'solicitor' in advancing your personal interests. You should consider the good repute of the profession – see rule 1 (core duties).

5.   It would be unfair to demand anything that is not recoverable through the proper legal process. This would include a letter of claim and any other communication with another party to the action. For instance, where you are instructed to collect a simple debt, you should not demand from the debtor the

cost of the letter of claim, since it cannot be said at that stage that such a cost is legally recoverable.

6. The following are some further examples of how you should act in order to ensure you comply with 10.01 and core duties 1.01 (integrity) and 1.07 (fairness):

    (a) If a person sends you documents or money subject to an express condition, you should return the documents or money if you are unwilling or unable to comply with the condition.

    (b) If you are sent documents or money on condition that they are held to the sender's order, you should return the documents or money to the sender on demand.

    (c) If you ask anyone to supply copies of documents, you should expect to pay a proper charge for them.

Agreeing costs with another party – 10.02

7. 10.02 applies to all types of work. Its application is clear in litigation matters but will also commonly be relevant to other matters, such as where a landlord's solicitor's costs for dealing with a request for a license to assign a lease are to be paid by the tenant.

8. You should expect to supply information about the basis of charging (for example an hourly rate or an estimate of the total amount) together with an indication of the nature of the elements of the work done or to be done.

Administering oaths – 10.03

9. You may administer oaths if you are:

    (a) a solicitor with a current practising certificate - see section 81(1) of the Solicitors Act 1974; or

    (b) an REL, under the Establishment Directive.

10. When administering oaths or affirmations or taking declarations, you must ensure the giver:

    (a) is present;

    (b) signs the document in your presence or, if the document is already signed, confirms that the signature is their own and that any attachments are correct; and

    (c) appears to understand what they are doing and that the purpose is to confirm that the contents of the document and any attachments are true.

11. You are not responsible for the contents of the document, but if you have a good reason to believe that the contents may be false, you should not proceed.

12. Solicitors Act 1974 section 81(2) and other related legislation prohibits you administering an oath where you are or your firm is acting for any party in the

matter. The effect of this section would, for example, prevent a solicitor administering an oath for the solicitor's own spouse where it arises out of a personal matter.

13. When the document has already been signed, it is sufficient for you to accept the giver's word that it is their signature, unless there is clear evidence to the contrary.

Contacting other party to a matter – 10.04

14. 10.04 requires that you do not contact another party to a matter, subject to exceptions, if that party is represented by a lawyer or a licensed conveyancer. It is not intended to prevent you from dealing with other types of representative, if appropriate. If you are asked to deal with such a representative you should ensure that you are not involved in possible breaches of the Solicitors Act 1974 (see guidance note 3 to this rule) and that to do so is in your client's best interest. For example, where the other party is disabled and vulnerable you may well think it appropriate to deal with a representative from a specialist advice organisation or a disability charity. To do so, may mean that the matter is dealt with more efficiently and that you derive some protection from an allegation that you are acting in breach of 10.01 (not taking unfair advantage). On the other hand, you would be unlikely to want to deal with a person purporting to represent another party who clearly does not have the relevant knowledge or skill.

15. Where an enquiry agent has been instructed, the agent may serve documents where the other party's lawyer or licensed conveyancer has refused to accept service, but should not take a statement or in any other way communicate with the other party.

16. Care should be taken if you are instructed in a dual capacity. For example, if you are additionally instructed as an estate agent for the seller, you may contact the buyer, but solely about estate agency matters.

17. The other party's lawyer or licensed conveyancer may consent explicitly to your contacting their client, or this may be implied, such as when a protocol is being followed or where it has been agreed that certain documents be sent to all parties.

18. It is not always easy to establish why another lawyer or licensed conveyancer involved in a matter is not responding to correspondence. If you reasonably consider that the other lawyer or licensed conveyancer may be refusing or failing to take instructions from their client, or may be refusing or failing to communicate your requests or correspondence to their client, then a warning should give them the opportunity to object if an incorrect conclusion has been drawn. If there is no valid objection, then you should be able to advance the matter by directly contacting the other client.

19. It is recommended that any communications permitted by 10.04 between you and another lawyer or licensed conveyancer's client be in writing.

20. 10.04 extends to your contact with the in-house lawyers or licensed conveyancers of organisations. For example, if you are acting for a client in a matter concerning a local authority, and you have express or implied notice that the authority's solicitor has been instructed to act in the matter, you must not

discuss that matter directly with the appropriate committee chair, any individual councillor or any political group on the authority. You can be involved in political lobbying of individual councillors or a political group on the local authority on behalf of a client, even if you know that the authority's solicitor has been instructed to deal with the legal issues.

21.   Where the other party is an organisation, you will not breach 10.04 by contacting employees who are not responsible for the giving of instructions because they are not regarded as the client for the purpose of 10.04. However, you should have regard to any contractual obligations employees may have to their employer. It may be appropriate to notify the employer or its lawyer or licensed conveyancer of your intention to contact the employee. This would enable the employee to be advised as to the appropriate response.

22.   Lawyers or licensed conveyancers employed by organisations carrying out a statutory function, such as the Law Society or the Land Registry, may properly deal with represented clients.

23.   There may be other situations where it becomes necessary to communicate directly with a represented client. 10.04(d) refers to these as "exceptional circumstances". Such circumstances would include where you are contacted by the client of another lawyer or licensed conveyancer. Care should be taken to avoid taking unfair advantage of this situation but it is acceptable for you to deal with that client's request, if appropriate, and explain that in future they should contact you through their own lawyer or licensed conveyancer.

Undertakings – 10.05

24.   An undertaking is any statement, made by you or your firm, that you or your firm will do something or cause something to be done, or refrain from doing something, given to someone who reasonably relies upon it (see rule 24 – interpretation). It can be given orally or in writing and need not include the word 'undertake'. However, it is recommended that oral undertakings be confirmed or recorded in writing for evidential purposes.

25.   An agreement to pay a trading debt such as your electricity bill is not normally an undertaking. Once an undertaking is given and the recipient has relied upon it, it can only be withdrawn by agreement.

26.   You are not obliged to give or accept undertakings.

27.   In 10.05(1)(b) "person within the firm" includes anyone held out by the firm as representing the firm, as well as locums, agents, consultants and other employees.

28.   It is important that there be a time frame within which an undertaking should be fulfilled. In the event that no specific time is referred to when the undertaking is given, fulfilment "within a reasonable time" will be expected. What amounts to a "reasonable time" will depend on the circumstances but the onus is on the giver to ensure that the recipient is kept informed of the likely time-scale and any delays to it.

29.   Failure to fulfil an undertaking may result in disciplinary action. However, neither the Law Society nor the Solicitors Disciplinary Tribunal may order

compensation to be paid to an aggrieved party or bring about performance of the terms of the undertaking.

30.   If an undertaking requires the recipient to take certain steps and the recipient fails to do so, the giver may ask the Law Society to give notice to the recipient that unless these steps are taken within a period of time they will not then consider a complaint.

31.   All undertakings given by solicitors and RELs can be enforced by the court. (See court rules for the appropriate procedure to be followed.)   The Law Society will not investigate complaints of breaches of undertakings given to the court.

32.   Where you undertake to pay the costs of another party or a professional agent's costs, unless a specific amount is agreed, the term "costs" will mean 'proper costs'.   This allows you to request an assessment of the costs by the court.

33.   If a complaint is made to the Law Society concerning an alleged breach of an undertaking and it is found that the undertaking was procured by fraud, deceit or, in certain circumstances, innocent misrepresentation, the Law Society is unlikely to take any action in respect of the alleged breach.

34.   The Law Society will generally interpret an ambiguous undertaking in favour of the recipient.

35.   If you give an undertaking 'on behalf' of a client it will usually fall within the definition of an undertaking (see rule 24 – interpretation) and its performance would, therefore, be your responsibility.   If this is not what you intend, you should ensure that liability is disclaimed or it is made clear that you are simply informing the other party about your client's intentions.

36.   A promise to give an undertaking is normally treated as an undertaking and will be binding.

37.   Where an undertaking has been breached, the aggrieved party may seek compensation.   Your firm's insurance as required by the Solicitors' Indemnity Insurance Rules should cover valid claims.   If you are in in-house practice, you should consider whether your employer has appropriate insurance.   You will remain personally liable in conduct, and may also be financially liable, regardless of whether you have adequate insurance.

38.   An undertaking is binding even if it is to do something outside your control. For example, if you undertake to make a payment out of the proceeds of sale of an asset, unless you clearly state to the contrary, you will be expected to make the payment even if the fund (gross or net) is insufficient.

39.   If you have received written instructions from your client that are expressed as irrevocable, they are nonetheless revocable, until you have acted on them in such a way as to change your personal position.

40.   Certain areas of work, particularly conveyancing, involve the use of tandard undertakings.   Care should be taken when using standard undertakings to ensure that they suit the specific circumstances.   For further details, please refer to a specialist publication.

41. Guidance on undertakings can be obtained from the Law Society's Professional Ethics department.

Seller's solicitor dealing with more than one prospective buyer – 10.06

42. When you are asked to "deal" with more than one prospective buyer you must comply with 10.06. "Deal" means any communication you have with any of the relevant parties intended to progress the matter – for example, the sending of a draft contract or a plan of the property. Communicating information of an estate agency nature, such as sending out particulars of sale or showing prospective buyers around a property, would not amount to "dealing" for the purposes of 10.06.

43. This requirement is sometimes known as the 'contract races' rule. This has created the impression that when a transaction is proceeding under such terms, whichever party presents their contract ready for exchanging first is the 'winner'. In fact, the terms of the arrangement are entirely at the discretion of the parties and speed may or may not be a factor. You should be careful to agree the terms of the arrangement.

44. If you are required to inform another conveyancer of your intention to proceed with two or more prospective buyers, you should do so immediately by the most suitable means. If the information is given in person or on the telephone, there is no requirement that the details be confirmed in writing but this is advisable.

45. Special care should be taken when dealing with unqualified conveyancers or unrepresented buyers. See notes 2 and 3 above.

Fees of lawyers of other jurisdictions – 10.07

46. 10.07 does not apply when you merely introduce or refer a client to a lawyer of another jurisdiction. However, when you instruct such a lawyer, you will be accepting the liability to pay the lawyer's proper fees unless one of the exceptions in 10.07 applies. For example, if you do not hold money on account and your client is declared bankrupt, you may have to pay the lawyer's proper fee out of your own funds.

47. The fees of a lawyer of another jurisdiction may be regulated by a scale approved by the relevant bar association or law society. You can contact the International Unit of the Law Society for advice.

48. 10.07 is intended in part to give effect to article 5.7 of the CCBE Code. In the event that a dispute arises concerning the payment of the fees of a lawyer of an Establishment Directive state, rule 16 (European cross-border practice) should be consulted and the necessary action taken before starting any proceedings.

Rule 11 – Litigation and advocacy

Introduction

Rule 11 imposes additional duties on you if you are a solicitor, an REL or an RFL whenever you exercise a right to conduct litigation or act as an advocate. "Court" in this rule has a wide meaning – see rule 24 (Interpretation). References to appearing or acting as an advocate apply when you are exercising rights of audience before any court, not just if you have been granted rights of audience in the higher courts. The rule only applies in a modified form to overseas practice – see 15.11.

Rule 11 – Litigation and advocacy

11.01 Deceiving or misleading the court

You must never deceive or knowingly mislead the court.

11.02 Obeying court orders

You must comply with any properly made court order requiring you or your firm to take, or refrain from taking, a particular course of action.

11.03 Contempt of court

You must not become in contempt of court.

11.04 Refusing instructions to act as advocate

(1)   You must not refuse to act as an advocate for any person on any of the following grounds:

(a)   that the nature of the case is objectionable to you or to any section of the public;

(b)   that the conduct, opinions or beliefs of the prospective client are unacceptable to you or to any section of the public; or

(c)   that the source of any financial support which may properly be given to the prospective client for the proceedings is unacceptable to you.

(2)   You are not required to act as an advocate:

(a)   under a conditional fee agreement; or

(b)   if you reasonably consider that you are not being offered a proper fee having regard to:

(i)   the circumstances of the case;

(ii)   the nature of your practice; or

       (iii)   your experience and standing.

11.05 Appearing as an advocate

(1)   If you are appearing as an advocate:

    (a)   you must not say anything which is merely scandalous or intended only to insult a witness or any other person;

    (b)   you must avoid naming in open court any third party whose character would thereby be called into question, unless it is necessary for the proper conduct of the case;

    (c)   you must not call into question the character of a witness you have cross-examined unless the witness has had the opportunity to answer the allegations during cross-examination; and

    (d)   you must not suggest that any person is guilty of a crime, fraud or misconduct unless such allegations:

        (i)   go to a matter in issue which is material to your client's case; and

        (ii)   appear to you to be supported by reasonable grounds.

(2)   You must not appear as an advocate at a trial if it is clear that you, or anyone within your firm, will be called as a witness at the trial, unless you are satisfied that this will not prejudice your independence as an advocate, the interests of your client or the interests of justice.

11.06 Payments to witnesses

You must not make, or offer to make, payments to a witness dependent upon the nature of the evidence given or upon the outcome of the case.

11.07 Recordings of child witnesses' evidence

If you are acting in the defence or prosecution of an accused and you have in your possession a copy of an audio or video recording of a child witness which has been identified as having been prepared to be admitted in evidence at a criminal trial in accordance with the relevant provisions of the Criminal Justice Act 1991 or the Youth Justice and Criminal Evidence Act 1999, you must:

    (a)   not make or permit any person to make a copy of the recording;

    (b)   not release the recording to the accused;

    (c)   not make or permit any disclosure of the recording or its contents to any person except when, in your opinion, it is necessary in the course of preparing the prosecution, defence or appeal against conviction and/or sentence;

    (d)   ensure that the recording is always kept in a locked, secure container when not in use; and

(e)   return the recording when you are no longer instructed in the matter.

Guidance to rule 11 – Litigation and advocacy

General

1.   If you are an RFL you do not have any rights of audience or right to conduct litigation (or the right to supervise or assume responsibility for the exercise of any such right) other than those rights which are not reserved by law to any category of persons but are open to any individual. See also 12.03(5) and note 4 of the guidance to rule 12 (framework of practice).

2.   If you are an REL you can conduct litigation or appear as an advocate provided you are instructed in conjunction with a solicitor or barrister who is entitled to perform that service. The role of the solicitor or barrister is not to supervise you or take responsibility for your work, but to assist the court in the event of a problem arising. You can appear as an advocate in those courts and cases in which all solicitors can exercise a right of audience. Like solicitors, you are eligible to acquire extended rights of audience by obtaining one of the Law Society's higher courts qualifications.

3.   When acting for a client requiring advocacy services you should always consider whether the interests of the client would be best served by you, another lawyer from the same firm or another advocate providing these services. Factors to be taken into consideration include the nature and complexity of the case, your experience and ability, and the nature of your practice.

4.   As an officer of the court you should take all reasonable steps to assist in the smooth running of the courts but only in so far as this is consistent with your duties to your client, in particular the duty of confidentiality. For example, if your client fails to attend a hearing you may properly state that you are without instructions, but could not disclose information about the client's whereabouts.

5.   You should be cautious about communicating with judges outside the courtroom, in respect of matters in which you are appearing before them, unless you are invited to do so in the presence of the solicitor or counsel for the other side or party.

Attending advocates at court

6.   Whenever you instruct an advocate – whether counsel or a solicitor advocate – you will need to decide whether it is in the interests of your client and the interests of justice for you, or a responsible representative of your firm, to attend the proceedings. In reaching this decision you will need to consider what is necessary for the proper conduct of the case, taking into account the nature and complexity of the case and the capacity of the client to understand the proceedings. For example, you, or your representative, should normally attend:

(a)   where the client is charged with an offence classified pursuant to section 75(2) of the Supreme Court Act 1981 as class 1 or 2 (such as murder, manslaughter or rape);

(b)   in cases of complex or serious fraud;

(c)   where the client may have difficulty in giving or receiving instructions or in understanding the proceedings, for example if the client is a child, has inadequate knowledge of English, or suffers from a mental illness or some other disability;

(d)   where the client is likely to disrupt proceedings if the advocate appears alone;

(e)   where the advocate is representing more than one party to the hearing;

(f)   where there are a substantial number of defence documents at a trial;

(g)   where there are a large number of witnesses in the case;

(h)   on the day on which the client is to be sentenced, particularly where the client is likely to receive a custodial sentence; or

(i)   where issues are likely to arise which question the client's character or your conduct of the case.

7.   Where you decide that an advocate should not be attended you should inform the advocate and deliver a full and detailed brief sufficiently early for the advocate to consider the papers and to decide whether it would be appropriate for the advocate to attend alone. You should also inform the client that the advocate will be unattended and how instructions may be given.

Statements to the media

8.   Before making a statement to the media you should consider:

(a)   whether it is in the client's best interests to do so;

(b)   whether the client has consented to this course of action; and

(c)   the legal position, for example contempt of court (see 11.03 and guidance note 18 below).

Deceiving or misleading the court – 11.01

9.   11.01 makes a distinction between deceiving the court, where knowledge is assumed, and misleading the court, which could happen inadvertently. You would not normally be guilty of misconduct if you inadvertently misled the court. However, if during the course of proceedings you become aware that you have inadvertently misled the court, you must, with your client's consent, immediately inform the court. If the client does not consent you must stop acting. 11.01 includes attempting to deceive or mislead the court.

10.   You might deceive or mislead the court by, for example:

(a)   submitting inaccurate information or allowing another person to do so;

(b)   indicating agreement with information that another person puts forward which you know is false;

    (c)   calling a witness whose evidence you know is untrue;

    (d)   seeking to persuade a witness to change their evidence; or

    (e)   not immediately disclosing a document you have become aware of during the course of a case, which should have been, but was not, disclosed.

11.   Whilst a person can call themselves by whatever name they choose, you must (in the context of court proceedings) be satisfied that the client is not adopting a different name or date of birth to avoid previous convictions becoming known to the court, or to deceive the court in any other way.

12.   If you are acting for a defendant, you need not correct information given to the court by the prosecution or any other party which you know may allow the court to make incorrect assumptions about the client or the case, provided you do not indicate agreement with that information.

13.   Where a client admits to having committed perjury or having misled the court in any material matter relating to ongoing proceedings, you must not act further in those proceedings unless the client agrees to disclose the truth to the court.

14.   If, either before or during the course of proceedings, the client makes statements to you which are inconsistent, this is not of itself a ground for you to stop acting. Only where it is clear that the client is attempting to put forward false evidence to the court should you stop acting. In other circumstances it would be for the court, and not for you, to assess the truth or otherwise of the client's statement.

15.   There are some types of information which you are obliged to disclose to the court, whether or not it is in the best interests of the client to do so. Failure to disclose such information could amount to a breach of 11.01. For example:

    (a)   The advocates on both sides must advise the court of relevant cases and statutory provisions. If one of them omits a case or provision or makes an incorrect reference to a case or provision, it is the duty of the other to draw attention to it even if it assists the opponent's case.

    (b)   Except when acting or appearing for the prosecution, if you know of facts which, or of a witness who, would assist the adversary you are not under any duty to inform the adversary, or the court, of this to the prejudice of your own client. However, if you know that a relevant document has been filed in the proceedings and is therefore notionally within the knowledge of the court, you must inform the judge of its existence.

16.   You are permitted, even when acting as an advocate, to interview and take statements from any witness or prospective witness at any stage in the proceedings, whether or not that witness has been interviewed or called as a witness by another party. You must not tamper with the evidence of a witness or attempt to pressurise the witness into changing their evidence. To avoid such allegations it would be wise, when seeking to interview a witness for the other side, to offer to interview them in the presence of the other side's representative.

Obeying court orders – 11.02

17.   You have a responsibility to ensure that you comply with properly made court orders. This responsibility extends to your relationship with your client. Therefore, you must not aid and abet a client where the client refuses to obey a properly made court order.

Contempt of court – 11.03

18.   You could, for example, become in contempt of court by making a statement to the press which is calculated to interfere with the fair trial of a case which has not been concluded.

Refusing instructions to act as advocate – 11.04

19.   In addition to complying with 11.04 you must comply with rule 6 (avoiding discrimination) in your dealings with clients, staff, other lawyers and third parties.

20.   11.04(2)(b) states that you may refuse to act if you are not being offered a proper fee. In the case of publicly funded matters this means that if the fee likely to be received from the Legal Services Commission is lower than your normal charging rate, you may decline to act.

Appearing as an advocate – 11.05

21.   11.05(1) sets out a number of issues relating to the way in which you conduct yourself in court. There may be other restrictions, such as rules of court, which affect the way a case may be presented in court and you should familiarise yourself with these.

22.   It is not the intention of 11.05(1) to prevent you robustly defending your client's position.

23.   The circumstances in which it will be proper for you to appear as an advocate at a trial at which you are also a witness will be extremely rare. Factors you will need to consider include:

(a)   the nature of the evidence you are being asked to give, its importance to the case and in particular whether it is likely to be contested or is purely formal;

(b)   whether the situation would give rise to a conflict between you or your firm and your client. For example, it would not be appropriate for you to give evidence for another party (or, in a criminal case, the prosecution); and

(c)   how your client would be affected if, having already accepted instructions to act, you were to stop acting.

24.   Provided the evidence is unlikely to be contested on a factual basis, it will normally be acceptable for you to act as an advocate if a member of your firm is to give evidence. For example, if an employee of your firm has advised a client at a police station, and is required to give evidence as to the reasons for

advising the client to exercise the right to silence, it would not be improper for you to act as an advocate in the case.

25.   You will need to consider your client's interests when asked to act in a matter in which there is a significant risk that you, or a member of your firm, will be called as a witness in the case. You should not accept instructions to act for a client in circumstances where you could not act if you had already been called – for example, if you had witnessed events which were material to the issue being tried. On the other hand there is always a degree of risk that events you witnessed at a police station, such as the client exercising the right to silence or an identity parade, will become an issue at the trial. However this would not normally prevent you appearing as an advocate.

26.   11.05 would not normally prevent you giving evidence at a pre-trial hearing, for example by making a witness statement which is purely concerned with procedural issues, provided your evidence is unlikely to be contested at the trial.

Payments to witnesses – 11.06

27.   There is no objection to your paying reasonable expenses to witnesses and reasonable compensation for loss of time attending court.

Recording of child witnesses' evidence – 11.07

28.   The Law Society recommends that you use the following form of undertaking in order to comply with 11.07:

"I/We acknowledge receipt of the recording marked 'evidence of ...'.

I/We undertake that whilst the recording is in my/our possession I/we shall:

(a)   not make or permit any other person to make a copy of the recording;

(b)   not release the recording to [name of the accused];

(c)   not make or permit any disclosure of the recording or its contents to any person except when in my/our opinion it is necessary in the course of preparing the prosecution, defence, or appeal against conviction and/or sentence;

(d)   ensure that the recording is always kept in a locked, secure container when not in use; and

(e)   return the recording to you when I am/we are no longer instructed in the matter."

29.   Recordings should preferably be delivered to third parties by hand but where this is not possible the recording should be sent by recorded delivery. To avoid the risk of theft the contents of the package should not be apparent from the outside. If you personally collect, or a member of staff personally collects, a recording, you or they should be able to produce a proper form of identification.

30.   Although 11.07 does not specifically define "locked, secure container" a locked car cannot be considered as such and a recording should never be left unattended in a car.

31.   You may be asked to give an undertaking in the form recommended by the Home Office, which is similar to that recommended by the Law Society. As with the giving of any undertaking, you should first ensure that you can comply with its terms.

Rule 12 – Framework of practice

Introduction

This rule sets out the types of business through which solicitors, RELs, RFLs and recognised bodies may practise under the regulation of the Law Society. The restrictions are necessary to ensure that members of the public receiving services from solicitors, RELs and their firms have all the client protections provided under the current statutory framework, and so that the Law Society can adequately regulate the firm within its current statutory powers. The guidance signposts the reader to other rules which deal with particular types of business in more detail.

Rule 12 – Framework of practice

12.01 Solicitors

Practice from an office in England and Wales

(1) You may practise as a solicitor from an office in England and Wales in the following ways only:

    (a) as a sole principal;

    (b) as a partner in a partnership consisting of:

        (i) solicitors, with or without RELs and/or recognised bodies;

        (ii) solicitors and RFLs, with or without RELs;

        (iii) solicitors, RELs and non-registered European lawyers, with or without RFLs; or

        (iv) solicitors, RELs, non-registered European lawyers and recognised bodies;

    (c) as a director, member or shareowner of a company which is a recognised body;

    (d) as a member of an LLP which is a recognised body;

    (e) in the employment of any firm in which a solicitor or an REL would be permitted to participate under this rule as a sole principal, partner, director, member or shareowner, for practice from an office in England and Wales; or

    (f) in any other employment, provided that you undertake work only for your employer, or as permitted by rule 13 (in-house practice).

(2) You must not, as a solicitor:

    (a) be a partner in a partnership which has a separate legal identity, if the partnership has an office in England and Wales; or

   (b)   be a director, member or owner of a body corporate which has an office in England and Wales and is not a recognised body, unless you do so as an in-house solicitor.

Practice from an office outside England and Wales

(3)   You may practise as a solicitor from an office outside England and Wales in the following ways only:

   (a)   as a sole principal;

   (b)   as a partner in a partnership consisting of:

      (i)   practising lawyers; and/or

      (ii)   bodies corporate wholly owned and directed by lawyers for the purpose of practising law; and/or

      (iii)   partnerships which have separate legal identity, whose partners are all lawyers;

   (c)   as a partner in a partnership consisting of persons under (b) above, together with other persons, provided that:

      (i)   the partnership has no office in England and Wales;

      (ii)   a controlling majority of the partners are persons under (b) above;

      (iii)   the involvement of non-lawyers in the partnership does not put the lawyers in breach of any applicable local rules; and

      (iv)   if the partnership has an office in an Establishment Directive state, the rules applying in that jurisdiction would permit local lawyers to enter into a partnership with similar involvement of non-lawyers;

   (d)   as a director or owner of a body corporate wholly owned and directed, for the purpose of practising law, by:

      (i)   practising lawyers; and/or

      (ii)   bodies corporate wholly owned and directed by lawyers for the purpose of practising law; and/or

      (iii)   partnerships which have separate legal identity, whose partners are all lawyers;

   (e)   as a director or owner of a body corporate wholly owned and directed, for the purpose of practising law, by persons under (d) above, together with other persons, provided that:

      (i)   the body corporate has no office in England and Wales;

      (ii)   a controlling majority of the directors and of the owners are persons under (d) above;

(iii)   the involvement of non-lawyers in the body corporate does not put the lawyer directors or owners in breach of any applicable local rules; and

(iv)   if the body corporate has an office in an Establishment Directive state, the rules applying in that jurisdiction would permit local lawyers to practise through a body corporate with similar involvement of non-lawyers;

(f)   in the employment of any firm in which a solicitor or an REL would be permitted to participate under this rule as a sole principal, partner, director or owner, for practice as a solicitor from an office outside England and Wales or as a lawyer of an Establishment Directive state from an office in Scotland or Northern Ireland; or

(g)   in any other employment, provided that you undertake work only as permitted by 15.13 (in-house practice overseas).

12.02   RELs

If you are an REL:

Practice from an office in England and Wales

(1)   You may practise as a lawyer of an Establishment Directive state from an office in England and Wales in the following ways only:

(a)   as a sole principal;

(b)   as a partner in a partnership consisting of:

(i)   RELs, with or without solicitors and/or recognised bodies;

(ii)   RELs and RFLs, with or without solicitors;

(iii)   RELs and non-registered European lawyers, with or without solicitors and/or RFLs; or

(iv)   RELs, non-registered European lawyers and recognised bodies, with or without solicitors;

(c)   as a director, member or shareowner of a company which is a recognised body;

(d)   as a member of an LLP which is a recognised body;

(e)   in the employment of any firm in which an REL or a solicitor would be permitted to participate under this rule as a sole principal, partner, director, member or shareowner, for practice from an office in England and Wales; or

(f)   in any other employment, provided that you undertake work only for your employer, or as permitted by rule 13 (in-house practice).

(2)   You must not, as a lawyer of an Establishment Directive state:

   (a)   be a partner in a partnership which has a separate legal identity, if the partnership has an office in England and Wales; or

   (b)   be a director, member or owner of a body corporate which has an office in England and Wales and is not a recognised body, unless you do so as an in-house lawyer.

Practice from an office in Scotland or Northern Ireland

(3)   You may practise as a lawyer of an Establishment Directive state from an office in Scotland or Northern Ireland in the following ways only:

   (a)   as a sole principal;

   (b)   as a partner in a partnership consisting of:

      (i)   practising lawyers; and/or

      (ii)   bodies corporate wholly owned and directed by lawyers for the purpose of practising law; and/or

      (iii)   partnerships which have separate legal identity, whose partners are all lawyers;

   (c)   as a partner in a partnership consisting of persons under (b) above, together with other persons, provided that:

      (i)   the partnership has no office in England and Wales;

      (ii)   a controlling majority of the partners are persons under (b) above;

      (iii)   the involvement of non-lawyers in the partnership does not put the lawyers in breach of any applicable local rules; and

      (iv)   the rules applying in that jurisdiction would permit local lawyers to enter into a partnership with similar involvement of non-lawyers;

   (d)   as a director or owner of a body corporate wholly owned and directed, for the purpose of practising law, by:

      (i)   practising lawyers; and/or

      (ii)   bodies corporate wholly owned and directed by lawyers for the purpose of practising law; and/or

      (iii)   partnerships which have separate legal identity, whose partners are all lawyers;

   (e)   as a director or owner of a body corporate wholly owned and directed, for the purpose of practising law, by persons under (d) above, together with other persons, provided that:

      (i)   the body corporate has no office in England and Wales;

       (ii)   a controlling majority of the directors and of the owners are persons under (d) above;

       (iii)   the involvement of non-lawyers in the body corporate does not put the lawyer directors or owners in breach of any applicable local rules; and

       (iv)   the rules applying in that jurisdiction would permit local lawyers to practise through a body corporate with similar involvement of non-lawyers;

   (f)   in the employment of any firm in which an REL or a solicitor would be permitted to participate under this rule as a sole principal, partner, director, or owner, for practice as a lawyer of an Establishment Directive state from an office in Scotland or Northern Ireland or as a solicitor from an office outside England and Wales; or

   (g)   in any other employment, provided that you undertake work only as permitted by 15.13 (in-house practice overseas).

12.03 RFLs

Practice in the capacity of an RFL

(1)   In these rules, practice as a foreign lawyer in the capacity of an RFL is confined to:

   (a)   practice as a partner in an MNP which has an office in England and Wales and which consists of:

       (i)   solicitors and/or RELs, together with RFLs; or

       (ii)   RELs, RFLs and non-registered European lawyers, with or without solicitors;

   (b)   practice as a director of a company which is a recognised body; and

   (c)   practice as a member of an LLP which is a recognised body;

and if you practise in that capacity you will be subject to these rules and to regulation by the Law Society.

Practice in another capacity than as an RFL

(2)   If you provide services as a foreign lawyer in any of the following ways, you will not be practising in the capacity of an RFL:

   (a)   as a sole principal;

   (b)   as a partner in a partnership in which none of the partners is a solicitor, or an REL;

   (c)   as a director of a company, or a member of an LLP, which is not a recognised body; or

(d)   as the employee of a business which is not the practice of a solicitor, an REL or a recognised body;

and you must not be held out or described in that context as an RFL, or as regulated by or registered with the Law Society.

(3)   You must not be held out or described as an RFL, or as regulated by or registered with the Law Society, in the context of:

(a)   employment in the practice of a solicitor, an REL or a recognised body; or

(b)   participation in any firm which operates wholly outside England and Wales.

(4)   If you have a practice under (1) above, and another business under (2) above, the latter is a "separate business" for the purpose of these rules and you must therefore comply with rule 21 (separate businesses).

Scope of practice of an RFL

(5)   Whether practising in your capacity as an RFL or not, you must not:

(a)   undertake work which you are not qualified or entitled to undertake by the law of England and Wales; or

(b)   appear as advocate before any court or tribunal in England and Wales in which you have no right of audience.

12.04 Recognised bodies

Practice from an office in England and Wales

(1)   A recognised body may practise from an office in England and Wales in the following ways only:

(a)   as a stand-alone firm;

(b)   as a body corporate wholly owned by, and providing services in conjunction with:

(i)   the practice of a solicitor or an REL as a sole principal;

(ii)   a partnership consisting of:

(A)   solicitors and/or RELs and/or recognised bodies;

(B)   solicitors and/or RELs together with RFLs;

(C)   RELs and non-registered European lawyers, with or without solicitors and/or RFLs; or

(D)   RELs, non-registered European lawyers and recognised bodies, with or without solicitors;

        (iii)   another recognised body;

    (c)   as a partner in a partnership consisting of

        (i)   recognised bodies, with or without solicitors and/or RELs; or

        (ii)   recognised bodies, RELs and non-registered European lawyers, with or without solicitors;

    (d)   as a member or shareowner of another recognised body.

(2)   A recognised body must not practise as:

    (a)   a partner in a partnership which has a separate legal identity, if the partnership has an office in England and Wales; or

    (b)   a director, member or owner of a body corporate which has an office in England and Wales and is not a recognised body.

Practice from an office outside England and Wales by a recognised body incorporated in England and Wales

(3)   A recognised body which is incorporated in England and Wales may practise from an office outside England and Wales in the following ways only:

    (a)   as a stand-alone firm;

    (b)   as a partner in a partnership consisting of:

        (i)   practising lawyers; and/or

        (ii)   bodies corporate wholly owned and directed by lawyers for the purpose of practising law; and/or

        (iii)   partnerships which have separate legal identity, whose partners are all lawyers;

    (c)   as a partner in a partnership consisting of persons under (b) above together with other persons, provided that:

        (i)   the partnership has no office in England and Wales;

        (ii)   a controlling majority of the partners are persons under (b) above;

        (iii)   the involvement of non-lawyers in the partnership does not put the lawyers in breach of any applicable local rules; and

        (iv)   if the partnership has an office in an Establishment Directive state, the rules applying in that jurisdiction would permit local lawyers to enter into a partnership with similar involvement of non-lawyers;

    (d)   as a member or shareowner of another recognised body;

(e)   as a director or owner of a body corporate which is wholly owned and directed, for the purpose of practising law, by:

    (i)   practising lawyers; and/or

    (ii)   bodies corporate wholly owned and directed by lawyers for the purpose of practising law; and/or

    (iii)   partnerships which have separate legal identity, whose partners are all lawyers; or

(f)   as a director or owner of a body corporate wholly owned and directed, for the purpose of practising law, by persons under (e) above, together with other persons, provided that:

    (i)   the body corporate has no office in England and Wales;

    (ii)   a controlling majority of the directors and of the owners are persons under (e) above;

    (iii)   the involvement of non-lawyers in the body corporate does not put the lawyer directors or owners in breach of any applicable local rules; and

    (iv)   if the body corporate has an office in an Establishment Directive state, the rules applying in that jurisdiction would permit local lawyers to practise through a body corporate with similar involvement of non-lawyers.

Practice from an office outside England and Wales by a recognised body incorporated outside England and Wales

(4)   (a)   In relation to practice from an office outside England and Wales, a recognised body incorporated outside England and Wales is not subject to these rules except as specified in this paragraph.

    (b)   The recognised body is subject to:

        (i)   this paragraph;

        (ii)   1.10 (profession);

        (iii)   rule 14 (incorporated practice); and

        (iv)   rule 15 (overseas practice), but only to the extent that rule 15 specifically applies any provision of these rules to a recognised body incorporated outside England and Wales.

    (c)   If a provision of these rules does not apply to a recognised body incorporated outside England and Wales, 14.01(4) will not apply to a director, member or shareowner of the recognised body or a person employed to work in the practice of the recognised body, in relation to that rule.

12.05 Definition of "lawyer" in this rule

In this rule, "lawyer" means a member, and entitled to practise as such, of:

(a) a legal profession covered by the Establishment Directive, including a solicitor and a barrister of England and Wales; or

(b) a legal profession not covered by the Establishment Directive, but excluding a lawyer whose registration under s.89 of the Courts and Legal Services Act 1990 is suspended or whose name has been struck off the register.

Guidance to rule 12 – Framework of practice

1. Rule 12 imposes restrictions on the type of business through which you may practise as a lawyer regulated by the Law Society. The main prohibitions can be summarised as follows:

(a) A solicitor may not practise from an office in England and Wales:

(i) in any partnership which has a separate legal identity;

(ii) through any body corporate which is not a recognised body; or

(iii) in partnership with any individual who is not directly regulated by the Law Society, except where there is an REL in the partnership, in which case non-registered European lawyers may also be partners.

Examples of partnerships which have separate legal identities are a general partnership formed under the law of Scotland, and a limited liability partnership formed under Californian law. Examples of partnerships which do not have separate legal identities are a general partnership formed under the law of England and Wales, and a limited liability partnership formed under the law of New York. Further guidance as to limited liability partnerships formed under the laws of various US states is available from the Professional Ethics department of the Law Society.

(b) A solicitor may practise with other lawyers from an office outside England and Wales in almost any kind of partnership or body corporate. Subject to strict limitations, a solicitor may also practise in partnership, or share ownership of a corporate firm with:

(i) an individual who is not a lawyer;

(ii) a body corporate which is not wholly owned and directed by lawyers; and

(iii) a partnership with a separate legal identity, whose partners are not all lawyers.

(c) A recognised body must have one office in England and Wales, under 14.06(1). It is subject to restrictions in relation to its English and Welsh office(s) similar to those which apply to a solicitor – but, unlike a solicitor, a recognised body is not allowed to practise in England and Wales in partnership with an RFL. A recognised body which provides services direct to clients and is paid for the service provided is a "stand-alone firm" for the purpose of 12.04(1)(a). An executor, trustee or nominee company which is owned by a partnership is providing services in conjunction with a firm for the purpose of 12.04(1)(b). See notes 15 and 16 of the guidance to rule 14 (incorporated practice).

(d)   In relation to the practice of a recognised body from offices outside England and Wales, rule 12 applies differently according to whether the recognised body is incorporated in, or outside, England and Wales. All recognised bodies are subject to rule 14 (incorporated practice) as to their own internal structure. A recognised body incorporated outside England and Wales can be a partner in a partnership which does not have an office in England and Wales, or share ownership of a corporate firm which does not have an office in England and Wales, without restriction. Although the rule allows a recognised body to participate in another firm which includes non-lawyers such a firm would have to be separate from the recognised body's practice from its office(s) in England and Wales.

(e)   An REL is subject to the same restrictions as a solicitor in relation to practice from an office in England and Wales, or in Scotland or Northern Ireland, but is not subject to rule 12 in relation to practice from an office outside the UK. Although the rule would allow an REL to practise from an office in Scotland or Northern Ireland in a firm which includes non-lawyers, the rules governing Scottish solicitors and Northern Irish solicitors do not currently allow it.

(f)   Partnerships between solicitors and RFLs, or between RELs and RFLs, are called multi-national partnerships (MNPs). An MNP cannot have a recognised body as a partner. An information pack on RFLs/MNPs is available from the Professional Ethics department of the Law Society. An RFL is subject to rule 12 only in relation to practice in England and Wales in partnership with a solicitor or an REL, or as a director of a recognised body which is a company, or as a member of a recognised body which is an LLP, except that:

(i)   12.03(2) applies to prohibit an RFL from being held out or described as an RFL or as regulated by or registered with the Law Society in the context of participation in a business which is not a firm; and

(ii)   12.03(3) applies to prohibit an RFL from being held out or described as an RFL or as regulated by or registered with the Law Society in the context of employment in a firm, or participation in a firm with no office in England and Wales.

2.   12.03(3)(a) does not prevent you from being described as an RFL or order to show that you are entitled to be held out as a "partner" of an LLP – see notes 33 - 36 of the guidance to rule 7 (publicity).

3.   Other rules govern, or restrict, certain specific types of practice, as follows:

(a)   Rule 13 (in-house practice) sets out the limited circumstances in which, as an in-house solicitor or in-house REL in England and Wales, you can provide services to persons other than your employer.

(b)   Rule 14 (incorporated practice) governs the internal structure of a recognised body. The provisions of rule 14 link with the prohibitions in rule 12 on practising from an office in England and Wales through a body corporate which is not a recognised body. The Recognised Bodies Regulations set out the formalities relating to applying for recognition, etc.

(c)   Rule 15 (overseas practice) governs practice as a solicitor from an office outside England and Wales, or an REL's practice as a lawyer of an Establishment Directive state from an office in Scotland or Northern Ireland. It also governs the overseas practice of a recognised body. Rule 15 applies or modifies other rules in relation to overseas practice. Sometimes a provision does not apply at all, or is replaced with a more flexible requirement suitable to practice in other jurisdictions.

(d)   Rule 8 (fee sharing) sets out the limited circumstances in which you may share fees with non-lawyers. Fee sharing with non-lawyers is not generally allowed, except with a partner permitted for overseas practice under rule 12, or for the purpose of raising capital or obtaining services for the firm. Note in particular, that:

(i)   fee sharing with non-lawyers remains prohibited in relation to European cross-border practice (see rule 16);

(ii)   a firm cannot share its fees even with an overseas partnership or overseas corporate firm which is permitted under rule 12, if that other firm includes non-lawyers.

(e)   Rule 21 (separate businesses) prohibits you from providing some services through a business which is not regulated by the Law Society. If you practise in England and Wales you are generally required to provide legal services as a practising lawyer regulated by the Law Society. If you provide other 'solicitor-like' services through a business which is not regulated by the Law Society you must put in place safeguards to prevent confusion arising from your professional status. For example:

(i)   under 21.04 you may have a separate business as an estate agent but you must comply with all the safeguards set out in 21.05.

(ii)   under 21.02 you may not have a separate business which provides trustee, executor or nominee services in England and Wales, so such a trustee, executor or nominee company must be a recognised body.

4.   You should note the following matters of law:

(a)   If you are an REL you have the same rights of audience, rights to conduct litigation and rights to draft litigation documents as a solicitor, but you must act in conjunction with a solicitor and/or barrister. You may not do or supervise reserved conveyancing or probate work unless you are qualified to do that work under regulation 12 or 13 of the European Communities (Lawyer's Practice) Regulations 2000. At present:

(i) RELs qualified in Cyprus, the Czech Republic, Denmark, Finland, Hungary, Iceland, the Irish Republic, Liechtenstein, Norway, Slovakia and Sweden are entitled to do reserved conveyancing work in England and Wales; and

(ii) RELs qualified in Austria, Cyprus, Denmark, Finland, Germany, Iceland, the Irish Republic, Liechtenstein, Norway, Slovakia and Sweden are entitled to do reserved probate work in England and Wales.

(b) If you are an RFL you are not a "qualified person" under the Solicitors Act 1974. Becoming an RFL does not confer any right of audience, right to conduct litigation or right to do or supervise reserved conveyancing, probate, trust or litigation work. An RFL who is a partner in an MNP cannot even do certain work which an employee of the MNP could do – appearing in chambers as a solicitor's clerk, or doing reserved conveyancing, probate, trust or litigation work under the supervision of a solicitor. However, an RFL who is a director of a recognised body which is a company or a member of a recognised body which is an LLP can do reserved conveyancing, probate, trust or litigation work under the supervision of a "qualified person" in the recognised body. If the recognised body is a company that person must be a co-director and if the recognised body is an LLP that person must be a fellow member.

(c) RFLs and MNPs exist by virtue of the Courts and Legal Services Act 1990. Under section 89 of and Schedule 14 to that Act:

(i) a solicitor or barrister of England and Wales, even if not practising as such, cannot be an RFL;

(ii) only a person who is a member, and entitled to practise as such, of a legal profession regulated within a jurisdiction outside England and Wales can become an RFL;

(iii) before a lawyer can be registered as an RFL the Law Society must have approved that lawyer's profession for the purpose (the Law Society's booklet on RFLs lists the professions already approved); and

(iv) the applicant must be of good standing, there must be no other circumstances to make registration undesirable, and the applicant's own profession must not prohibit practice in partnership with English solicitors in England and Wales (the Law Society's booklet on RFLs lists the professional bodies which have already confirmed that their rules do not prohibit practice in partnership with solicitors in England and Wales).

(d) Under the Immigration and Asylum Act 1999, immigration advice and immigration services may be provided by a firm, on the basis that the service is either provided by or supervised by:

(i) a solicitor;

(ii)   a lawyer of an Establishment Directive state, including an REL; or

(iii) an RFL who is a partner in an MNP, a director of a recognised body which is a company, or a member of a recognised body which is an LLP; or

(iv)   a legal executive (FILEX) employee of the firm.

(e)   If you are an REL or an RFL, legal restrictions on your right to do or to supervise certain types of work do not prevent you from being the person in a firm who is "qualified to supervise" for the purpose of 5.02. However, under 5.01(1)(a) you would have to ensure that unqualified employees do not do reserved work unless supervised by a solicitor, or by an REL who is entitled to undertake and supervise that work. See also notes 8 and 41 of the guidance to rule 5 (business management).

5.   Rule 12 governs the types of business through which you may practise, but disgraceful conduct outside your practice may put you in breach of 1.10 (profession).

Rule 13 – In-house practice

Introduction

If you are a solicitor or an REL you may practise from an office in England and Wales as the employee of a business which is not the practice of a solicitor, an REL or a recognised body (rule 12 - framework of practice). You are subject to these rules, and your employer is your client. In addition, you must comply with rule 13. An in-house solicitor or in-house REL acting for a member of the public cannot provide the same protections for that client as a solicitor or REL practising through a firm. For this reason, and in order to reduce the scope for conflicts of interest, rule 13 limits and sets conditions upon your ability to act for persons other than your employer. The rule, except for 13.04, does not apply to your overseas practice, but you must comply with 15.13.

Rule 13 – In-house practice

13.01 Conditions applying at all times

(1)   You must not act for a client other than your employer under 13.02 to 13.12 if to do so would compromise:

    (a)   your professional independence or integrity;

    (b)   your duty to act in the best interests of that client;

    (c)   your duty to comply with rule 3 (conflict of interests);

    (d)   your duty to keep information about that client's affairs confidential from your employer (unless the other client consents to disclosure, or you are acting under 13.11 as the employee of a foreign law firm); or

    (e)   your ability to discharge any other duty owed to that client under these rules.

(2)   (a)   In order to act for a client other than your employer under 13.04, 13.07, 13.09 and 13.11, you must have professional indemnity insurance cover.

    (b)   In all other cases you must consider whether your employer has appropriate indemnity insurance or funds to meet any award made as a result of a claim in professional negligence against you, for which your employer might be vicariously liable. If not, you must inform the client in writing that you are not covered by the Law Society's insurance scheme.

13.02 Fellow employees

(1)   Subject to the provisos in 13.02(2), you may act for a person who is, or was formerly:

    (a)   a fellow employee;

    (b)   a director, the company secretary, a board member or (if the employer is an LLP) a member of your employer;

    (c)   an employee, a director, the company secretary, a board member, a trustee or (if the related body is an LLP) a member of a related body of the employer within the meaning of 13.03(1) or 13.08(c); or

    (d)   a contributor to a programme or periodical publication, broadcast or published by your employer (or by a related body within the meaning of 13.03(1) or 13.08(c)), but only where the contributor is a defendant or potential defendant in a defamation case.

(2)   You may act under (1) above only if:

    (a)   the matter relates to or arises out of the work of the employee, director, company secretary, board member, trustee, member or contributor in that capacity;

    (b)   the matter does not relate to a claim arising as a result of a personal injury to the employee, director, company secretary, board member, trustee, member or contributor;

    (c)   you are satisfied that the employee, director, company secretary, board member, trustee, member or contributor does not wish to instruct some other lawyer or qualified conveyancer; and

    (d)   no charge is made for your work unless those costs are recoverable from another source.

(3)   Where acting in a conveyancing transaction under (1)(a) to (c) above you may also act for a joint owner/buyer and for a mortgagee.

13.03 Related bodies

(1)   You may act for:

    (a)   the employer's holding, associated or subsidiary company;

    (b)   a partnership, syndicate, LLP or company by way of joint venture in which the employer and others have an interest;

    (c)   a trade association of which the employer is a member; or

    (d)   a club, association, pension fund or other scheme operated for the benefit of employees of the employer.

(2)   If you are employed in local government, (1)(a) and (b) above do not apply.

13.04 *Pro bono* work

(1)   You may, in the course of your employment, conduct work on a *pro bono* basis for a client other than your employer provided:

(a) the work is covered by professional indemnity cover reasonably equivalent to that required under the Solicitors' Indemnity Insurance Rules; and

(b) no fees are charged.

(2) (1) above does not apply to you if you are employed by a law centre, charity or other non-commercial advice service.

13.05 Associations

If you are employed by an association you may act for a member provided:

(a) the membership of the association is limited to persons engaged or concerned in a particular trade, occupation or activity or otherwise having a community of interest;

(b) the association is one formed *bona fide* for the benefit of its members and not formed directly or indirectly for your benefit or primarily for securing assistance in legal proceedings; and

(c) there is no charge to the member in non-contentious matters, and in contentious matters the association indemnifies the member in relation to your costs and disbursements insofar as they are not recoverable from any other source.

13.06 Insurers

(1) If you are employed by an insurer subrogated to the rights of an insured in respect of any matter you may act on behalf of the insurer in relation to that matter in the name of the insured, and also:

(a) act on behalf of the insured in relation to uninsured losses in respect of the matter;

(b) act in proceedings both for the insured and for a defendant covered by another insurer where the insurers have agreed an apportionment of liability; and/or

(c) act in the matter on behalf of the employer and another insurer in the joint prosecution of a claim.

(2) If you are employed by a legal expenses insurer you may, provided that the insured has given specific consent, act for an insured in any proceedings which are covered by the legal expenses insurance policy, provided that the proceedings do not include:

(a) a personal injury claim (whether made by or for the insured); or

(b) a civil claim for damages which

(i) exceeds the small claims limit from time to time in operation in the county court; and/or

(ii) is allocated or re-allocated to the fast track or the multi-track.

13.07 Commercial legal advice services

If you are employed by a commercial organisation providing a telephone legal advice service you may advise enquirers, provided:

(a)   the advice comprises telephone advice only, together with a follow up letter to the enquirer when necessary; and

(b)   you are satisfied that there is indemnity cover reasonably equivalent to that required under the Solicitors' Indemnity Insurance Rules.

13.08 Local government

If you are employed in local government you may act:

(a)   for another organisation or person to which or to whom the employer is statutorily empowered to provide legal services;

(b)   for a member or former member of the local authority, provided that:

(i)   the matter relates to or arises out of the work of the member in that capacity;

(ii)   the matter does not relate to a claim arising as a result of a personal injury to the member;

(iii) you are satisfied that the member does not wish to instruct some other lawyer; and

(iv) no charge is made for your work unless those costs are recoverable from some other source;

(c)   for a company limited by shares or guarantee of which:

(i)   the employer or nominee of the employer is a shareholder or guarantor; or

(ii)   you are, or an officer of the employer is, appointed by the employer as an officer of the company;

provided the employer is acting in pursuance of its statutory powers;

(d)   for lenders in connection with new mortgages arising from the redemption of mortgages to the local authority, provided:

(i)   neither you nor any other employee acts on behalf of the borrowers; and

(ii)   the borrowers are given the opportunity to be independently advised by a qualified conveyancer of their choice;

(e)   for a charity or voluntary organisation whose objects relate wholly or mainly to the employer's area, provided that there is no charge to the charity or voluntary organisation in non-contentious matters, and in contentious matters the employer indemnifies the charity or voluntary organisation in relation to your costs insofar as they are not recoverable from any other source;

(f)   for a patient who is the subject of a Court of Protection Order where you are acting for a fellow employee (under 13.02) who is appointed as receiver for the patient; or

(g)   for a child or young person subject to a Care Order in favour of the employer on an application to the Criminal Injuries Compensation Authority.

13.09 Law centres, charities and other non-commercial advice services

(1)   If you are employed by a law centre or advice service operated by a charitable or similar non-commercial organisation you may give advice to and otherwise act for members of the public, provided:

(a)   no funding agent has majority representation on the body responsible for the management of the service, and that body remains independent of central and local government;

(b)   no fees are charged save:

(i)   where the client is publicly funded; or

(ii)   where the organisation indemnifies the client in relation to your costs insofar as they are not recoverable from any other source;

(c)   all fees you earn and costs you recover are paid to the organisation for furthering the provision of the organisation's services;

(d)   the organisation is not described as a law centre unless it is a member of the Law Centres Federation; and

(e)   the organisation effects indemnity cover reasonably equivalent to that required under the Solicitors' Indemnity Insurance Rules.

(2)   (1) above does not apply to an association formed for the benefit of its members.

13.10 The Crown, non-departmental public bodies, and the Legal Services Commission

If you are employed by the Crown, a non-departmental public body, or the Legal Services Commission (or any body established or maintained by the Legal Services Commission), you may give legal advice to, and act for, other persons if in doing so you are carrying out the lawful functions of the employer.

13.11 Lawyers of other jurisdictions

(1)   You may provide legal services to your employer's clients, subject to the conditions set out in (2) below, if you are a solicitor or an REL employed by:

(a)   a practising lawyer of another jurisdiction who:

(i)   is not struck off or suspended from the register of foreign lawyers or the register of European lawyers, and

(ii)   is not practising in that context as a solicitor or as an REL; or

(b)   a business (including a body corporate) whose principals (or owners and directors) are all practising through that business as lawyers of jurisdictions other than England and Wales, but do not include any principal, owner or director who:

(i)   is struck off or suspended from the register of foreign lawyers or the register of European lawyers; or

(ii)   is practising through or in the context of that business a solicitor or as an REL.

(2)   You must meet the following conditions if acting for anyone other than your employer.

(a)   Even if you are qualified to do such work for your employer, you must not do, or supervise or assume responsibility for doing any of the following:

(i)   drawing or preparing any instrument or papers, or making any application or lodging any document relating to litigation reserved to qualified persons by the Solicitors Act 1974; or

(ii)   exercising any right of audience, or right to conduct litigation, for which a solicitor would have to rely on his or her qualification as a solicitor; or

(iii)   providing any immigration advice or immigration services, unless the employer, or a senior fellow employee, is registered with the Immigration Services Commissioner.

(b)   You must ensure that the work is covered by professional indemnity insurance reasonably equivalent to that required under the Solicitors' Indemnity Insurance Rules.

(c)   You must inform your client that your employer is not regulated by the Law Society and that the Law Society's insurance scheme does not apply; and either give or confirm this information in writing, if you are a solicitor, and you are held out to a client as a solicitor (or as an English or Welsh lawyer) in connection with work you are doing for that client.

(d)   You must ensure that if you are identified on the notepaper as a solicitor (or as an English or Welsh lawyer) the notepaper also states that your employer is not regulated by the Law Society.

(3)   (2)(c) and (d) above should also be read as referring to an REL being held out or identified as a lawyer, or under the REL's home title.

13.12 Regulatory bodies

If you are employed by a regulatory body you may in carrying out the function of the employer give legal advice to other persons and in the case of statutory functions may act generally for such persons.

Guidance to rule 13 – In-house practice

1. If you are a solicitor working in-house (whether in or outside England and Wales) you must comply with 20.01, and therefore will need a practising certificate. Examples of situations where you will be practising as a solicitor, and will therefore need a practising certificate, include:

    (a) you are employed as a solicitor;

    (b) you are held out, on stationery or otherwise, as a solicitor for your employer;

    (c) you administer oaths;

    (d) you appear before a court or tribunal in reliance upon your qualification as a solicitor;

    (e) you instruct counsel;

    (f) you undertake work which is prohibited to unqualified persons by the Solicitors Act 1974, unless you are supervised by, and acting in the name of, a solicitor with a practising certificate or another qualified person; or

    (g) your only qualification as a lawyer is that you are a solicitor, and

        (i) you are employed or held out as a lawyer;

        (ii) you undertake work in another jurisdiction which is reserved to lawyers;

        (iii) you are registered in a state other than the UK under the Establishment Directive; or

        (iv) you are a registered foreign legal consultant in another jurisdiction.

2. In England and Wales a number of statutory exceptions apply to qualify this. Certain in-house government solicitors are allowed to practise as solicitors without practising certificates. Some reserved work can be undertaken by non-solicitors working for local government, and therefore by non-practising solicitors working for local government. See also rule 20 (requirements of practice) and the guidance to it.

3. A solicitor acting only as a justices' clerk in England and Wales is not practising as a solicitor and can instruct counsel without a practising certificate.

4. Although the guidance to this rule will generally apply to practice in and outside England and Wales unless otherwise stated, the only provision of rule 13 which

applies to practice outside England and Wales is 13.04 (*pro bono* work). However, you must also comply with the provisions of 15.13 (in-house practice overseas) in relation to your in-house practice, if you are employed at an office outside England and Wales (or if you are an REL, employed at an office in Scotland or Northern Ireland).

5. If you are an in-house solicitor or in-house REL you are personally bound by undertakings given in the course of your professional duties – see 10.05 (or, if you practise overseas, 15.10(2)(a)).

6. When you act in your capacity as an in-house solicitor or in-house REL you should not communicate with third parties who you know are represented by another lawyer, except with that lawyer's consent. Any communication should be made through the lawyer acting for the third party.

7. You may use the stationery of, or stationery including the name of, your employer for professional work, provided:

    (a) the letterhead or the signature makes it clear that the stationery is being used by an in-house solicitor or in-house REL on legal professional business and that person is responsible for the contents of the letter; and

    (b) the stationery is being used for the business of the non-lawyer employer or for third parties in circumstances permitted by rule 13 or 15.13.

8. You may, as an in-house solicitor or in-house REL, use a style of stationery or description which appears to hold you out as a principal in a firm. However, if you are held out as a principal on notepaper and you hold or receive clients' money, you will be required to pay the full contribution to the Compensation Fund.

9. If you are an in-house solicitor the address of your employer's legal department is the place (or one of the places) where you practise and must therefore be notified to the Law Society.

Accounts rules and accountants' reports

10. If you are an in-house solicitor or in-house REL employed in England and Wales, and you receive or hold clients' money, you must comply with the Solicitors' Accounts Rules 1998. If you pay in or endorse over a cheque made out in your favour, you receive clients' money and must deal with it in accordance with the relevant rules (see note (viii) to rule 35 of the accounts rules). For the name of a client account, see rule 14(3) of the accounts rules. Even if a cheque is simply endorsed over to your employer, you will need to keep a record (see rule 32 of the accounts rules), submit an accountant's report, and pay the full contribution to the Solicitors' Compensation Fund. If you receive only your employer's money you can try to ensure that all cheques are made payable to the employer. If you are an in-house solicitor or in-house REL employed overseas, the accounts rules do not apply but you must comply with similar requirements which are set out in 15.27.

11. An in-house accountant (working for the same employer) may not prepare an accountant's report for an in-house solicitor or in-house REL (see rule 37(2)(a) of the accounts rules).

12. If you only undertake a small number of transactions or handle a small volume of clients' money in a year, you can apply to the Registration department of the Law Society for a dispensation from the obligation to deliver an accountant's report. However, dispensations are not given as a matter of course.

13. If you are:

(a) a solicitor or REL practising as an employee of:

(i) a local authority;

(ii) statutory undertakers;

(iii) a body whose accounts are audited by the Comptroller and Auditor General;

(iv) the Duchy of Lancaster;

(v) the Duchy of Cornwall;

(vi) the Church Commissioners;

(b) a solicitor practising as the Solicitor of the City of London; or

(c) a solicitor or REL carrying out the functions of:

(i) a coroner or other judicial office; or

(ii) a sheriff or under-sheriff,

you need not comply with the accounts rules (see rule 5 of those rules) or submit an accountant's report. However, if you hold or receive clients' money, you must pay the full Compensation Fund contribution, but this will not apply if you come within (c) above and are not practising as a solicitor.

Separate practice through a firm

14. If you are an in-house solicitor or in-house REL you can also be a principal in a firm. However, you must effect indemnity insurance for the firm in accordance with the Solicitors' Indemnity Insurance Rules, and notify the Law Society of the address of the firm.

15. The firm must not act for a private client where there is any conflict between the interests of that client and the interests of your employer.

16. For details regarding arrangements for the referral of clients, see rule 9 (referrals of business).

17. If you hold or receive clients' money as a principal in a firm in England and Wales you must comply with the Solicitors' Accounts Rules 1998.

18. You may agree to reimburse your employer for that proportion of your salary and of the employer's other overhead expenses which is attributable to any work carried out in the employer's time for your firm, on the employer's premises and/or with the assistance of staff and materials provided by the

employer. You must make sure that this allowance for overheads is properly calculated, otherwise there could be a breach of rule 8 (fee sharing).

Industrial action by in-house solicitors or in-house RELs

19. It is not professional misconduct for you to strike or take other industrial action, but you must have regard to your duties to the court and third parties. Before deciding to take such action you must:

(a) ensure that no client for whom you act is prejudiced by the action in any crucial way, e.g. by missing a time limit;

(b) ensure that steps are taken to cover all court engagements;

(c) ensure compliance with your professional undertakings; and

(d) promptly arrange to notify persons who may be affected by the proposed action.

Costs recovered from third parties

20. When you put forward a claim for costs against a third party, you must, as an in-house solicitor or in-house REL, have regard to the proper indemnity basis for costs.

21. Where you act for your employer, there is no presumption that it is any cheaper to employ an in-house lawyer than to retain a firm. The court will, therefore, normally regard it as proper for your bill to be drawn on the usual principles applicable to firms. There may, however, be special cases where it is clear that a bill drawn on this basis would improperly remunerate the employer and should therefore be disallowed (see Henderson v. Merthyr Tydfil U.D.C. [1900] 1 Q.B. 434 and Re Eastwood (deceased) [1975] Ch. 112). There seems no reason in principle why such an approach should not also be applicable to non-contentious business, or to matters where you act for someone other than the employer.

22. Under certain circumstances rule 13 allows you to act for someone other than your employer, as part of your employment. In such cases there will be no breach of rule 8 (fee sharing) when you account to your employer for costs paid either by the client, the client's opponent or another third party (see rule 8).

Direct access to client

23. If you are the senior legal adviser of a company or a local authority you should have direct access to the board or to the council and its committees, and should try to ensure that your terms of employment provide for such access. "Direct access" does not mean that all instructions and advice must pass directly to and from the council, committee or board, but you must have direct access where necessary.

Insurers and commercial legal advice services

24.   If you are employed as a solicitor or REL by an insurer which runs a commercial legal telephone advice service, the restrictions in 13.07 will not apply to prevent you acting for an insured under a legal expenses insurance policy in accordance with 13.06.

Law centres, charities and other non-commercial advice services

25.   If you are employed as a solicitor or REL by a law centre or advice service operated by a charitable or similar non-commercial organisation, you can advise and act for members of the public provided you comply with 13.09. This contains important provisions relating to (for example) professional indemnity, the charging of fees, and the independence of the body responsible for the management of the service. A solicitor or REL who works as a volunteer for such an advice service must comply with the Solicitors' Indemnity Insurance Rules unless exempted by a waiver.

Lawyers of other jurisdictions

26.   In-house practice in England and Wales includes any employment by a business with no principal, owner or director who is a solicitor or REL practising as such in the context of that business (see rule 24 - interpretation). As the in-house employee of a lawyer of another jurisdiction, you are not as free to act for your employer's clients as you would be if you were employed in England and Wales by a solicitor, an REL or a recognised body. Under 13.11 you may not do reserved work for clients, or (unless your employer is separately authorised) immigration work. You must also comply with special requirements as to insurance and 'health warnings'. Note also, that if you are employed by a foreign law firm and a principal, owner or director of the firm is a solicitor, 13.11 will not apply unless the solicitor is dually qualified and is practising only as a lawyer of another jurisdiction in the context of that business.

27.   By contrast, employment *overseas* by a foreign law firm will not usually fall within the definition of in-house practice in rule 24 (interpretation) if your employer is a lawyer or a law firm, provided that none of the lawyer principals or owners of the firm have been struck off or suspended from the Law Society's register of foreign lawyers.

Rule 14 – Incorporated practice

Introduction

Under the Solicitors Act 1974 a body corporate – that is, a company or an LLP – may not carry on the practice of a solicitor unless it is a recognised body. A solicitor or an REL may only practise from an office in England and Wales through a body corporate if it is a recognised body.

Rule 14 sets out the requirements which apply specifically to a recognised body and its members, directors, shareowners and employees. There are provisions which exclude non-lawyers from being directors, members or shareowners of a recognised body. These are necessary because section 9 of the Administration of Justice Act 1985 restricts the management and control of recognised bodies to lawyers.

Rule 14 – Incorporated practice

14.01 General

Compliance duties

(1)   A recognised body must:

   (a)   comply with rule 14; and

   (b)   so far as possible ensure that its directors, members and shareowners comply with 14.03, 14.04 and 14.05.

(2)   A director of a recognised body which is a company must so far as possible ensure that the body complies with rule 14.

(3)   A member of a recognised body which is an LLP must take all reasonable steps to ensure that the body complies with rule 14.

(4)   A director, member or shareowner of a recognised body and a person employed to work in the practice of a recognised body must not cause, instigate or connive at any breach of these rules.

Mental Health Act equivalents

(5)   In rule 14, references to a "patient" as defined by section 94 of the Mental Health Act 1983, , a person made the subject of emergency powers, and a receiver appointed under that Act include equivalents in other Establishment Directive states.

14.02 Scope of practice

General business of a recognised body

(1)   The business of a recognised body may consist only of professional services of the sort provided by individuals practising as solicitors and/or lawyers of other jurisdictions.

Conveyancing and probate

(2)   A recognised body must not undertake any work which includes a conveyancing or probate service reserved to qualified persons by the Solicitors Act 1974, unless:

   (a)   if the recognised body is a company, at least one director is a solicitor with a practising certificate or an REL qualified to provide that service under regulation 12 or 13 of the European Communities (Lawyer's Practice) Regulations 2000; and, if the company is a societas Europaea with a two-tier system, at least one member of both the management organ and the supervisory organ is such a person; or

   (b)   if the recognised body is an LLP, at least one member is a solicitor with a practising certificate, an REL qualified to provide that service under regulation 12 or 13 of the European Communities (Lawyer's Practice) Regulations 2000, or a recognised body qualified to undertake the work under (a) above.

14.03 Directors of a company

Persons who may be directors

(1)   A recognised body which is a company must ensure that at all times:

   (a)   all the directors are solicitors with practising certificates, RELs, RFLs and/or non-registered European lawyers; and

   (b)   at least one director is a solicitor with a practising certificate or an REL, and, if the company is a societas Europaea with a two-tier system, at least one member of both the management organ and the supervisory organ is a solicitor with a practising certificate or an REL.

Death of director

(2)   If a director dies and this would put a company in breach of (1)(b) above, the company must ensure that a director who is a solicitor with a practising certificate or an REL is appointed within 14 days. If this is done the company will be deemed to have remained in compliance with (1)(b) above, and to that extent will not be liable to have its recognition revoked under regulation 7.2(b) of the Recognised Bodies Regulations.

Director incapacitated, abandoning the practice, etc.

(3)   If the company's only, or last remaining, director who is a solicitor with a practising certificate or an REL or, if the company is a societas Europaea with a two-tier system, the only or last remaining member of either the management organ or the supervisory organ who is a solicitor with a practising certificate or an REL:

   (a)   is committed to prison in civil or criminal proceedings;

   (b)   becomes and continues to be unable to attend to the practice of the company because of incapacity caused by illness, accident or age;

(c) becomes and continues to be a "patient" as defined by section 94 of the Mental Health Act 1983 or is made the subject of powers exercised under section 98 of that Act and continues to be subject to those powers;

(d) abandons the practice of the company; or

(e) the director's practising certificate or registration is made subject to a condition which would be breached by continuing as a director,

the company must ensure that an additional or replacement director who is a solicitor with a practising certificate or an REL is appointed within 14 days.

14.04 Members and shareowners of a company

Persons who may be members or shareowners

(1) A recognised body which is a company must ensure that all members and all shareowners are:

(a) solicitors with practising certificates;

(b) RELs;

(c) RFLs;

(d) non-registered European lawyers;

(e) recognised bodies; and/or

(f) European corporate practices.

(2) A recognised body which is a company with shares must have at least one shareowner who is a solicitor with a practising certificate, an REL, a recognised body, or a European corporate practice which is at least partly owned by a solicitor with a practising certificate or an REL.

(3) A recognised body which is a company without shares must have at least one member who is a solicitor with a practising certificate, an REL, a recognised body, or a European corporate practice which is at least partly owned by a solicitor with a practising certificate or an REL.

Prohibition on creating third party interests

(4) A member or shareowner must not create any charge or other third party interest over his or her interest in the company, except by holding a share as nominee for a non-member shareowner who is eligible to be a member or shareowner under (1) above.

Record of non-member shareowners

(5) (a) A recognised body which is a company with shares must keep a record of any non-member shareowners, and retain the record for at least three years after their ownership ceases; and

(b)   A member who holds a share as nominee for a non-member shareowner must keep the recognised body informed of all facts necessary to keep an accurate and up-to-date record.

Death of member or shareowner of a company

(6)   (a)   If a member or shareowner of a company with shares dies and is eligible to be a member or shareowner at the date of death, then, whether or not the personal representatives are themselves eligible to be members or shareowners, the personal representatives may replace the deceased member or shareowner in their capacity as personal representatives, provided that:

(i)   no vote may be exercised by or on behalf of a personal representative (and no such vote may be accepted) unless all the personal representatives are eligible to be members or shareowners;

(ii)   no personal representative may hold or own a share in that capacity for longer than 12 months from the date of death;

(iii)   within 12 months of the death the recognised body must cancel or acquire the shares or ensure that they are held and owned by persons eligible to be members and shareowners, but without this resulting in RFLs being the only shareowners; and

(iv)   no vote may be exercised by or on behalf of any personal representative (and no such vote may be accepted) after the 12 month period has expired.

(b)   If, following the death of a member or shareowner, a company meets the requirements of (a) above the company will be deemed to have remained in compliance with (1) above as to membership and share ownership, and to that extent will not be liable to have its recognition revoked under regulation 7.2(b) of the Recognised Bodies Regulations.

Member or shareowner ceasing to be eligible to be a member or shareowner

(7)   (a)   If a member or shareowner of a recognised body which is a company with shares ceases to be eligible to be a member or shareowner, or ceases to exist as a body corporate, then:

(i)   no vote may be exercised or accepted on the shares held by or on behalf of that member or shareowner;

(ii)   in the case of a member or shareowner becoming ineligible, a trustee in bankruptcy or liquidator may (whether or not eligible to be a member or shareowner) replace that member or shareowner in the capacity of trustee or liquidator for a period which must not exceed six months from the date the member or shareowner became ineligible; and

(iii)   the company must cancel or acquire the shares within six months, or within that time ensure that the shares are held and owned by persons eligible to be members and shareowners, but without this resulting in RFLs being the only shareowners.

(b)   If (a) above applies and a company meets its requirements, the company will be deemed to have remained in compliance with (1) above as to membership and share ownership, and to that extent will not be liable to have its recognition revoked under regulation 7.2(b) of the Recognised Bodies Regulations.

Member or shareowner becoming insolvent but not ineligible

(8)   (a)   If a member or shareowner of a recognised body which is a company with shares becomes insolvent but remains eligible to be a member or shareowner, then the trustee in bankruptcy or liquidator (whether eligible or not) may replace the insolvent member or shareowner in the capacity of trustee in bankruptcy or liquidator, provided that:

    (i)   no vote may be exercised by or on behalf of a trustee in bankruptcy or liquidator (and no such vote may be accepted) unless the trustee or liquidator is eligible to be a member or shareowner;

    (ii)   no trustee in bankruptcy or liquidator may hold or own a share in that capacity for longer than six months from the date of the insolvency;

    (iii)   within six months of the insolvency the company must cancel or acquire the shares or ensure that they are held and owned by persons eligible to be members and shareowners, and without this resulting in RFLs being the only shareowners; and

    (iv)   no vote may be exercised by or on behalf of any trustee in bankruptcy or liquidator (and no such vote may be accepted) after the six month period has expired.

(b)   If (a) above applies and a company meets its requirements, the company will be deemed to have remained in compliance with (1) above as to membership and share ownership, and to that extent will not be liable to have its recognition revoked under regulation 7.2(b) of the Recognised Bodies Regulations.

Mental health receiver for a member or shareowner in a company

(9)   (a)   A receiver appointed under the Mental Health Act 1983 may be a member or shareowner in that capacity, without breach of these rules, provided that:

    (i)   the "patient" (as defined in the Mental Health Act 1983) remains eligible to be a member or shareowner; and

    (ii)   if the receiver is not eligible to be a member or shareowner, no vote is exercised or accepted on the shares.

(b)   If (a) above applies and a company meets its requirements, the company will be deemed to have remained in compliance with (1) above as to membership and share ownership, and to that extent will not be liable to have its recognition revoked under regulation 7.2(b) of the Recognised Bodies Regulations.

Proxies and corporate representatives

(10) Only a solicitor with a practising certificate, an REL, an RFL or a non-registered European lawyer may be appointed as a proxy or corporate representative for the purpose of attending and voting at meetings.

14.05 Members of an LLP

Persons who may be members

(1) A recognised body which is an LLP must ensure that all the members are:

    (a) solicitors with practising certificates;

    (b) RELs;

    (c) RFLs;

    (d) non-registered European lawyers;

    (e) recognised bodies; and/or

    (f) European corporate practices.

(2) (a) A recognised body which is an LLP must have at least two members.

    (b) If a death results in an LLP having fewer than two members, but a person within (1) above becomes a member within six months, the LLP will be deemed to have remained in compliance with (a) above and to that extent will not be liable to have its recognition revoked under regulation 7.2(b) of the Recognised Bodies Regulations.

(3) (a) A recognised body which is an LLP must have at least one member who is:

    (i) a solicitor with a practising certificate;

    (ii) an REL;

    (iii) a recognised body which is a company with a director who is a solicitor with a practising certificate or an REL; or

    (iv) a recognised body which is an LLP with a member who is a solicitor with a practising certificate or an REL.

    (b) If a member dies and this would put the company in breach of (a) above, but a person within (a) above becomes a member within 14 days, the LLP will be deemed to have remained in compliance with (a) above as to membership, and to that extent will not be liable to have its recognition revoked under regulation 7.2(b) of the Recognised Bodies Regulations.

Member incapacitated, abandoning the practice, etc.

(4) If the last remaining solicitor or REL within (3)(a) above:

   (a) is committed to prison in civil or criminal proceedings;

   (b) becomes and continues to be unable to attend to the practice of the LLP because of incapacity caused by illness, accident or age;

   (c) becomes and continues to be a "patient" as defined by section 94 of the Mental Health Act 1983 or is made the subject of powers exercised under section 98 of that Act and continues to be subject to those powers;

   (d) abandons the practice of the LLP; or

   (e) the member's practising certificate or registration (or director's, as the case may be) is made subject to a condition which would be breached by continuing as a member or director;

   the LLP must ensure that an additional or replacement solicitor with a practising certificate or REL within (3)(a) above is in place within 14 days.

Prohibition on creating third party interests

(5) A member must not create any charge or other third party interest over the member's interest in the LLP.

14.06 Practising address and registered office of a recognised body

(1) A recognised body must have at least one practising address in England and Wales.

(2) A recognised body must have its registered office at a practising address in England and Wales if the recognised body is registered in England and Wales:

   (a) under Part I of the Companies Act 1985;

   (b) under the Limited Liability Partnerships Act 2000; or

   (c) as a societas Europaea.

14.07 Information and documentation

(1) A recognised body must supply any information and documentation relating to the ownership, structure, directors, members or shareowners of the recognised body as and when requested to do so by the Law Society.

(2) A recognised body must notify the Law Society immediately of any change to:

   (a) its name;

   (b) its registered office and/or any of its practising addresses; or

   (c) its directors, members and/or shareowners.

(3)   A recognised body must notify the Law Society immediately if it is an unlimited company and it is re-registered as limited under the Companies Act 1985.

(4)   If a recognised body's recognition expires automatically under regulation 8.2 of the Recognised Bodies Regulations, the directors (if it is a company) or the members (if it is an LLP) must notify the Law Society immediately.

(5)   If a recognised body which is an oversea company or a societas Europaea registered outside England, Wales and Scotland is subject to an event in its country of incorporation analogous to a winding-up order or administration order under Part II of the Insolvency Act 1986, a resolution for voluntary winding-up, or the appointment of an administrative receiver, the directors must notify the Law Society immediately.

Guidance to rule 14 – Incorporated practice

The legal and regulatory framework

1.   A body corporate through which a solicitor or REL practises must be a recognised body if it is to have an office in England and Wales. If a solicitor or an REL provides services to the public from an office in England and Wales through a company or an LLP which is not a recognised body, there is a breach of rule 12 (framework of practice). If the company or LLP includes a solicitor there is also a criminal offence under the Solicitors Act 1974.

2.   A recognised body is a body corporate recognised by the Law Society under the Administration of Justice Act 1985 (AJA), rule 14 and the Recognised Bodies Regulations. Recognition will only be granted if a body corporate is:

(a)   a company (including a societas Europaea) incorporated in England and Wales or in Scotland;

(b)   a company incorporated in another Establishment Directive state and registered in England and Wales or in Scotland as an oversea company;

(c)   an LLP incorporated in England and Wales or in Scotland; or

(d)   a societas Europaea incorporated outside England, Wales and Scotland.

If you would like an information booklet on incorporating your practice as a company or as an LLP, contact the Professional Ethics department of the Law Society.

3.   A recognised body is, for the purposes of practice, in the same position as a solicitor or a partnership of solicitors, and subject to similar legal and professional requirements. Schedule 2 to the AJA, the Solicitors' Incorporated Practices Order 1991 (SI 1991 no. 2684) and the Solicitors' Incorporated Practices (Amendment) Order 2001 (SI 2001 no. 645) apply provisions in the Solicitors Act 1974 and other legislation to recognised bodies, sometimes modified. The Solicitors' Disciplinary Tribunal has power to revoke recognition for misconduct.

4. Under 14.03 to 14.05 a solicitor must have a current practising certificate in order to be a director, a member or a shareowner in a recognised body. Under section 1A of the Solicitors Act 1974, a solicitor must have a current practising certificate in order to work for a recognised body in England and Wales in connection with the provision of legal services.

5. Under 14.06(1) every recognised body must have at least one practising address in England and Wales. Under 14.06(2) a recognised body incorporated in England and Wales must have its registered office in England or in Wales, and must practise from that office.

6. A recognised body can be a member of another recognised body or own a share in another recognised body. It can practise in England and Wales in partnership with solicitors, RELs, or other recognised bodies, but not with RFLs (see 12.04).

7. A recognised body may practise outside England and Wales as well as in England and Wales. If a recognised body is incorporated in England and Wales, its practice from offices outside England and Wales will be subject to all the rules of conduct which apply to a solicitor practising from offices outside England and Wales. A recognised body incorporated outside England and Wales is subject only to certain rules in relation to overseas practice – see 23.01(d)(ii), 12.04(4) and 15.01(2)(a).

8. If you practise through a corporate firm which has no office in England and Wales it does not have to be a recognised body – and indeed cannot be a recognised body because a recognised body has to have at least one practising address in England or Wales.

The Recognised Bodies Regulations

9. The Recognised Bodies Regulations ("the regulations") are rules made under section 9 of the AJA. They govern the formalities of applications and appeals relating to recognition. They are not part of these rules. Under the regulations, the Law Society may only grant recognition if it is satisfied that the applicant body is registered in England and Wales or in Scotland, or is a societas Europaea, complies with or is exempt from the Solicitors' Indemnity Insurance Rules, has a name which is not misleading, and complies with rule 14 in its internal structure. The regulations also provide, amongst other things, that:

    (a) once granted recognition, a recognised body will be placed on a list kept by the Law Society and issued with a certificate of recognition;

    (b) recognition is renewable every three years but expires automatically if a recognised body becomes insolvent; and

    (c) the Law Society may revoke recognition if:

        (i) the renewal date passes and no application is made for renewal;

        (ii) the Law Society is satisfied that recognition was granted as a result of mistake or fraud; or

        (iii) the Law Society is satisfied that a recognised body would not be eligible if applying for initial recognition – though this power is tempered by a number of the provisions of rule 14. For example, recognition could be revoked if the only director who is a solicitor or REL dies, and the company fails to remedy the position within the 14 days' grace allowed under 14.03(2).

Compliance with rules

10. A recognised body's practice in England and Wales is subject to all the rules and requirements of conduct which apply to solicitors. Under 14.01, reciprocal responsibilities are laid upon a recognised body and its directors and members to oversee each others' compliance with the provisions of rule 14. A solicitor or REL who is a director, member, shareowner or employee of a recognised body must not 'turn a blind eye' or otherwise connive at a breach of any of these rules.

11. In addition to these rules, a recognised body must comply with the Solicitors' Indemnity Insurance Rules, the Solicitors' Accounts Rules and the statutory requirements to submit an accountant's report and to make a contribution to the Compensation Fund. The following matters should be borne in mind:

   (a) *Indemnity insurance*

   The Solicitors' Indemnity Insurance Rules apply to a recognised body, and recognition will not be granted or renewed unless the Law Society is satisfied that the body complies with or will comply with the indemnity rules. These require a recognised body to have "qualifying insurance" from a "qualifying insurer" in accordance with the minimum terms and conditions set out in the Solicitors' Indemnity Insurance Rules. For a recognised body with limited liability (i.e. a limited company or an LLP) the minimum level of cover is £3 million. For an unlimited company the minimum level is £2 million. A limited company which is a nominee company only may be exempt from the additional £1 million cover – see note 16(d) below. A recognised body may be eligible for full or partial exemption from the requirement to have "qualifying insurance". This is obtained only on application and only if the recognised body has at least one director, member or owner who is an REL, and has equivalent cover under the rules of the REL's home state (see Appendix 4 of the Solicitors' Indemnity Insurance Rules). A recognised body may also have additional "top-up" cover, from any insurer.

   (b) *Accountants' reports*

   If a recognised body holds or receives client money or controlled trust money, it will in due course have to deliver an accountant's report to the Law Society. This obligation also extends to the directors of a company and to the members of an LLP. The names of these individuals as well as the name of the recognised body must appear on the accountant's report, as well as the names of any assistant or consultant solicitor (or REL) who has held or received the money or operated a client's own account as signatory.

   (c) *Compensation Fund contributions*

   Recognised bodies must pay a contribution to the Compensation Fund on initial recognition and every three years thereafter, when recognition is renewed. Solicitors, RELs and RFLs who practise through a recognised body also have to pay individual contributions on a yearly basis when renewing their practising certificates or registration. If the recognised body has (directly or indirectly) held or received client money or controlled trust money, the individual members', directors' and shareowners' contributions will be assessed at full rate.

Ownership and direction

12. A recognised body must be owned and directed by solicitors and/or RELs, although ownership and direction can be shared with other lawyers. In general, a director, member or shareowner who is not a solicitor or an REL must be an RFL. However, lawyers of Establishment Directive states who are based outside England and Wales ("non-registered European lawyers") may also share in the ownership and direction of a recognised body, and "European corporate practices" as defined in rule 24 (interpretation), may be members or shareowners. The company secretary need not be a lawyer.

   (a) A body corporate cannot be a director. At all times at least one of the directors of a recognised body which is a company must be a solicitor or an REL. A similar restriction applies to ensure that at least one solicitor or REL is involved in the membership of a recognised body which is an LLP.

   (b) Every recognised body must be at least partly owned by a solicitor or an REL. No recognised body can, for example, be wholly owned by RFLs.

13. 14.03 to 14.05 require steps to be taken to regularise a recognised body's position following various events which would otherwise put the recognised body in breach of a provision of the rule. There are strict time limits for taking such action, and if the recognised body meets these there is no breach of the rule. For example, the death of the only director of a company who is a solicitor or REL would put the recognised body in breach of 14.03(1)(b), but if a new solicitor or REL director is appointed within 14 days there is no breach. It is very important to meet such time limits because breach of any provision of rule 14 can result in the recognised body losing its right to practise. The articles of association of a company and the members' agreement of an LLP must therefore allow for speedy action to be taken in such circumstances.

Charging a member's interest in a recognised body – 14.04(4) and 14.05(5)

14. A member of a recognised body (whether it is a company or an LLP) may not create any charge or other third party interest in the body, except, in the case of a company, that a member may hold a share as nominee for a person who is eligible under the rules to own a share. The purpose is to ensure that control of the recognised body remains solely in the hands of persons who are eligible to be members. The prohibitions in 14.04(4) and 14.05(5) do not, however, prevent a member's bank taking a charge or assignment on a member's right to receive back his or her capital invested in a recognised body.

Executor, trustee and nominee companies

15. If you wish to operate an executor, trustee or nominee company in conjunction with your main practice you should bear the following matters in mind:

(a) An *English* executor, trustee or nominee company itself provides the executor, trustee or nominee service. If run in conjunction with your practice it is a "business" for the purpose of rule 21 (separate businesses), whether or not it is dormant for Companies Act purposes and whether or not a charge is made for its services. If you are practising from an office in England and Wales the company must therefore be a recognised body, or you will breach rule 21 - see 21.02(1)(g) and guidance note 8 to rule 21.

(b) An *overseas* executor, trustee or nominee company cannot be a recognised body. It can be run in accordance with rule 12, as an overseas practice. Alternatively, it can be operated as a "separate business" provided that you comply with rule 21 or with 15.21 (separate businesses), as appropriate, in relation to the company. See also guidance note 9 to rule 21.

16. In relation to an English executor, trustee or nominee company, you should also note that:

(a) a recognised body, when holding money or receiving dividends *as nominee*, acts as a controlled trustee; and if the company holds client money or controlled trust money as defined in the Solicitors' Accounts Rules 1998 or in rule 24 (interpretation) it must have its own client account, in its own name;

(b) a single set of accounting records may be used for the company and the main practice and a single accountant's report can be delivered for both, if the relevant accounting periods are the same, and provided the accountant deals with the accounts for each separately;

(c) a wholly owned executor, trustee or nominee company can be covered by the same policy of qualifying insurance as your main practice, but only if the company is named on the policy and certificate of insurance as a separate insured; and

(d) a nominee company may be exempt from the requirement to have an extra £1 million qualifying insurance if it can show that:

(i) it is a nominee company only;

(ii) it is wholly owned by your main practice;

(iii) it holds assets only for clients of your main practice;

(iv) it can act only as agent for your main practice; and

(v) all fees accrue to the benefit of your main practice.

Service companies

17. A firm may have a service company to carry out administrative functions concerned with the running of the firm, such as the employment of qualified and unqualified staff, the hiring of premises, furniture and equipment and

general maintenance. If the service company is wholly owned by the firm and provides services only to the firm and not to clients, it does not need to be a recognised body. The books of the company must be made available if the Law Society requires an inspection of accounts. See also notes 10 and 11 of the guidance to rule 21 (separate businesses).

Rule 15 – Overseas practice

Introduction

Rule 15 is specific to overseas practice, which is defined in rule 24 to mean the practice of a solicitor or a recognised body from an office or offices outside England and Wales; and the practice of an REL from an office or offices in Scotland or Northern Ireland.

Rule 15 applies the provisions of these rules to your overseas practice. Sometimes rule 15 disapplies one of these rules, or a provision in one of the rules, and in some cases substitutes alternative provisions.

Rule 15 also makes specific provisions in relation to accounts, deposit interest and professional indemnity, because the equivalent domestic rules do not apply to your overseas practice.

The purpose of applying different provisions to overseas practice is to ensure similar protection for clients but by way of rules which are more adaptable to conditions in other jurisdictions.

Rule 15 – Overseas practice

15.01 Core duties (rule 1) application, and conflicts of rules

The core duties

(1) Rule 1 (core duties) applies to your overseas practice.

Application, and conflicts of rules

(2) These rules and the principles of professional conduct apply to the practice of a solicitor or a recognised body from an office outside England and Wales, and to the practice of an REL from an office in Scotland or Northern Ireland, with the following exceptions:

    (a) a recognised body incorporated outside England and Wales is subject only to the following of these rules in relation to its practice outside England and Wales:

        (i) 1.10 (profession);

        (ii) 12.04(4) (framework of practice);

        (iii) rule 14 (incorporated practice); and

        (iv) if a controlling majority of the owners are, or are controlled by, solicitors, 15.07(b)(ii) (letterhead), 15.15 (deposit interest), 15.27 (accounts), and rule 20 (requirements of practice);

    (b) if this rule states that a rule or a provision of these rules does not apply to your overseas practice, you may disregard that rule or provision in relation to your overseas practice, but you must comply with any alternative provision which is substituted by this rule; and

(c) if compliance with any provision of these rules would result in your breaching local law, you may disregard that provision to the extent necessary to comply with that local law.

(3) In this rule, in relation to practice from an office in Scotland or Northern Ireland, all references to a firm with a controlling majority of partners or owners who are, or which are controlled by, solicitors must be read as referring to a controlling majority of partners or owners who are, or which are controlled by, solicitors and/or RELs.

15.02 Client relations (rule 2)

(1) Rule 2 does not apply to your overseas practice but you must comply with (2) to (4) below.

(2) (a) You must pay to your clients any commission received, unless:

    (i) the client, having been told the amount of the commission (or an approximate amount if the precise amount is not known) has agreed that you or your firm may keep the commission; or

    (ii) in all the circumstances it is not reasonable to pay the commission to the client.

(b) In deciding whether it is reasonable to pay a commission to your client you must have regard to all the circumstances, including the law governing the retainer and the prevailing custom of lawyers in the jurisdiction in which you are practising.

(3) If you are a principal or a recognised body you must not exclude or attempt to exclude by contract all liability to your clients. However, you may limit your civil liability, provided that such limitation is not below the minimum level of cover you would need in order to comply with 15.26 below, and the agreement is in writing.

(4) (a) (i) You must not enter into an arrangement to receive a contingency fee for work done in prosecuting or defending any contentious proceedings before a court of England and Wales, a British court martial or an arbitrator hearing a matter in England and Wales, except as permitted by statute or the common law.

    (ii) If you enter into a conditional fee agreement with a client in relation to such proceedings, you must explain, both at the outset and, where appropriate, as the matter progresses:

        (A) the circumstances in which your client may be liable for your costs, and whether you will seek payment of these from the client, if entitled to do so; and

        (B) if you intend to seek payment of any or all of your costs from your client, you must advise your client of their right to an assessment of those costs.

(b) You must not enter into an arrangement to receive a contingency fee for work done in prosecuting or defending any contentious proceedings before a court of an overseas jurisdiction or an arbitrator hearing a matter overseas except to the extent that a lawyer of that jurisdiction would be permitted to do so.

15.03 Conflict of interests (rule 3)

Rule 3 applies to your overseas practice, except that you do not have to comply with 3.07 to 3.22 (provisions relating to conveyancing of land) if the land in question is situated outside England and Wales.

15.04 Confidentiality (rule 4)

Rule 4 applies to your overseas practice.

15.05 Business management (rule 5)

(1) Rule 5 does not apply to your overseas practice but you must comply with (2) and (3) below.

(2) (a) You must not set up as a sole principal unless you have been entitled to practise as a lawyer for a minimum of 36 months within the last 10 years.

    (b) If you are:

        (i) a partner in a partnership with a controlling majority of partners who are, or which are controlled by, solicitors; or

        (ii) a director of a body corporate with a controlling majority of owners who are, or which are controlled by, solicitors;

    you must ensure that the partnership has at least one partner, or the body corporate has at least one director if it is a company, or at least one member if it is an LLP, who has been entitled to practise as a lawyer for a minimum of 36 months within the last 10 years.

(3) If you are:

    (a) a sole principal;

    (b) a partner in a partnership with a controlling majority of partners who are, or which are controlled by solicitors; or

    (c) a director of a company or a member of an LLP with a controlling majority of owners who are, or which are controlled by, solicitors;

you must ensure that the firm is managed and supervised with a view to ensuring that its affairs are properly conducted at all times; and that clients' matters receive proper attention, and are supervised so as to ensure that the quality of the work is checked with reasonable regularity by suitably experienced and competent persons within the firm.

15.06 Avoiding discrimination (rule 6)

Rule 6 does not apply to your overseas practice, but rule 1 (core duties) will always apply.

15.07 Publicity (rule 7)

Rule 7 applies to your overseas practice, except that:

(a)   rule 7 does not apply to the website, e-mails, text messages or similar electronic communications of any practice you conduct from an office in an EU state other than the UK; and

(b)   7.07 (letterhead) does not apply, but:

(i)   if an REL is named on the letterhead (including a fax heading) of an office in Scotland or Northern Ireland, the letterhead must also identify:

(A)   the European jurisdiction(s) – local or national as appropriate – under whose professional title the REL is practising;

(B)   the REL's professional title(s), expressed in an official language of the European state concerned; and

(C)   the fact that the REL is registered with the Law Society of England and Wales; and

(ii)   if you are a partner in a partnership with a controlling majority of partners who are, or which are controlled by, solicitors, or a director of a company or member of an LLP with a controlling majority of owners who are, or which are controlled by, solicitors, you must make clear on the firm's letterhead (including a fax heading) that it is the letterhead of a law firm.

15.08 Fee sharing (rule 8)

Rule 8 applies to your overseas practice.

15.09 Referrals of business (rule 9)

(1)   Rule 9 does not apply to your overseas practice, but you must comply with (2) below.

(2)   When you accept referrals of business from other persons and when you refer business to other persons, you must ensure that there is no breach of rule 1 (core duties) or any other applicable provision of these rules.

15.10 Relations with third parties (rule 10)

(1)   Rule 10 applies to your overseas practice except as provided in (2) and (3) below.

(2)   10.05 (undertakings) does not apply, but:

(a) you must fulfil an undertaking which you give:

    (i) in the course of practice;

    (ii) outside the course of practice, but as a "solicitor"; or

    (iii) if you are an REL based at an office in Scotland or Northern Ireland, and you give the undertaking within the UK, outside your practice as an REL, but as a lawyer of an Establishment Directive state;

(b) you must fulfil an undertaking within a reasonable time; and

(c) if you give an undertaking which is dependent upon the happening of a future event, you must notify the recipient immediately if it becomes clear that the event will not occur; and

(3) 10.06 (dealing with more than one prospective buyer in a conveyancing transaction) applies only if the land in question is situated in England and Wales.

15.11 Litigation and advocacy (rule 11)

Rule 11 applies to your overseas practice in relation to litigation or advocacy conducted before a court, tribunal or inquiry in England and Wales or a British court martial. Rule 11 does not apply to your overseas practice in relation to litigation or advocacy conducted before a court or tribunal in another jurisdiction, but rule 1 (core duties) will always apply.

15.12 Framework of practice (rule 12)

Rule 12 applies to your overseas practice.

15.13 In-house practice overseas (rule 13)

(1) 13.04 applies to your overseas practice. The other provisions of rule 13 do not apply to your overseas practice, but you must comply with (2) below.

(2) (a) subject to (b) below, you may act as an in-house lawyer, but only for:

    (i) your employer;

    (ii) a company or organisation controlled by your employer or in which your employer has a substantial measure of control;

    (iii) a company in the same group as your employer;

    (iv) a company which controls your employer; or

    (v) an employee (including a director or a company secretary) of a company or organisation under (i) to (iv) above, provided that the matter relates to or arises out of the work of that company or organisation, does not relate to a claim arising as a result of a personal injury to the employee, and no charge is made for your work unless those costs are recoverable from another source.

(b)   if you are a solicitor registered in another state under the Establishment Directive with the professional body for a local legal profession you may practise in-house to the extent that a member of that legal profession is permitted to do so.

15.14 Incorporated practice (rule 14)

(1) (a)   Rule 14 applies to a recognised body in relation to the recognised body's overseas practice.

      (b)   Rule 14 applies to the overseas practice of the directors, members and shareowners of a recognised body, but 14.01(4) applies in relation to a recognised body incorporated outside England and Wales only where the provision in question is specifically applied to the recognised body by 15.01(2)(a).

(2)   If you are a solicitor or an REL you are not required to comply with rule 14 in order to practise through a body corporate which has no office in England and Wales, but you must comply with 12.01(3) or 12.02(3).

15.15 Deposit interest

(1)   You must comply with (2) below, if:

      (a)   you have held client money as a sole principal;

      (b)   you are a partner in a partnership which has held client money and

            (i)   the partnership has no separate legal identity and either a controlling majority of partners are, or are controlled by, solicitors, or UK lawyers form the largest group of lawyers in the partnership; or

            (ii)   the partnership has a separate legal identity and a controlling majority of partners are or are controlled by solicitors; or

      (c)   You are a director or owner of a body corporate which has held client money, and a controlling majority of the owners are, or are controlled by, solicitors.

(2)   If interest ought, in fairness, to be earned for the client on client money held under (1) above, you must ensure that:

      (a)   the client money is dealt with so that proper interest is earned upon it, and that the interest is paid to the client;

      (b)   the client is paid a sum equivalent to the interest that would have been earned if the client money had earned proper interest; or

      (c)   any alternative written agreement with the client setting out arrangements regarding the payment of interest on that money is carried out.

(3)   In deciding whether interest ought, in fairness, to be earned for a client on client money, you must have regard to all the circumstances, including:

(a) the amount of the money;

(b) the length of time for which you are likely to hold the money; and

(c) the law and prevailing custom of lawyers practising in the jurisdiction in which you are practising.

15.16 European cross-border practice (rule 16)

Rule 16 applies to your overseas practice, to the extent that such practice is European cross-border practice as defined in 16.01(1).

15.17 Insolvency practice (rule 17)

Rule 17 does not apply to your overseas practice except in relation to appointments appertaining to orders made in the courts of England and Wales.

15.18 Property selling (rule 18)

Rule 18 applies to your practice from offices in Scotland or Northern Ireland but not to your practice from offices outside the UK.

15.19 Financial services (rule 19)

(1) Rule 19 does not apply to your overseas practice except as provided in (2) below.

(2) Rule 19 applies to regulated activities you conduct

(a) from an office in Scotland or Northern Ireland; or

(b) into the UK from an office outside the UK.

15.20 Requirements of practice (rule 20)

Rule 20 applies to your overseas practice.

15.21 Separate businesses (rule 21)

(1) (a) Rule 21 applies to you if you practise from an office in England and Wales and you have a separate business, wherever the separate business is situated.

(b) If you do not practise from an office in England and Wales but you practise from an office outside England and Wales and you have a separate business, rule 21 does not apply but you must comply with (2) below, wherever the separate business is situated.

(2) In relation to your separate business:

(a) you must do nothing in the course of practice, or in the course of making referrals to the business or accepting referrals from the business, which would contravene rule 1 (core duties);

(b) you must not allow the separate business to be held out or described in such a way as to suggest that it is carrying on the practice of a lawyer regulated by the Law Society;

(c) you must ensure that all paperwork, documents, records or files relating to the separate business and its customers are kept separate from those of any firm or in-house practice, even where a customer of the separate business is also a client of the firm or in-house practice;

(d) you must not allow the client account used for any firm or in-house practice to be used to hold money for the separate business, or for customers of the separate business in their capacity as such; and

(e) you must ensure that if you or your firm refer a client to the separate business, the client is first informed of your interest in the separate business, that the separate business is not regulated by the Law Society, and that the statutory protections attaching to clients of a lawyer regulated by the Law Society are not available to clients of the separate business.

15.22 Waivers (rule 22)

Rule 22 applies to your overseas practice.

15.23 Application (rule 23)

Rule 23 applies to your overseas practice.

15.24 Interpretation (rule 24)

Rule 24 applies to your overseas practice.

15.25 Commencement and repeal (rule 25)

Rule 25 applies to your overseas practice.

15.26 Professional indemnity

(1) You must comply with (2) below in relation to your overseas practice, unless you are practising only in-house in compliance with 15.13.

(2) (a) You must ensure that in relation to your overseas practice you are at all times covered by insurance or other indemnity against professional liabilities.

(b) The extent and amount of the insurance or other indemnity need not exceed the current requirements of the Solicitors' Indemnity Insurance Rules or any other current rules made by the Council under section 37 of the Solicitors Act 1974 but must be reasonable having regard to:

(i) the nature and extent of the risks you incur in your overseas practice;

(ii) the local conditions in the jurisdiction in which you are practising; and

(iii)   the terms upon which insurance or other indemnity is available.

15.27 Accounts

(1)   You must comply with (3) to (5) below if you have held or received client money or controlled trust money:

    (a)   as the sole principal of a firm which has held or received client money or controlled trust money;

    (b)   as a named trustee; or

    (c)   as a partner in a partnership which has held or received client money or controlled trust money, if the partnership has no separate legal identity and:

        (i)   a majority of the partners are or are controlled by solicitors; or

        (ii)   UK lawyers form the largest group of lawyers in the partnership.

(2)   You must also comply with (3) to (5) below as if you have held or received client money or controlled trust money as a principal, if you are

    (a)   a director or owner of a body corporate which has held or received client money or controlled trust money, if a controlling majority of the body's owners are or are controlled by solicitors; or

    (b)   a partner in a partnership with separate legal identity which has held or received client money or controlled trust money, if a controlling majority of the partners are or are controlled by solicitors.

Dealings with client money

(3)   In all dealings with client money, you must ensure that:

(a)   it is kept separate from money which is not client money or controlled trust money in a client account;

(b)   on receipt, it is paid without delay into a client account and kept there, unless the client has expressly or by implication agreed that the money shall be dealt with otherwise;

(c)   it is not paid or withdrawn from a client account except on the specific authority of the client or where the payment or withdrawal is properly required:

    (i)   for a payment to or on behalf of the client;

    (ii)   for or towards payment of a debt due to the firm from the client or in reimbursement of money expended by the firm on behalf of the client; or

    (iii)   for or towards payment of costs due to the firm from the client, provided that a bill of costs or other written intimation of the amount of the costs incurred has been delivered to the client and it has thereby (or otherwise in writing) been made clear to the client that the money held will be applied in payment of the costs due;

(d) accounts are kept at all times, whether by written, electronic, mechanical or other means, to:

    (i) record all dealings with client money in any client account;

    (ii) show all client money received, held or paid, distinct from any other money, and separately in respect of each client; and

    (iii) ensure that the firm is able at all times to account, without delay, to each and every client for all money received, held or paid on that client's behalf; and

(e) all accounts, books, ledgers and records kept in relation to the firm's client account(s) are preserved for at least six years from the date of the last entry therein.

Dealings with controlled trust money

(4) If you hold or receive money subject to a controlled trust of which you are a trustee, you must:

(a) keep it separate from money which is not client money or controlled trust money in a client account;

(b) pay controlled trust money without delay into a client account and keep it there, unless you pay it straight over to a third party in the execution of the trust;

(c) make no payment or withdrawal of controlled trust money out of a client account, except in proper execution of the trust under which it is held;

(d) keep accounts at all times, whether by written, electronic, mechanical or other means, to:

    (i) show all your dealings with money received, held or paid on account of controlled trusts;

    (ii) record all your dealings separately in respect of each controlled trust of which you are a trustee; and

    (iii) distinguish money you have received, held or paid subject to a controlled trust from money you have received, held or paid for some other reason;

and either keep such accounts together, centrally, or maintain a central register of controlled trusts of which you are a trustee; and

(e) preserve all accounts, books, ledgers and records of your dealings with money you receive, hold or pay which is subject to a controlled trust for at least six years from the date of the last entry therein.

Accountants' reports

(5)   (a)   You must deliver an accountant's report in respect of any period during which you or your firm have held or received client money or controlled trust money and you were subject to (3) or (4) above.

      (b)   The accountant's report must be signed by the reporting accountant, who must be an accountant qualified in England and Wales or in the overseas jurisdiction where your office is based, or by such other person as the Law Society may think fit. The Law Society may for reasonable cause disqualify a person from signing accountants' reports.

      (c)   The accountant's report must be based on a sufficient examination of the relevant documents to give the reporting accountant a reasonable indication whether or not you have complied with (3) and/or (4) above, as appropriate, during the period covered by the report, and must include the following:

           (i)   your name, practising address(es) and practising style and the name(s) of your partner(s), and those details for a body corporate through which you practise if relevant;

           (ii)   the name, address and qualification of the reporting accountant;

           (iii)   an indication of the nature and extent of the examination the reporting accountant has made of the relevant documents;

           (iv)   a statement of the total amount of money held at banks or similar institutions on behalf of clients and controlled trusts, and of the total liabilities to clients and controlled trusts, on any date selected by the reporting accountant (including the last day), falling within the period under review; and an explanation of any difference between the total amount of money held for clients and controlled trusts and the total liabilities to clients and controlled trusts;

           (v)   if the reporting accountant is satisfied that (so far as may be ascertained from the examination) you have complied with (3) and/or (4) above, as appropriate, during the period covered by the report, except for trivial breaches, or situations where you have been bound by a local rule not to comply, a statement to that effect; and

           (vi)   if the reporting accountant is not sufficiently satisfied to give a statement under (v) above, details of any matters in respect of which it appears to the reporting accountant that you have not complied with (3) and/or (4) above, as appropriate.

      (d)   You need not deliver an accountant's report until after the end of any period of 12 months, ending 31 October, during which you or your firm first held or received client money or controlled trust money subject to (3) or (4), if you, or your firm, had not held or received any such money in the 12 months immediately preceding that period, provided that the accountant's report then delivered includes the period when such money was first held or received.

Guidance to rule 15 – Overseas practice

How these rules apply to overseas practice

1. These rules affect solicitors, RELs, RFLs and recognised bodies differently as regards overseas practice.

    (a) Solicitors, and recognised bodies incorporated in England and Wales, are subject to these rules in relation to practice from offices outside England and Wales.

    (b) RELs are subject to these rules in relation to practice from offices in Scotland and Northern Ireland, but not in relation to practice from offices outside the UK.

    (c) recognised bodies incorporated outside England and Wales are not subject to these rules in relation to practice from offices outside England and Wales, *except* as set out in 15.01(2)(a).

    (d) RFLs are not directly subject to these rules outside England and Wales, except for 1.10 and 12.03(2) and (3). However, an RFL will be affected by the rules in relation to overseas offices, if practising as a partner in an MNP, a director of a recognised body which is a company, or a member of a recognised body which is an LLP, to the extent that other partners or the recognised body is subject to them.

2. You are "practising from an office outside England and Wales" if you are a partner in a partnership with an office outside England and Wales, even if you are not based there. If you are an owner or director of an overseas body corporate which practises law, you are "practising from an office outside England and Wales" even if you are not based there – see rule 24 (interpretation).

Core duties – 15.01(1)

3. Rule 1 (core duties) applies to your overseas practice because these duties are fundamental to your profession. However, although lawyers' professional cultures are usually similar, legal and professional requirements vary from jurisdiction to jurisdiction, and therefore the specific expectations of clients, local lawyers and the courts will be different. It may be necessary to clarify in advance what rules you are bound by, in relation to your dealings with your client, the opposing party and the opposing party's lawyer.

    (a) For example, in Belgium, France, Greece, Italy, Luxembourg, Portugal and Spain communications between lawyers (written or by word of mouth) are normally regarded as confidential as between the lawyers, and may not be disclosed to the lawyers' own clients. Such communications are often marked *confidentiel* or *sous la foi du Palais*. The legal and professional requirements on solicitors, as reflected in these rules, include a duty to disclose all relevant information to your client. You may be working under a legal requirement to comply with the local rule, or you may not, so you will need to make the basis on which correspondence can be sent or received clear in advance.

(b) Similarly, although most lawyers are subject to rules requiring them to keep their clients' affairs confidential, the way in which those rules and conventions operate may vary. In some jurisdictions the concept of a 'without prejudice' offer is alien, and if you wish to make such an offer to an opposing party's lawyer you may need to clarify in advance whether it can be received as such.

Conflicts of rules – 15.01(2)(c)

4. A rule is applicable if you are required by law to comply with it. A conflict of rules can arise when you are required to comply with two applicable rules, but if you comply with one rule you will breach the other. This situation can arise when you are required by local or EU legislation to comply with the rules of the local legal profession. This may occur, for instance, where:

(a) you are a solicitor registered in another jurisdiction under the Establishment Directive, and there is a conflict between one of the local rules and one of the Law Society's rules; or

(b) you are practising under dual title, e.g. as a solicitor and as a New York attorney, and a rule of the New York Bar conflicts with one of the Law Society's rules.

5. If a local rule applies, you cannot choose to comply only with that rule, if you can also comply with the Law Society's rule. You must comply with both, which will mean meeting the stricter standard. However, 15.01(2) addresses the possibility of a conflict of rules by disapplying any Law Society rule to the extent (and no more) that it conflicts with an applicable local rule. In a situation where compliance with both rules might be possible but perhaps create a bizarre result, application can be made to the Law Society for a waiver.

6. Rule 15 modifies the provisions of other rules to allow for adaptation to the legal and professional framework of the jurisdiction in which you are practising. Sometimes more general provisions are substituted, in recognition of the fact that legal and market conditions may be very different in other jurisdictions.

7. Where a rule relates closely to the legal or regulatory framework in England and Wales it may be disapplied by rule 15 without a substitute. If a rule applies in part – for example rule 3 (conflict of interests) – or in full – for example rule 4 (confidentiality and disclosure), you will need to refer to that rule and its guidance, as well as the provisions in rule 15 and this guidance. Even if rule 15 has completely replaced the provisions of another rule, the guidance on the corresponding rule may help you to understand how you are expected to act.

Client relations – 15.02

8. This provision embodies three general principles.

(a) You must account to your client for any commission or secret profit, unless your client agrees otherwise in full knowledge of the amount or approximate amount involved. However, the requirement does not apply if, in all the circumstances, it is not reasonable to pay the commission to the client, taking account of the wide differences in conditions outside England and Wales. For example, the general custom, or the custom in legal practice in that jurisdiction might make it reasonable to deal with commissions in a different way.

(b)   You must not seek to limit your firm's liability below the minimum level of insurance you are required to maintain under 15.26.

(c)   You must not enter into an unlawful contingency fee arrangement (see also the guidance to 2.04).

Avoiding discrimination – 15.06

9.   Because rule 6 is largely based on UK statutes its detailed requirements are unsuitable for application outside the jurisdiction. However rule 1 (core duties) applies to your overseas practice, and 1.07 requires that "You must treat others fairly, reasonably and without unlawful discrimination." This would include compliance with the anti-discrimination provisions of the jurisdiction(s) in which you practise.

Publicity – 15.07

10.   The requirements of rule 7 on publicity apply except as regards the emails, websites etc. of an office in an EU state other than the UK, and the requirements of 7.07 (letterhead) which are replaced by 15.07(b) in relation to your overseas practice. When considering your publicity in relation to the guidance to rule 7 you should bear in mind that the law of the jurisdiction in which your overseas office is based will apply rather than the law of England and Wales; and that you may also be directly subject to local rules. You should therefore interpret the guidance to rule 7 in the light of the following:

(a)   Publicity intended for a jurisdiction outside England and Wales must comply with:

(i)   any applicable law or rules regarding lawyers' publicity in the jurisdiction in which your office is based;

(ii)   the applicable provisions of rule 7 and 15.07; and

(iii)   if the publicity is intended for a third jurisdiction, the rules in force in the "target" jurisdiction governing lawyers' publicity.

(b)   Your publicity will not breach rule 7 through being incidentally received in a jurisdiction where it is not permitted (this is important in relation to a website, which can be accessed world-wide).

(c)   Your website must comply with the E-Commerce Directive and, if you are established anywhere within the EU, with the relevant implementing legislation and the rules which apply to you by virtue of your establishment in an EU state other than the UK.

Fee sharing – 15.08

11.   In general, you must not share your professional fees with a non-lawyer other than your partner, a retired or predecessor partner, an employee, a director or owner of your firm or a body corporate carrying on the practice of lawyers and wholly owned by lawyers. You may, however, share your professional fees with

a non-lawyer for the purpose of facilitating the introduction of capital and/or the provision of services to your firm, though not in relation to European cross-border practice – see rules 8 (fee sharing) and 16 (European cross-border practice) and the attached guidance. Because, subject to the requirements of rule 12 (framework of practice), you are allowed to practise overseas in partnership with non-lawyers, you are also allowed to share fees with a non-lawyer partner. This does not, however, extend to non-lawyers who are not your partners, so you are not allowed to share fees with another solicitor's or REL's firm which has non-lawyer partners or owners.

Undertakings – 15.10(2)

12. The obligation on you as a principal to comply with undertakings given by your firm does not apply to you if you practise from an office outside England and Wales, because your other partners may not be subject to the regulatory powers of the Law Society. You are, however, required to comply with any undertaking you give yourself, and 15.10(2) is not intended to absolve you from any responsibilities you have as a principal.

Framework of practice – 15.12

13. Rule 12 applies in full to your overseas practice. An overseas firm – that is, a firm which has no office in England and Wales – may have lawyer principals, directors and owners who are not registered with the Law Society but would need to be registered if the firm had an office in England and Wales. An overseas firm may also have non-lawyer principals, directors and/or owners, provided there is majority control by lawyers and no breach of applicable local rules, or rules applying in an Establishment Directive state.

In-house practice – 15.13

14. If you are employed at an office outside England and Wales (or in Scotland or Northern Ireland if you are an REL) 15.13 replaces rule 13 with more general requirements. In-house practice overseas is defined differently from in-house practice in England and Wales – see rule 24 (interpretation). If your employer is structured in a way which would allow a solicitor or an REL to be a partner, director or owner under 12.01(3) and 12.02(3) you will be practising in a firm as defined in rule 24 (interpretation) and will not be practising in-house.

15. Note also that if you are registered with another regulatory body under the Establishment Directive 15.13(2)(b) allows you to practise in-house to the extent allowed to the profession governed by that regulatory body. This may be more or less restrictive than the requirements of these rules.

Deposit interest – 15.15

16. In relation to overseas practice, you are not bound by the deposit interest requirements in the accounts rules, but by those in 15.15. You must ensure that a client gets proper interest – but this is subject to the proviso that the circumstances must be such that interest ought, in fairness, to be earned for the client. This might not be so if the interest is or would be negligible, or it is customary in that jurisdiction to deal with interest in a different way. It is also open to you to enter into a written agreement with the client regarding the payment of interest.

European cross-border practice – 15.16

17. The requirements of rule 16 (European cross-border practice) are applied in full. European cross-border practice is:

   (a) any professional activity in an Establishment Directive state other than the UK, whether or not you are physically present in that Establishment Directive state; and

   (b) any professional contact with a lawyer of an Establishment Directive state other than the UK.

   The Establishment Directive states are the EU states and Iceland, Liechtenstein, Norway and Switzerland.

18. For the purpose of rule 16, "professional contacts" and "professional activities" taking place within a firm or in-house practice and "professional contacts" within the UK with RELs and other lawyers established in the UK under the Establishment Directive do not constitute European cross-border practice. However, "professional contacts" with solicitors established in other Establishment Directive states do constitute European cross-border practice.

19. RELs' activities within the UK are not European cross-border practice in themselves.

Separate businesses – 15.21

20. Rule 21 (separate businesses) and 15.21 do not regulate your separate business, but regulate the interface between a firm or in-house practice and a business which is not regulated by the Law Society, wherever the separate business is situated or carries on business. Therefore, if you have a separate business but have no office in England and Wales only 15.21 will apply. However, if you also practise from an office in England and Wales, the more detailed provisions of rule 21 will apply.

21. 15.21 completely replaces the provisions of rule 21 (separate businesses) if you practise wholly outside England and Wales. It applies a lighter regime than rule 21. The requirements of 15.21 are mainly designed to ensure that:

   (a) your compliance with rule 1 (core duties) as a practising lawyer regulated by the Law Society is not compromised by your involvement with the separate business;

   (b) you keep the separate business truly separate from any firm or in-house practice; and

   (c) you ensure that people who obtain services from the separate business know it is not carrying on the practice of a lawyer regulated by the Law Society.

Professional indemnity – 15.26

22. In relation to overseas practice, you are not bound by the Solicitors' Indemnity Insurance Rules but by 15.26, which requires that you must be covered by insurance if you are a principal or employee of a firm. The insurance must be

reasonable, and it is not "reasonable" insurance to have none at all. The extent and amount of the insurance under 15.26 need not exceed the minimum requirements for practice from an office in England and Wales, but local law may apply more onerous requirements.

Accounts – 15.27

23. In relation to overseas practice, you are not bound by the Solicitors' Accounts Rules but by 15.27, which imposes similar but more general provisions. If an applicable local rule conflicts with a provision of 15.27, you will still be expected to comply with any other provisions of 15.27 that do not conflict.

24. Although the accounts rules do not apply, they may provide useful information about keeping accounts, the kind of checks an accountant might make, and the preparation of accountants' reports. Also, if your firm has offices in and outside England and Wales, a single accountant's report may be submitted covering your practice from offices both in, and outside, England and Wales.

25. 15.27 will apply to you if:

    (a) you have held or received client money or controlled trust money as a sole principal;

    (b) you have held or received client money or controlled trust money as a named trustee;

    (c) you are a partner in a partnership which has no separate legal identity and the partnership has held or received client money or controlled trust money, provided that:

        (i) a majority of the partners are solicitors, bodies corporate controlled by solicitors or partnerships with separate legal identity controlled by solicitors; or

        (ii) UK lawyers form the largest national group of lawyers in the partnership;

    (d) you are a partner in a partnership which has a separate legal identity and which has held or received client money or controlled trust money, provided that a controlling majority of the partners are solicitors, bodies corporate controlled by solicitors or partnerships with separate legal identity controlled by solicitors; or

    (e) you are a director and/or owner of a body corporate (including a recognised body) which has held or received client money or controlled trust money if:

        (i) a controlling majority of the owners of the firm are solicitors, bodies corporate controlled by solicitors or partnerships with separate legal identity controlled by solicitors; or

        (ii) the body is a recognised body incorporated in England and Wales.

    The accounting requirements and the obligation to deliver an accountant's report in 15.27 are designed to apply to you in relation to money held or received by your firm unless it is primarily the practice of lawyers of other jurisdictions. The fact that they do not apply in certain cases is not intended to allow a lower standard of care in the handling of client money and controlled trust money – simply to prevent the Law Society's rules applying 'by the back door' in a disproportionate or inappropriate way.

Rule 16 – European cross-border practice

Introduction

The purpose of rule 16 is to apply the provisions of the CCBE Code to European cross-border practice. This is necessary to provide a system of mutual professional understanding for professional relations between lawyers of different Establishment Directive states. Although the CCBE Code contains a large number of requirements, rule 16 contains only those requirements which are not replicated elsewhere in these rules.

Rule 16 – European cross-border practice

16.01 Definition and application

Definition

(1)   (a)   European cross-border practice is:

        (i)   any professional activity in an Establishment Directive state other than the UK, whether or not you are physically present in that Establishment Directive state; and

        (ii)   any professional contact with a lawyer of an Establishment Directive state other than the UK.

   (b)   For the purposes of this rule:

        (i)   a professional contact with a lawyer registered under the Establishment Directive with any of the Law Societies or Bars of the UK is a professional contact with a UK lawyer;

        (ii)   a professional contact with a UK lawyer who is registered under the Establishment Directive in an Establishment Directive state other than the UK is a professional contact with a lawyer of that state; and

        (iii)   professional contacts and professional activities taking place within a firm or in-house legal department are not European cross-border practice.

Application of this rule

(2)   (a)   If you are a solicitor this rule applies to your European cross-border practice from an office in, or outside, England and Wales;

   (b)   if you are an REL this rule applies to your European cross-border practice from an office within the UK;

   (c)   if you are an RFL and you are a partner in an MNP, a director of a recognised body which is a company, or a member of a recognised body which is an LLP, this rule applies to your European cross-border practice from an office in England and Wales;

(d) this rule applies to a recognised body incorporated in England and Wales in relation to its European cross-border practice from an office in, or outside, England and Wales; and

(e) this rule applies to a recognised body incorporated outside England and Wales in relation to its European cross-border practice from an office in England and Wales.

16.02 Occupations considered incompatible with legal practice

(1) If you act in legal proceedings or proceedings before public authorities in an Establishment Directive state other than the UK, you must, in that state, comply with any rules regarding occupations incompatible with the practice of law, as if you were a lawyer of that state.

(2) If you are a solicitor based at an office in an Establishment Directive state other than the UK, you must respect any rules regarding participation in commercial or other activities not connected with the practice of law, as they are applied to lawyers of that state.

16.03 Fee sharing with non-lawyers

(1) If you are practising from an office in the UK, whether or not you are physically present at that office, you must not share your professional fees from that practice with a non-lawyer situated in another Establishment Directive state except to pay a fee, commission or other compensation to a deceased lawyer's heirs, or to a retired lawyer, in respect of taking over the deceased or retired lawyer's practice.

(2) If you are practising from an office in an Establishment Directive state other than the UK, whether or not you are physically present at that office, you must not share your professional fees from that practice with a non-lawyer, except:

(a) within a firm which is permitted under rule 12 (framework of practice); or

(b) to pay a fee, commission or other compensation to a deceased lawyer's heirs, or to a retired lawyer, in respect of taking over the deceased or retired lawyer's practice.

(3) If you are practising from an office in a state which is not covered by the Establishment Directive, whether or not you are physically present at that office, you must not share your professional fees from that practice with a non-lawyer situated in an Establishment Directive state other than the UK, except:

(a) within a firm which is permitted under rule 12 (framework of practice); or

(b) to pay a fee, commission or other compensation to a deceased lawyer's heirs, or to a retired lawyer, in respect of taking over the deceased or retired lawyer's practice.

16.04 Co-operation between lawyers of different member states

(1)   If you are approached by a lawyer of an Establishment Directive state other than the UK to undertake work which you are not competent to undertake, you must assist that lawyer to obtain the information necessary to find and instruct a lawyer capable of providing the service asked for.

(2)   When co-operating with a lawyer of an Establishment Directive state other than the UK you must take into account the differences which may exist between your respective legal systems and the professional organisations, competencies and obligations of lawyers in your respective states.

16.05 Correspondence between lawyers in different member states

(1)   if you want to send to a lawyer in an Establishment Directive state other than the UK a communication which you wish to remain "confidential" or "without prejudice", you must, before sending the communication, clearly express your intention in order to avoid misunderstanding, and ask if the lawyer is able to accept the communication on that basis; and

(2)   if you receive from a lawyer in another Establishment Directive state a communication which is stated to be "confidential" or "without prejudice", but which you are unable to accept on the basis intended by that lawyer, you must return it without revealing the contents to others.

16.06 Paying referral fees to non-lawyers

You must not pay a fee, commission or any other compensation to a non-lawyer as a consideration for referring a client to you:

(a)   if the non-lawyer is situated in an Establishment Directive state other than the UK; or

(b)   if you are practising from an office in an Establishment Directive state other than the UK, whether or not you are physically present at that office.

16.07 Disputes between lawyers of different member states

(1)   If you consider that a lawyer of an Establishment Directive state other than the UK has acted in breach of a rule of professional conduct you must draw the breach to the other lawyer's attention.

(2)   If a professional dispute arises between you and a lawyer of an Establishment Directive state other than the UK, you must attempt to settle the dispute in a friendly way.

(3)   In either case, you must inform the Law Society and the other lawyer's bar or law society prior to commencing any form of proceedings against the other lawyer, for their assistance in resolving the matter.

Guidance to rule 16 – European cross-border practice

1. The Law Society has adopted the CCBE Code in relation to European cross-border practice in the Establishment Directive area. The Establishment Directive states are the EU states and Iceland, Liechtenstein, Norway and Switzerland.

2. If you comply with these rules in relation to your practice generally, and with rule 16 in relation to European cross-border practice, you will also comply with the requirements of the CCBE Code, as interpreted in the light of article 1 of the CCBE Code and the CCBE's Explanatory Memorandum and Commentary dated May 1989.

Incompatible occupations – 16.02

3. 16.02(1) prohibits you from pursuing any occupation prohibited to local lawyers as incompatible with the practice of law, in another Establishment Directive state in which you act in legal proceedings or proceedings before a public authority. This does not prevent you from pursuing such an occupation in the UK if it is permitted under these rules, or in another Establishment Directive state where it is allowed.

4. 16.02(2) requires you to "respect" the rules regarding incompatible occupations in a state where you are established. If you are subject to the Establishment Directive and established in an Establishment Directive state, any provisions regarding incompatible occupations which bind the local legal profession will apply to you directly. If you are established in an Establishment Directive state, but you are not subject to the Establishment Directive, for example, because you are not an EU national, you will not be subject to the host state rule but rule 16 will apply. "Respect" for a rule is not the same as an obligation to comply with that rule, but the Law Society would expect you to comply with the spirit of such a rule where it is not unreasonable to do so.

Fee sharing – 16.03

5. Although rule 8 (fee sharing) allows you to share fees with a non-lawyer in some circumstances, this is prohibited under rule 16 in respect of European cross-border practice, except within a firm which is permitted under rule 12 (framework of practice).

6. Interpreting how the prohibition applies to a firm in the UK sharing fees with a non-lawyer fee sharer operating in more than one state, and how it applies to a firm of solicitors practising in more than one state, may be complex. For example:

    (a) rule 16 would prohibit your firm from sharing fees with a non-lawyer company whose principal place of business is in an Establishment Directive state other than the UK, or with a non-lawyer company's branch establishment in an Establishment Directive state other than the UK; and

    (b) if your firm has its main office in the UK and a branch office in another Establishment Directive state, the fees of the branch office cannot be shared with a non-lawyer, so the firm cannot share a percentage of its fees as a whole with a non-lawyer. However, the firm could share a percentage of the fees of its UK office, and of any office outside the Establishment Directive area, with a non-lawyer fee sharer, provided:

(i)   the fee sharer is situated in the UK or outside the Establishment Directive area; and

(ii)   the requirements of rule 8 (fee sharing) are met.

Correspondence between lawyers in different member states – 16.05

7.   Differences between the ways in which client business is conducted in different states can give rise to misunderstandings between lawyers, and this provision is designed to help avoid such misunderstandings. Terms such as *confidential, confidentiel, sous la fois du Palais* or *without prejudice* are not of universal application throughout the Establishment Directive area. For example, in some jurisdictions, *confidentiel* means confidential as between lawyers and excluding the client. The following examples, based on the CCBE's Explanatory Memorandum and Commentary dated May 1989, illustrate some of these differences.

(a)   In the UK and the Irish Republic there is a general duty to keep clients informed, and "confidentiality" is understood to refer to lawyers' duties to keep their client's affairs confidential. Communications between lawyers made in order to attempt to settle a dispute and marked "without prejudice" are normally discussed with the client but are not to be used as evidence prior to an order being made.

(b)   In Belgium, France, Greece, Italy, Luxembourg, Portugal and Spain, communications marked *confidentiel* or *sous la foi du Palais* between lawyers are normally regarded as confidential as between the lawyers, and not to be disclosed even to the lawyers' clients.

(c)   In Denmark the lawyer's duty to keep the client informed about all important correspondence generally applies whether or not a letter is marked "without prejudice" or "confidential", but as an exception, lawyers may exchange views (normally by word of mouth only) with a view to finding an amicable settlement, on the mutual understanding that such communications are not disclosed to the clients. A lawyer is not legally bound by such a confidence, but to break it would prejudice future participation in such confidential exchanges.

(d)   In the Netherlands legal recourse based on communications between lawyers may not be sought, unless the interest of the client requires it, and only after prior consultation with the lawyer for the other party. If such consultation does not lead to a solution, the advice of the dean should be sought before recourse to law. The content of settlement negotiations between lawyers may not be communicated to the court without the permission of the lawyer for the other party, unless the right to do so was expressly reserved when the settlement proposal in question was made. There is however no general rule preventing a lawyer from sending copies of such communications to the client.

(e)   In Germany communications between lawyers are not confidential. The lawyer has an obligation to communicate them to the client and they may be admitted as evidence in court.

Referral fees – 16.06

8. Although rule 9 (referrals of business) allows you to have an arrangement for the referral of clients with a non-lawyer, and, subject to disclosure, to pay the introducer, this is prohibited under rule 16 in respect of European cross-border practice.

9. As with the prohibition on fee-sharing with a non-lawyer, there are complexities involved in interpreting how the prohibition applies to a firm practising in more than one state, and to an arrangement with a non-lawyer introducer operating in more than one state. For example:

    (a) rule 16 would prohibit your firm from paying for a referral from a non-lawyer company whose principal place of business is in an Establishment Directive state other than the UK, or from a non-lawyer company's branch establishment in an Establishment Directive state other than the UK; and

    (b) if your firm has its main office in the UK and a branch office in another Establishment Directive state, the branch office cannot pay for referrals from a non-lawyer, but the UK office, and any office outside the Establishment Directive area, could do so provided that:

        (i) the introducer is situated in the UK or outside the Establishment Directive area; and

        (ii) the requirements of rule 9 (referrals of business) are met.

Rule 17 – Insolvency practice

Introduction

If you are a solicitor or an REL, and an insolvency practitioner in a firm, rule 17 applies to you when you accept appointments and act as an appointment holder. Rule 17 should be read in conjunction with The Practice of Insolvency: a Guide to Professional Conduct and Ethics produced by the Joint Insolvency Committee and adopted by all recognised professional bodies (RPBs) including the Law Society. The purpose of this Guide is to ensure your independence and objectivity when acting as an appointment holder and that you can identify and avoid conflicts of interest. The rule does not apply to your overseas practice except in relation to appointments appertaining to orders made in the courts of England and Wales.

Rule 17 – Insolvency practice

17.01

If you are a solicitor or an REL you must, when accepting an appointment or acting as an appointment holder as an insolvency practitioner, comply with *The Practice of Insolvency: a Guide to Professional Conduct and Ethics* produced by the Joint Insolvency Committee and adopted by the Law Society.

Guidance to rule 17 – Insolvency practice

1. You must comply with the requirements of the Insolvency Act 1986 and other relevant legislation in relation to accepting appointments and acting as an appointment holder.

2. You should have regard to the other guidance and best practice promulgated from time to time by the Law Society as an RPB on all issues relating to appointment holding, including professional independence.

Rule 18 – Property selling

Introduction

This rule sets out requirements for providing property selling services through your firm. Requirements for providing property selling services through a separate business are dealt with under rule 21 (separate businesses).

The seller is your client, and any property selling work you do is, in addition to this rule, subject to the same law and professional rules binding on you in relation to your other work.

The rule applies to your overseas practice from offices in Scotland or Northern Ireland but not to your overseas practice from offices outside the UK.

Rule 18 – Property selling

18.01 Standards of property selling services

(1) When providing property selling services through your firm, you must:

    (a) ensure that you, or the relevant staff, are competent to carry out the work;

    (b) not seek from any prospective buyer a pre-contract deposit in excess of any prescribed limit; and

    (c) promptly send to your client written accurate details of any offer you have received from a prospective buyer in respect of an interest in the property (other than those of a description which your client has indicated in writing that they do not want to receive).

(2) In 18.01(1) above:

    (a) "competent" includes meeting any standards of competence set by the Secretary of State under s.22 of the Estate Agents Act 1979; and

    (b) "prescribed limit" means any limit prescribed by the Secretary of State under s.19 of the Estate Agents Act 1979.

18.02 Statement on the cost

(1) When accepting instructions to act in the sale of a property, you must, at the outset of communication between you and the client, or as soon as is reasonably practicable, and before the client is committed to any liability towards you, give the client a written statement setting out your agreement as to:

    (a) the identity of the property;

    (b) the interest to be sold;

    (c) the price to be sought;

(d) the amount of your fee or the method of its calculation;

(e) the circumstances in which your fee is to become payable;

(f) regarding any payments to be made to others, and charged separately:

(i) the amount, or the method by which they will be calculated; and

(ii) the circumstances in which they may be incurred; and

(g) the incidence of VAT.

(2) You must also, within the written statement:

(a) state whether or not you are to have "sole agency" or "sole selling rights". The statement must also include a clear explanation of the intention and effect of those terms, or any similar terms used; and

(b) if the statement refers to a "ready, willing and able" buyer (or similar term), include a clear explanation of the term.

18.03 Conflict of interests

(1) In addition to your duties under rule 3 (conflict of interests), when selling property you must comply with the following requirements.

(a) If you or any connected person has, or is seeking to acquire, a beneficial interest in the property or in the proceeds of sale of any interest in the property, you must promptly inform your client in writing.

(b) If you act in the sale of property, even if not in the conveyancing, you must not act for the buyer in the negotiations.

(c) If a prospective buyer makes an offer for a client's property, you must promptly inform the client in writing if, to your knowledge, you or any connected person has been instructed, or is to be instructed by the buyer to sell an interest in land, and that sale is necessary to enable the buyer to buy from the client or results from that prospective purchase.

(d) If you have, or to your knowledge any connected person has, a beneficial interest in a property or in the proceeds of sale of any interest in it, you must promptly inform in writing any person negotiating to acquire or dispose of any interest in that property. You must make this disclosure before entering into any negotiations with a prospective buyer.

(e) You must not discriminate against a prospective buyer because they are unlikely to instruct you to sell an interest in land, which sale is necessary to enable the buyer to buy from your client or results from that prospective purchase.

(f) When acting for a seller, you must restrict communication with the buyer to your property selling function. In particular:

(i) you must communicate about legal matters so far as possible only through the buyer's solicitor; and

      (ii)   you must not lead the buyer to believe that they are receiving legal advice from you.

    (g)   When acting for a seller, if you arrange for a mortgage to be available on the property in order to facilitate the sale, you may inform prospective buyers of the availability of the mortgage (subject to the buyer's status) but, unless exempted by rule 3 (conflict of interests) you must also inform prospective buyers in writing:

      (i)   that you cannot advise or act for the prospective buyer in respect of the mortgage;

      (ii)   that the mortgage may not be the only one available; and

      (iii)   that the prospective buyer should consult their own lawyer or licensed conveyancer.

(2)   In 18.03(1) above:

    (a)   "connected person" means:

      (i)   spouse, former spouse, reputed spouse, brother, sister, uncle, aunt, nephew, niece, direct descendant, parent or other direct ancestor;

      (ii)   any employee of your firm, and any member of your employee's family;

      (iii)   any owner or employee of an associated firm defined in rule 24 (interpretation) or any member of their families;

      (iv)   any company of which you are a director or employee, or any LLP of which you are a member or employee, or any company in which you, either alone or with any other connected person or persons are entitled to exercise, or control the exercise of, one-third or more of the voting power at any general meeting;

      (v)   any company of which any of the persons mentioned in (i) to (iii) above is a director or employee, or any LLP of which any of them is a member or employee, or any company in which any of them, either alone or with any other connected person or persons, is entitled to exercise, or control the exercise of, one-third or more of the voting power at any general meeting; and

      (vi)   any other "associate" as defined in s.32 of the Estate Agents Act 1979; and

    (b)   "you" includes anyone with whom you carry on a joint property selling practice, and owners of an associated firm as defined in rule 24 (interpretation).

18.04 Waivers

Notwithstanding rule 22 (waivers), the Council of the Law Society shall not have power to waive any of the provisions of this rule.

Guidance to rule 18 – Property selling

General – business structures and property selling

1.   You may sell property through a separate business – see notes 8 and 9 below and rule 21 (separate businesses) – or as part of the general work of your firm, or through a firm formed especially for that purpose, either alone or with other firms. If you form a property selling firm with solicitors from other firms, it will be a distinct firm for all purposes.

2.   A jointly owned property selling firm may be incorporated as a SEAL (Solicitors' Estate Agency Limited). A SEAL is defined in 3.12. See rule 3 (conflict of interests) for the position of a SEAL regarding conflicts of interests.

3.   A further alternative for firms wishing to co-operate in selling property is a joint Property Display Centre (PDC), where the principal activity carried on is publicising properties in the sale of which an individual participating firm is instructed. It is also possible for a single firm to establish its own PDC. A PDC:

   (a)   is not itself a firm, and is not a separate entity; it is an administrative extension of the practices of the participating firms, and its address should be notified to the Law Society's Registration department;

   (b)   can have no clients; it may merely carry out certain activities on behalf of the participating firms (only individual participating firms may be instructed in the sale of a property);

   (c)   is a place where the principal activity carried on is the display and dissemination of information about properties which the individual participating firms have for sale; and

   (d)   cannot carry on any part of your professional practice. In particular no negotiations may be conducted at the PDC; prospective buyers must be referred to the individual participating firm instructed in the sale of the property in question. Instructions to sell a property may only be accepted at offices of participating firms. To avoid problems with rule 3 (conflict of interests), the participating firms must operate totally independently so far as their professional business, including property selling, is concerned.

4.   You and the other participating firms may wish to establish a joint service company to carry out support functions connected with the running of the PDC, e.g. hiring premises and equipment. The service company (as with a service company established by an individual firm of solicitors) cannot carry on any legal practice or have any dealings with the property selling or property buying public.

5.   As no part of the professional practice of the participating firms is carried out at the PDC, rule 5 (business management) does not apply. Nor would rule 5

apply to a PDC established by a single firm. The participating firms, or the single firm, would nevertheless be responsible for the activities of its PDC staff and would have a duty to supervise them.

6.   If you sell property you may share your professional fees with an estate agent who is your sub-agent for a sale – see 8.01(j).

7.   You may properly provide structural surveys and formal valuations of property through your firm. You must ensure that you, or relevant staff, have the appropriate level of competence.

8.   You may provide property selling services through a separate business – see 21.04(1)(c). If so, you must comply with the safeguards in 21.05. Note also that a separate business will not fall within the exemption in s.1 of the Estate Agents Act 1979 (see note 10 below). The effect of this is that your separate business providing property selling services will be subject to all the provisions of the Estate Agents Act 1979.

9.   If you are selling a property through a separate business, your firm may do the seller's conveyancing, but may not normally do the buyer's conveyancing unless you comply with 21.05(2)(f), and:

   (a)   your firm is not doing the seller's conveyancing; or

   (b)   your firm is allowed to act for both buyer and seller under rule 3 (conflict of interests).

Your separate business may, however, provide mortgage related services to the buyer even if your firm is doing the seller's conveyancing.

Standards of property selling services – 18.01

10.   S.1(2)(a) of the Estate Agents Act 1979 exempts from that Act "things done in the course of his profession by a practising solicitor or a person employed by him." This exemption is on the basis that certain standards, set out in the Act, are already required of you under the rules of professional conduct. These standards are contained in rule 18 and in other rules of professional conduct, all of which remain applicable when you are selling property.

11.   These standards are:

   (a)   a requirement of competence, imposed by 18.01(a); this also reflects 1.06 (competence);

   (b)   a prohibition on making false statements as set out in s.1 of the Property Misdescriptions Act 1991 - "a false or misleading statement about a prescribed matter" (s.1(1)). A prescribed matter is "any matter relating to land which is specified in an order made by the Secretary of State" (s.1(5)). A statement can be made by pictures as well as words. Any false statement will be a breach of 1.01 (integrity);

   (c)   a prohibition on seeking a pre-contract deposit in excess of the prescribed limit, imposed by 18.01(1)(b);

(d)   requirements for the holding of clients' money and the keeping of client accounts, which are imposed on you under the Solicitors' Accounts Rules 1998;

(e)   requirements relating to the provision of information to clients, imposed on you by 18.01(1)(c) and 18.02; this also reflects rule 2 (client relations); and

(f)   requirements relating to conflict of interests. Some of these are imposed on you by 18.03, and some by rule 3 (conflict of interests). In addition to the general provisions on conflict of interests (3.01 to 3.06), you should also have regard to the provisions specifically on conveyancing, property selling and mortgage related services (3.07 to 3.22). Note that there are also special conflict provisions where you sell property through a separate business – see notes 8 and 9 above and 21.05(2)(f).

Statement on the cost – 18.02

12.   Notes 13 to 16 below set out the detailed information requirements to help you comply with 18.02. These requirements correspond to those in the Estate Agents (Provision of Information) Regulations 1991 (SI 1991 no. 859) and the Schedule to it.

13.   A clear explanation of the intention and effect of the terms sole agency/sole selling rights or similar terms, given to clients will take the following form.

"*Sole agency*

You will be liable to pay a fee to us, in addition to any other costs or charges agreed, if unconditional contracts for the sale of the property are exchanged at any time:

with a buyer introduced by us with whom we had negotiations about the property in the period during which we have sole agency; or

with a buyer introduced by another agent during the period of our sole agency.

Sole selling rights

You will be liable to pay a fee to us, in addition to any other costs or charges agreed, in each of the following circumstances:

if unconditional contracts for the sale of the property are exchanged in the period during which we have sole selling rights, even if the buyer was not found by us but by another agent or by any other person, including yourself; or

if unconditional contracts for the sale of the property are exchanged after the expiry of the period during which we have sole selling rights but to a buyer who was introduced to you during that period or with whom we had negotiations about the property during that period."

14.   A clear explanation of the term "ready, willing and able" given to clients will take the following form.

"A buyer is a "ready, willing and able" buyer if he or she is prepared and is able to exchange unconditional contracts for the purchase of your property. You will be liable to pay a fee to us, in addition to any other costs or charges agreed, if such a buyer is introduced by us in accordance with your instructions and this must be paid even if you subsequently withdraw and unconditional contracts for sale are not exchanged, irrespective of your reasons."

15. If, by reason of the provisions of the statement in which any of the terms referred to above appear, any of the prescribed explanations is in any way misleading, you should alter the content of the explanation so as accurately to describe the liability of the client to pay a fee in accordance with those provisions. Subject to this requirement, you should reproduce the explanations prominently, clearly and legibly without any material alterations or additions. They should be given no less prominence than that given to any other information in the statement apart from the heading, firm names, names of the parties, numbers or lettering subsequently inserted.

16. You may quote or publicise a composite fee for property selling and conveyancing, but should be prepared to quote separate fees if asked. The separate fees may total more than the composite fee.

Conflict of interests – 18.03

17. The requirements of 18.03 are similar to those imposed on estate agents by the Estate Agents (Undesirable Practices) (No.2) Order 1991 (SI 1991 no. 1032).

18. It is important to read the requirements of 18.03 in close conjunction with rule 3 (conflict of interests).

19. The situation covered by 18.03(1)(d) is also a specific case of the application of 1.07 (fairness) and 10.01 (not taking unfair advantage).

Waivers – 18.04

20. The exemption from the Estate Agents Act 1979, explained in note 10 above, is on the basis that the standards in rule 18 are complied with in all circumstances. For this reason there is no power to waive rule 18.

Rule 19 – Financial services

Introduction

This rule sets out the requirements for ensuring that your independence is preserved when acting in connection with the provision of financial services for clients, both through your firm and through a separate business.

The rule applies to your overseas practice in relation to regulated activities you conduct from an office in Scotland or Northern Ireland and to regulated activities you conduct into the UK from an office outside the UK.

Rule 19 – Financial services

19.01 Independence

(1)　You must not, in connection with any regulated activity:

　　(a)　be an appointed representative; or

　　(b)　have any arrangement with other persons under which you could be constrained to recommend to clients or effect for them (or refrain from doing so) transactions:

　　　　(i)　in some investments but not others;

　　　　(ii)　with some persons but not others; or

　　　　(iii)　through the agency of some persons but not others; or

　　(c)　have any arrangement with other persons under which you could be constrained to introduce or refer clients or other persons with whom you deal to some persons but not others.

(2)　You must not have any active involvement in a separate business which is an appointed representative, unless it is the appointed representative of an independent financial adviser.

(3)　(1)(b) and (c) above shall not apply to arrangements in connection with any of the following types of investments:

　　(a)　regulated mortgage contracts;

　　(b)　general insurance contracts; or

　　(c)　pure protection contracts.

(4)　In this rule:

　　(a)　"appointed representative" has the meaning given in the Financial Services and Markets Act 2000;

(b)   "general insurance contract" is any contract of insurance within Part I of Schedule 1 to the Financial Services and Markets Act 2000 (Regulated Activities) Order 2001;

(c)   "investment" means any of the investments specified in Part III of the Financial Services and Markets Act 2000 (Regulated Activities) Order 2001;

(d)   "pure protection contract" has the meaning given in rule 8(1) of the Solicitors' Financial Services (Scope) Rules 2001;

(e)   "regulated activity" means an activity which is specified in the Financial Services and Markets Act 2000 (Regulated Activities) Order 2001; and

(f)   "regulated mortgage contract" has the meaning given by article 61(3) of the Financial Services and Markets Act 2000 (Regulated Activities) Order 2001.

Guidance to rule 19 – Financial services

1.   Independence is a core duty – see 1.02. However rule 19 sets out the exact scope of this duty when carrying on regulated activities.

2.   Note that under the Financial Services and Markets Act 2000 (the FSMA) the Financial Services Authority (FSA) is the single statutory regulator of financial services business. Under the FSMA, if you carry on "regulated activities" you will need either to be regulated by the FSA or to rely on the part XX exemption in the FSMA.

3.   The Law Society is, therefore, no longer able to authorise you to conduct investment business. However, part XX of the FSMA makes special provision for professional firms which do not carry on mainstream investment business but which may carry on regulated activities in the course of other work such as conveyancing, corporate, matrimonial, probate and trust work. Part XX enables firms of solicitors which meet certain conditions to be treated as exempt professional firms and to carry on activities known as exempt regulated activities. These firms will not need to be regulated by the FSA but will be able to carry on exempt regulated activities under the supervision of and regulation by the Law Society which is a Designated Professional Body.

4.   As a Designated Professional Body, the Law Society is required to make rules governing the carrying on of regulated activities by its members. In accordance with this requirement, the Law Society has made the Solicitors' Financial Services (Scope) Rules 2001 which set out the scope of the activities which may be undertaken by firms under the part XX exemption. You should refer to these rules and the Solicitors' Financial Services (Conduct of Business) Rules 2001 regarding the carrying on of regulated activities.

5.   This rule applies specifically in connection with regulated activities. It prohibits you from being an appointed representative (i.e. a tied agent) or from being actively involved in a separate business which is an appointed representative unless the separate business is the appointed representative of an independent financial adviser.

6.   It also prevents you from entering into any restrictive arrangements in connection with regulated activities that could constrain the advice you give to clients or the referrals that you make. However, it would not prevent you from regularly introducing clients to a particular broker, provided that you have not entered into any arrangement which could constrain you to use that broker.

7.   The prohibition on entering into restrictive arrangements does not apply to arrangements in connection with:

       (a)   regulated mortgage contracts;

       (b)   general insurance contracts, for example after the event insurance; or

       (c)   pure protection contracts, for example term assurance.

       This means that you would not be prevented from having an arrangement under which an introducer stipulates that you might only sell one particular insurance policy – for example, if there is a conditional fee agreement, provided that it is suitable for the client's needs and you have informed the client of the constraint. Although the prohibition in rule 19 does not apply to arrangements in connection with particular types of investments, you must still comply with the core duty of independence (see 1.02) and rule 9 (referrals of business).

Rule 20 – Requirements of practice

Introduction

Rule 20 sets out the requirements for certification, the types of work which you are permitted to do, and co-operation with, and provision of information to, the Law Society.

Rule 20 – Requirements of practice

20.01 Practising certificates

(1)　If you are practising as a solicitor you must:

　　(a)　have in force a practising certificate issued by the Law Society; or

　　(b)　be exempt under section 88 of the Solicitors Act 1974 from holding a practising certificate.

(2)　You will be practising as a solicitor if you are involved in legal practice and:

　　(a)　your involvement in the firm or the work depends on your being a solicitor;

　　(b)　you are held out explicitly or implicitly as a practising solicitor;

　　(c)　you are employed explicitly or implicitly as a solicitor; or

　　(d)　you are deemed by section 1A of the Solicitors Act 1974 to be acting as a solicitor.

(3)　In (2) above "legal practice" includes not only the practice of law but also the provision of business services such as are provided by solicitors.

(4)　If you are a solicitor who was formerly an REL, and you are practising from an office in the UK as a lawyer of an Establishment Directive state, you must have in force a practising certificate issued by the Law Society, even if you are not practising as a solicitor.

20.02 Reserved work

A firm may undertake activities reserved to solicitors under the Solicitors Act 1974 relating to the conveyancing of land or the administration of a deceased's estate only if:

　　(a)　the firm has a principal who is:

　　　　(i)　a solicitor;

　　　　(ii)　an REL qualified to provide that service under regulation 12 or 13 of the Establishment Directive Regulations; or

       (iii)   a recognised body qualified to provide that service under (b) below; or

  (b)   the firm is a recognised body which is:

       (i)   a company with a director who is a solicitor, or an REL qualified to provide that service under regulation 12 or 13 of the Establishment Directive Regulations; or

       (ii)   an LLP with a member who is:

           (A)   a solicitor;

           (B)   an REL qualified to provide that service under regulation 12 or 13 of the Establishment Directive Regulations;

           (C)   a recognised body which is a company with a director who is a solicitor, or an REL qualified to provide that service under regulation 12 or 13 of the Establishment Directive Regulations; or

           (D)   a recognised body which is an LLP with a member who is a solicitor, or an REL qualified to provide that service under regulation 12 or 13 of the Establishment Directive Regulations.

20.03 Duty to co-operate with the Law Society

(1)   You must deal with the Law Society in an open, prompt and co-operative way.

(2)   You must:

  (a)   provide the Law Society with information necessary in order to issue you with a practising certificate, or deal with renewal of registration or renewal of recognition, as appropriate; and

  (b)   during the period your practising certificate, registration or recognition is in force, notify the Law Society of any changes to relevant information about you or your firm or in-house practice.

20.04 Reporting serious misconduct and serious financial difficulty

You must (subject, where necessary, to your client's consent) report to the Law Society if:

  (a)   you become aware of serious misconduct by a solicitor, an REL, an RFL or a firm;

  (b)   you are a principal in a firm, and you become aware of serious misconduct by an employee of the firm;

  (c)   you have reason to doubt the professional integrity of a solicitor, an REL or an RFL; or

(d)   you have reason to believe that a solicitor, an REL, an RFL or a firm is in serious financial difficulty which could put the public at risk.

20.05 Obstructing complaints

(1)   You must not try to hinder or prevent a person who wishes to report your conduct to the Law Society from doing so.

(2)   You must not victimise a person for reporting your conduct to the Law Society.

(3)   You must not on your own or on your clients' behalf enter into an agreement which would attempt to preclude the Law Society from investigating any actual or potential allegation of professional misconduct.

(4)   Unless you can properly allege malice, you must not issue defamation proceedings in respect of a complaint to the Law Society.

20.06 Production of documents and information

(1)   You must promptly comply with a notice served by the Law Society in accordance with (2) below for the purpose of ascertaining whether a solicitor, an REL, an RFL or a recognised body is complying with or has complied with any provision of these rules, or of any other rules, codes or mandatory guidance made or issued by the Council of the Law Society.

Such notice will be to the effect that you must produce for inspection by the Law Society's appointee all documents held by you or held under your control and all information and explanations requested:

(a)   in connection with your practice; or

(b)   in connection with any trust of which you are, or formerly were, a trustee;

and you must promptly comply with any notice served under (2) below.

(2)   Notice served under this rule:

(a)   must be in writing;

(b)   must be left at, or sent by registered post or recorded delivery to, the most recent address held by the Law Society, or delivered by the Law Society's appointee; and

(c)   will be deemed to have been received upon proof of its having been delivered at your practising address or last known practising address (or, in the case of a recognised body, its registered office) 48 hours (excluding Saturdays, Sundays and Bank Holidays) after posting.

(3)   You must provide any necessary permissions for information to be given so as to enable the Law Society's appointee to:

(a)   prepare a report on the documents produced under (1) above; and

(b)   seek verification from clients, staff and the banks, building societies or other financial institutions used by you.

(4)　(a)　You must comply with all requests from the Law Society or its appointee as to:

　　　(i)　the form in which you produce any documents you hold electronically; and

　　　(ii)　photocopies of any documents to take away.

　　(b)　The Law Society's appointee is not entitled under 20.06 to take original documents away.

20.07 Dealing with claims

(1)　If you are a principal in a firm, a director of a recognised body which is a company, a member of a recognised body which is an LLP or a recognised body, and you discover an act or omission which could give rise to a claim, you must inform your client.

(2)　If a client makes a claim against you, or notifies an intention to do so, or if you discover an act or omission which could give rise to a claim, you must:

　　(a)　inform your client that independent advice should be sought (unless your client's loss, if any, is trivial and you promptly remedy that loss);

　　(b)　consider whether a conflict of interests has arisen, and if so not act further for your client in the matter giving rise to the claim; and

　　(c)　notify the qualifying insurer or the Assigned Risks Pool (ARP) Manager in accordance with the terms of the policy or, if appropriate, the Solicitors' Indemnity Fund (SIF).

Guidance to rule 20 – Requirements of practice

Requirements and exemptions under the Solicitors Act 1974 – 20.01

1.　20.01 includes, in rule form, the requirements of Section 1 of the Solicitors Act 1974. The section reads:

"No person shall be qualified to act as a solicitor unless –

　　(a)　he has been admitted as a solicitor, and

　　(b)　his name is on the roll, and

　　(c)　he has in force a certificate issued by the Society in accordance with the provisions of this Part authorising him to practise as a solicitor (in this Act referred to as a 'practising certificate')."

2.　If you practise as a solicitor without having a practising certificate, you will commit a criminal offence unless you are entitled to rely on a statutory exemption.

3. Section 88 of the Solicitors Act 1974 exempts from the requirement to hold a practising certificate the solicitor to certain public authorities, and a solicitor who is the "clerk" to such a solicitor. The section reads:

    "(1) Nothing in this Act shall prejudice or affect any rights or privileges of the solicitor to the Treasury, any other public department, the Church Commissioners or the Duchy of Cornwall, or require any such officer or any clerk or officer appointed to act for him to be admitted or enrolled or to hold a practising certificate in any case where it would not have been necessary for him to be admitted or enrolled or to hold such a certificate if this Act had not been passed.

    (1A) The exemption from the requirement to hold a practising certificate conferred by subsection (1) above shall not apply to solicitors who are Crown Prosecutors.

    (2) Sections 31 and 32(1) shall not apply to, and nothing in this Act shall prejudice or affect any rights or privileges which immediately before the commencement of this Act attached to the office of the Solicitor of the City of London."

4. Although section 88 of the Solicitors Act 1974 preserves certain pre-existing rights, privileges and exemptions, it does not say what these are. They are to be found in a number of statutory provisions of some age, each conferring different rights, privileges or exemptions on different persons. Some of the older provisions do not fit easily into modern conditions and it is not possible to provide a full list of exemptions. The view of the Law Society is as follows.

    (a) A solicitor is exempt if holding office as the solicitor (i.e. is the principal solicitor) to:

        (i)   the Treasury;

        (ii)   the Church Commissioners;

        (iii) the Duchy of Cornwall; or

        (iv)   any other public department.

    (b) There is no definition of "public department" in section 88 of the Solicitors Act 1974, but the Law Society takes the view that the term includes any department of central government in the UK, but not e.g. quangos, agencies, the National Assembly of Wales, or the Legal Services Commission.

    (c) A solicitor who is a clerk or officer appointed to act for one of the above is also exempt.

    (d) A solicitor who is a Crown Prosecutor is not exempt.

    (e) A solicitor without a practising certificate (and indeed, a non-solicitor) may conduct magistrates' court proceedings on behalf of a local authority if the solicitor is:

        (i)   a member or officer of the local authority; or

(ii)   a person, or the employee of a person, authorised by an order under the Deregulation and Contracting Out Act 1994 to exercise a function of the local authority.

(See section 223 of the Local Government Act 1972.)

Being held out as a practising solicitor – 20.01(2)(b)

5.   Being described on your firm's notepaper or website as a member of the Law Society is an example of being held out "implicitly" as a solicitor.

6.   There is a presumption that you are practising as a solicitor if you are held out (explicitly or implicitly) as a solicitor whilst providing lawyer-like services. The same presumption arises if you are described as a lawyer in such a context, if you have no other legal qualification to justify that description. It is possible in some circumstances to rebut the presumption by ensuring that some such words as "non-practising" are used whenever you are held out as a solicitor or lawyer. However, you cannot rebut the presumption if you rely on being a solicitor in the context of legal practice – for example in order:

(a)   to be a partner in a firm of lawyers;

(b)   to be employed as a solicitor or lawyer;

(c)   to do work in England and Wales which is reserved to solicitors;

(d)   to do work in another jurisdiction which is reserved to lawyers;

(e)   to be a registered foreign legal consultant in another jurisdiction; or

(f)   to be a registered lawyer in another European state under the Establishment Directive.

7.   If you are dually qualified you may be practising as a member of both professions simultaneously, either through a single combined practice, or through two separate practices. In the latter case you would need separate notepaper, etc., to distinguish the two practices.

8.   The context of a description can make a real difference as to whether you are held out as a practising solicitor or not. For example:

(a)   if you are running a web-based or telephone advice service, and describe yourself as a solicitor (without qualifying the description with words such as "non-practising"), you will need a practising certificate;

(b)   if your only work is as an academic and writer, and you have written a legal textbook in which you are described as a solicitor or as a lawyer on the title page, you will not need a practising certificate. This is because there is no context of services normally provided by practising solicitors.

Reserved work – 20.02

9.   Reserved work is work that is restricted, by statute or otherwise, to a limited category or categories of person, including solicitors.

10. The following activities are reserved work:

    (a)   *Litigation, advocacy, conveyancing and probate activities*

        Sections 20 to 22 and 23 to 24 of the Solicitors Act 1974 and sections 27 and 28 of the Courts and Legal Services Act 1990 reserve to solicitors (and certain other persons) the following essential steps in litigation, conveyancing and probate:

        (i)   conducting litigation;

        (ii)   appearing as an advocate before a court; and

        (iii)   unless the work is done free, or at the direction and under the supervision of a qualified employer or fellow employee:

            (A)   drawing or preparing instruments relating to legal proceedings;

            (B)   drawing or preparing instruments relating to real or personal estate, including the contract, conveyance and mortgage in a land transaction;

            (C)   making applications or lodging documents for registration at the Land Registry; and

            (D)   drawing or preparing papers upon which to found or oppose a grant of probate or letters of administration.

    (b)   *Oaths*

        Section 81 of the Solicitors Act 1974 extends the rights of Commissioners for Oaths to all solicitors with practising certificates. See also 10.03.

    (c)   *Instructing counsel*

        Instructing counsel is not restricted to any particular category of person by statute. However, barristers only accept instructions made professionally on behalf of clients from solicitors and limited categories of non-solicitors – see www.barcouncil.org.uk for details. If you instruct counsel as a solicitor, you will be practising as a solicitor and must have a practising certificate.

    (d)   *Immigration advice and immigration services*

        The Immigration and Asylum Act 1999 requires most persons providing immigration advice and services to be registered with the Office of the Immigration Services Commissioner. Solicitors' firms do not have to register because the Law Society regulates them in relation to such work. In order to rely on this exemption you must have a practising certificate. You should note that you may not provide immigration advice or services through a separate business – see 21.02(1)(d).

(e) *Financial services*

The Financial Services and Markets Act 2000 reserves the provision of "regulated activities" to persons authorised by the Financial Services Authority (FSA). Certain "regulated activities", ancillary to the provision of a professional service, are exempt from regulation by the FSA when carried out by solicitors' firms; but you must have a practising certificate to rely on this exemption. For the definition of "regulated activity" see 19.01(4).

Solicitors in firms

11. If you are a solicitor in a firm you will almost certainly need a practising certificate, for the following reasons:

(a) If you are a principal in a firm then, as a principal, you will be practising as a solicitor.

(b) If you are an owner of an interest in a corporate firm, whether it is a recognised body or an overseas body corporate, you will be practising through a body corporate – see rule 24 (interpretation). Also rule 14 (incorporated practice) does not allow solicitors without practising certificates to participate in a recognised body as members or shareowners.

(c) If you are an employee, consultant or locum employed in England and Wales in connection with the provision of legal services, then even if you are not held out as a solicitor, and even if you do no reserved work, you will need a practising certificate. Section 1A of the Solicitors Act 1974 states that:

"A person who has been admitted as a solicitor and whose name is on the roll shall, if he would not otherwise be taken to be acting as a solicitor, be taken for the purposes of this Act to be so acting if he is employed in connection with the provision of legal services –

(a) by any person who is qualified to act as a solicitor;

(b) by any partnership at least one member of which is so qualified; or

(c) by a body recognised by the Council of the Law Society under section 9 of the Administration of Justice Act 1985 (incorporated practices)."

Note that if you are a solicitor or REL director of a corporate firm you are an employee – see rule 24 (interpretation) – so section 1A will apply. Also rule 14 (incorporated practice) does not allow solicitors without practising certificates to participate in a recognised body as directors.

(d) If you are an employee of a firm and you are based at an office outside England and Wales, you are likely to be employed, explicitly or implicitly as a solicitor, and/or held out, explicitly or implicitly, as a solicitor or as a lawyer in connection with your employment.

12. Your job title alone may be insufficient to tell you whether you will fall within section 1A of the Solicitors Act 1974. If you are not employed as a solicitor, but you work in any capacity which involves your input into client matters, you will need a practising certificate. For example:

  (a) you will need a practising certificate if you are employed as the firm's librarian, and you undertake research for fee-earners in connection with a client matter; or

  (b) you will need a practising certificate if you are employed by a firm as a compliance manager, but also handle complaints from clients.

In-house solicitors

13. If you are an in-house solicitor, you must hold a practising certificate if:

  (a) you are held out as, or employed as, a solicitor or lawyer;

  (b) you do reserved work (other than at the direction and under the supervision of a fellow employee as provided in the Solicitors Act 1974);

  (c) you fulfil the role of a "person qualified to supervise" – see 5.02; or

  (d) you authorise the withdrawal of money from a client account, under rule 23(1)(a) of the Solicitors' Accounts Rules 1998.

Retirement from practice

14. You may continue to need a practising certificate after you retire, depending on how complete your retirement is. If you are in the process of closing your firm, but will continue to hold money for clients only while you tie up loose ends and submit bills of costs, you will still be subject to the accounts rules. However, if that is all you are doing you will not need a practising certificate, provided that a solicitor with a practising certificate authorises any withdrawals from your client account.

15. If you have retired but continue to do some work, you may need a practising certificate. For example:

  (a) you must have a practising certificate if you continue to work in a firm in connection with the provision of legal services. This would include being a consultant or supervising fee earners, even if you only 'help out' on an occasional basis or cover a professional colleague's holiday absences; or

  (b) you must have a practising certificate if you continue to undertake any reserved work.

16. If you are completely retired from all legal work you may still need a practising certificate if, for example:

  (a) you continue to be held out as a solicitor or lawyer by your former firm; or

  (b) your name appears on your firm's notepaper as a "consultant", unless it is made clear on the notepaper that you are not practising.

Duty to co-operate with the Law Society – 20.03

17. 20.03 requires you to deal with any communication from the Law Society properly. This means that you will need to respond promptly and substantively to communications when appropriate – for example, to a letter referring to a complaint made against you or a member of your firm.

18. The duty imposed by 20.03 may be limited by your legal obligations to your clients or others, for example your obligation to protect clients' confidentiality and privilege.

19. If you are a solicitor you should note that failure to comply with a request for an explanation of any matter in relation to your conduct may result in the imposition of conditions, or even refusal by the Law Society to issue a practising certificate (sections 12(1)(e) and 13A Solicitors Act 1974).

20. 1.01 (integrity) and 1.10 (profession) require you to act with integrity and to refrain from behaviour likely to damage the reputation of the profession. You should therefore, unless there is good reason to the contrary, comply with binding orders or requests for information from the Legal Services Ombudsman. Similarly, it may be appropriate, subject to any overriding duties, to assist the Bar Council or other regulatory body when they are investigating the conduct of a member of their profession.

21. Abusive communications and unreasonable attempts to delay an investigation or enquiry are inconsistent with the co-operation required by 20.03.

Reporting serious misconduct and serious financial difficulty – 20.04

22. The purpose of 20.04 is to protect the public and the integrity of the profession. Often, professional colleagues will be aware of serious misconduct and/or risk arising from a firm's financial problems before any complaint has been made, and if the Law Society is notified it can take timely action. The Law Society's Forensic Investigations Unit and Fraud Intelligence Officers will consider information of this nature on an anonymous basis if requested.

23. Unless you are required by law to report a matter, 20.04 does not apply to confidential and/or privileged information another lawyer discloses to you:

    (a)   as your client or the client of your firm; or

    (b)   when seeking advice from a confidential helpline.

    A solicitor may tell you, in confidence, of serious misconduct or serious financial difficulty when consulting you, either on a paying basis as the client of your firm, or in relation to a free advice service such as the Solicitors' Assistance Scheme, or when seeking advice from a helpline such as LawCare or the Professional Ethics department of the Law Society.

24. You will not breach 20.04 if you take no action because you know that someone else has already reported a matter of which you are aware.

25. Whether or not "misconduct" can be considered "serious", and whether or not a firm's financial difficulties could put the public at risk, will depend on the

circumstances. In general, any conduct involving dishonesty or deception or a serious arrestable offence (as defined by the Police and Criminal Evidence Act 1984) would amount to "serious misconduct". If in your judgement a firm's financial difficulties present a risk to its clients or to others, you should report the matter, and can do so on a confidential basis if you wish.

26. If you are an employee and you become aware of serious misconduct on the part of a fellow employee, you should bring the matter to the attention of the principal(s), director(s) or member(s) of the firm so they can report the matter under 20.04(b).

27. If reporting misconduct within your own firm which may give rise to a claim, you should also consider your obligations to your insurers. See also guidance note 54 to rule 3 (conflict of interests).

28. If making a report about another lawyer or firm would involve disclosing confidential information, you should obtain your client's consent before proceeding.

29. You should exercise care where there may be evidence of money laundering activities (see the Proceeds of Crime Act 2002, other relevant law and directives, and guidance issued by the Law Society on this subject).

Obstructing complaints – 20.05

30. No agreement, whether with a client or a third party, can affect the Law Society's right to investigate misconduct or to consider complaints. To attempt to make such an agreement is a breach of 20.05. Examples of situations that would breach 20.05 are:

   (a) accepting instructions to act for a client which involve any agreement preventing the Law Society from investigating your conduct or the conduct of a member of your firm;

   (b) improperly demanding, offering or accepting payment in return for not reporting alleged misconduct;

   (c) harassing or bringing improper pressure to bear on a complainant or potential complainant; and

   (d) issuing proceedings for defamation against a client or former client in relation to material contained in a complaint to the Law Society, unless you are alleging malice.

31. The following, however, would not breach 20.05:

   (a) proper attempts to persuade the client that the client's complaint is unfounded; and

   (b) in a case of inadequate professional services, genuine attempts to propose an agreement to compensate the aggrieved client.

Production of documents and information – 20.06

32. The Law Society will only exercise its powers under 20.06 in accordance with the law, in pursuit of a legitimate aim and proportionate to that aim.

33. The Law Society may use or disclose any information obtained under 20.06 and the report prepared by its appointee:

    (a) in proceedings before the Solicitors Disciplinary Tribunal;

    (b) to the police, the Crown Prosecution Service or the Serious Fraud Office for use in investigating the matter and in any subsequent prosecution, if it appears that you or any partner, employee, member or owner of your firm may have committed a serious criminal offence;

    (c) to your regulatory body in your home state or states if you are an REL or RFL;

    (d) to the regulatory body with which you are registered, if you are a solicitor registered under the Establishment Directive; and/or

    (e) to the professional body of which the accountant who has signed an accountant's report under 15.27 is a member, or by which the accountant is regulated (and the information and report may also be taken into account by the Council of the Law Society in relation to a possible disqualification of that person from signing an accountant's report in future).

Dealing with claims – 20.07

34. The aim of 20.07 is to ensure that a claim or a potential claim is dealt with fairly and efficiently. In particular, the client should be advised at the earliest possible opportunity of an act or omission which could give rise to a claim. "Claim" has the meaning given in the Solicitors' Indemnity Insurance Rules, Minimum Terms and Conditions, 8.3.

35. You must consider whether a conflict of interests has arisen between your interests and your client's. It will be rare for there to be no conflict. Where there is, you must refuse to act further in the matter.

36. Under 2.05 firms must operate a complaints handling procedure. Complaints should be dealt with under that procedure, where appropriate, rather than as claims. For example, if your client makes a complaint purely relating to poor service, it would rarely be appropriate to treat that complaint as a claim.

37. In order that a claim can be dealt with efficiently, you should consult the qualifying insurer or ARP Manager in accordance with the policy terms. In some circumstances, you may need to take limited steps to preserve your client's position.

38. Although there is no general duty for you to keep under review work which has been concluded, if you discover an act or omission which could give rise to a claim relating to a former client, you should notify the qualifying insurer or ARP

Manager (or, if appropriate, SIF) and seek their advice as to what further steps to take.

39. Under rule 46 of the Solicitors' Indemnity Insurance Rules a firm must provide details of its insurer to a person who asserts a claim against the firm. The details are the name and address of the qualifying insurer and the policy number. It is good practice for you also to provide these details to a potential claimant if you discover an act or omission which could give rise to a claim. The Law Society may disclose information regarding a firm's qualifying insurer where it considers it appropriate to do so to any person asserting a claim against the firm.

40. You and your insurers should also comply with the terms of the professional negligence pre-action protocol (available at http://www.lcd.gov.uk/civil/procrules_fin/cprofr.htm)

41. The aim of this protocol is to establish a framework in which there is an early exchange of information between the parties so that a claim can be fully investigated and, if possible, resolved without the need for litigation. This includes:

    (a) ensuring that the parties are on an equal footing;

    (b) saving expense;

    (c) dealing with the dispute in ways which are proportionate:

        (i) to the amount of money involved;

        (ii) to the importance of the case;

        (iii) to the complexity of the issues; and

        (iv) to the financial position of each party; and

    (d) ensuring that the claim is dealt with expeditiously and fairly.

42. The court can make an order for costs against a party for failure to comply with the protocol. While normally it would be a matter for the insurer to ensure that the protocol is complied with, you should be aware of it when asked to provide information to the insurer, and in the occasional circumstances where an insurer may agree to you handling the claim.

Rule 21 – Separate businesses

Introduction

A "separate business" is a business which is not regulated by the Law Society but which provides 'solicitor-like' services. The purpose of rule 21 is to ensure that members of the public are not confused or misled into believing that a business carried on by a solicitor or REL is regulated by the Law Society when it is not. The rule as it applies to your overseas practice is modified by 15.21.

Rule 21 – Separate businesses

21.01 General

(1) If you are practising from an office in England and Wales as a solicitor or an REL, or as an RFL who is a partner in an MNP, a director of a recognised body which is a company or a member of a recognised body which is an LLP, you must comply with the provisions of this rule in relation to:

    (a) services which may not be provided through a separate business;

    (b) services which may be provided through a separate business or (subject to these rules) through a firm or in-house practice; and

    (c) services which fall outside the scope of a solicitor's practice but which may be provided in conjunction with a firm or in-house practice.

(2) This rule applies to your involvement in any separate business whether the separate business is in England and Wales or outside the jurisdiction.

(3) This rule also applies to a recognised body in relation to an interest held in another body corporate which is not a recognised body.

(4) For the avoidance of doubt, in this rule "practising" includes practising as an in-house solicitor or an in-house REL.

21.02 Services which may not be provided through a separate business

(1) Subject to (2) below, you must not provide any of the following services through a separate business:

    (a) the conduct of any matter which could come before a court, tribunal or inquiry, whether or not proceedings are started;

    (b) advocacy before a court, tribunal or inquiry;

    (c) instructing counsel in any part of the UK;

    (d) immigration advice or immigration services;

(e)   any activity in relation to conveyancing, applications for probate or letters of administration, or drawing trust deeds or court documents, which is reserved to solicitors and others under the Solicitors Act 1974;

(f)   drafting wills;

(g)   acting as nominee, trustee or executor in England and Wales;

(h)   legal advice not included above; or

(i)   drafting legal documents not included above.

Exceptions

(2)   The provisions of (1) above do not apply to prohibit you from providing services through a separate business:

(a)   which carries on your practice as a lawyer of another jurisdiction;

(b)   which carries on your business as a trade mark agent, patent agent or European patent attorney;

(c)   which carries on your business as a parliamentary agent;

(d)   which is a wholly owned nominee company operated as a subsidiary but necessary part of the work of a separate business providing financial services;

(e)   which provides legal advice and/or drafts legal documents within (1)(h) and/or (i) above, as a subsidiary but necessary part of some other service which is one of the main services of the separate business; or

(f)   which has no office in England and Wales, does not receive customers directly or indirectly referred from any firm through which you carry on your practice in England and Wales, or from any in-house practice you have in England and Wales, does not provide any services in relation to the UK; and does not provide executor, trustee or nominee services anywhere.

However, you must comply with the requirements of 21.05 in relation to any such separate business.

21.03 Services which may be provided in conjunction with a firm or in-house practice

(1)   The following services extend beyond, or fall outside, the scope of a solicitor's practice but you may provide such services in conjunction with a firm or in-house practice:

(a)   practice as a qualified notary public;

(b)   educational activities; and

(c)   authorship, journalism or publishing.

(2)   A service provided in conjunction with a firm or in-house practice of a solicitor, an REL, an MNP or a recognised body is not provided through a separate business.

21.04 Services which may be provided (subject to these rules) either through a firm or in-house practice, or through a separate business

(1)   You may provide the following services either (subject to these rules) through a firm or in-house practice, or through a separate business:

  (a)   alternative dispute resolution;

  (b)   financial services;

  (c)   estate agency;

  (d)   management consultancy;

  (e)   company secretarial services;

  (f)   acting as a parliamentary agent;

  (g)   acting as a trade mark agent, patent agent or European patent attorney;

  (h)   practising as a lawyer of another jurisdiction;

  (i)   acting as an under-sheriff or bailiff;

  (j)   acting as nominee, trustee or executor outside England and Wales; or

  (k)   providing any other business, advisory or agency service which could be provided (subject to these rules) through a firm or in-house practice but is not included in 21.02.

(2)   If you provide any service listed in (1) above through a separate business you must comply with 21.05.

21.05 Safeguards in relation to a separate business

(1)   If you provide services through a separate business you must do nothing in the course of practice, or in the course of making referrals to the business or accepting referrals from the business, which would breach rule 1 (core duties).

(2)   Subject to (3) below you must ensure that the following safeguards are in place in relation to a separate business which offers or provides any of the services listed in 21.04(1):

  (a)   the separate business must not be held out or described in such a way as to suggest that the separate business is carrying on a practice regulated by the Law Society, or that any lawyer connected with your firm is providing services through the separate business as a practising lawyer regulated by the Law Society;

(b)   all paperwork, documents, records or files relating to the separate business and its customers must be kept separate from those of any firm or in-house practice, even where a customer of the separate business is also a client of the firm or in-house practice;

(c)   the client account used for any firm or in-house practice must not be used to hold money for the separate business, or for customers of the separate business in their capacity as such;

(d)   if the separate business shares premises, office accommodation or reception staff with any firm or in-house practice:

    (i)   the areas used by the firm or in-house practice must be clearly differentiated from the areas used by the separate business; and

    (ii)   all customers of the separate business must be informed that it is not regulated by the Law Society and that the statutory protections attaching to clients of a lawyer regulated by the Law Society are not available to them as customers of that business;

(e)   if you or your firm refer a client to the separate business, the client must first be informed of your interest in the separate business, that the separate business is not regulated by the Law Society, and that the statutory protections attaching to clients of a lawyer regulated by the Law Society are not available to clients of the separate business; and

(f)   if the separate business is an estate agency, then without prejudice to the provisions of these rules regarding conflicts of interests, neither you nor any firm through which you practise as a principal may act in the conveyance for the buyer of any property sold through the estate agency unless:

    (i)   the firm shares ownership of the estate agency with at least one other business in which neither you nor the firm have any financial interest;

    (ii)   neither you nor anyone else in the firm is dealing with or has dealt with the sale of the seller's property for the separate business; and

    (iii)   the buyer has given written consent to you or the firm acting, after your financial interest in the sale going through has been explained to the buyer.

Guidance to rule 21 – Separate businesses

1. A separate business is a business which is not a firm or in-house practice but which offers a service or services that could properly be offered by a firm or, subject to rule 13, an in-house practice.

2. Providing a service through a separate business means having any active involvement in a separate business which provides that service – see the definitions of "separate business" and "providing a service through a separate business" in rule 24 (interpretation). You are not providing services through a separate business solely by virtue of being a non-executive director of, or having an insignificant shareholding in, a company which provides, for example, financial services.

3. In England and Wales there is no legal impediment to a non-lawyer giving legal advice, drafting wills or administering estates, or running a business which provides such services. However, the client of a firm or in-house practice has the protections afforded by these rules, the Law Society's regulatory powers, the Solicitors' Compensation Fund and (if a firm provides the service) indemnity insurance under the Law Society's compulsory indemnity scheme. The customers of a business which is not a firm or in-house practice will not have the same protections. Rule 21 does two things:

    (a) it prohibits you, if you are practising in England and Wales as a solicitor or an REL, or as an RFL within the Law Society's regulation, from 'hiving off' the kind of services a member of the public would expect you to provide as a lawyer regulated by the Law Society, to a business which is not so regulated; and

    (b) it requires you to institute safeguards in relation to other services which you are allowed to 'hive off' (the kind of services a member of the public would not necessarily expect to be provided only by a lawyer regulated by the Law Society but which are 'solicitor-like' services).

    The purpose of the rule is to ensure that members of the public are not misled into believing that a business is regulated by the Law Society when it is not.

4. If you are practising wholly outside England and Wales, the provisions of this rule do not apply to you but you must comply with 15.21(2) in relation to your involvement in any separate business.

5. As an in-house solicitor doing work permitted by rule 13 (in-house practice) you are not providing services through a separate business; but if you have a separate business in addition to your in-house practice you must comply with rule 21 or, if you are employed outside England and Wales, with 15.21(2).

Business as a professional not regulated by the Law Society – 21.02(2)

6. Although you may not provide reserved litigation, advocacy, conveyancing and probate services, or immigration services, through a separate business, you may have a separate business as a parliamentary agent, trade mark agent, patent agent, European patent attorney, or as a lawyer of another jurisdiction. Such a business may undertake some of the activities listed in 21.02(1), but 21.02(2) states that you are not prohibited from having such a business. The

safeguards for such a separate business are intended to make it clear that the business is governed by a different legal and regulatory regime from services provided by solicitors.

Legal advice as a necessary and subsidiary part of another service

7.   The prohibitions on providing certain legal advice and drafting certain documents through separate businesses do not apply when the advice or drafting is merely a necessary but subsidiary part of another service which you are allowed to provide through a separate business. An example would be a management consultancy business giving ancillary advice on obligations under the Data Protection Act 1998.

Executor, trustee and nominee companies

8.   You are not allowed to provide executor, trustee or nominee services in England and Wales through a separate business. An executor, trustee or nominee company operated in conjunction with the practice of a firm must be a recognised body, because:

   (a)   a company has a separate legal identity, so if a firm owns a company, and the company provides a service to the firm's clients, it is the company and not the firm that provides the service; and

   (b)   a company providing a service for clients of a firm will constitute a "business" for the purpose of rule 21, even if the company is dormant for Companies Act purposes, and even if no charge is made to clients for its services.

9.   You are allowed to have a separate business which provides executor, trustee and nominee services *outside* England and Wales. If you do, you must put in place the safeguards required. You can, on the other hand, run an executor, trustee or nominee company which provides services only outside England and Wales as an overseas corporate firm within rule 12 (framework of practice).

Service companies

10.   A service company operated for the purpose of providing services only to carry out administrative functions concerned with the running of the firm which owns it, such as the employment of staff, the hiring of premises, furniture and equipment and general maintenance, is not a separate business.

11.   A company incorporated by an individual solicitor to provide that solicitor's services to a firm cannot be a separate business.

Marketing and description of a separate business

12.   Under 21.05(2) your separate business must not be held out or described in such a way as to suggest that the separate business is carrying on a practice regulated by the Law Society, or that any lawyer connected with your firm is providing services through the separate business as a practising lawyer regulated by the Law Society. Unlike the more specific safeguards in 21.05(b) to (f), this prohibition has a wide application and amounts to an absolute requirement to take all necessary steps to ensure that customers and third parties dealing with the separate business are not misled. However, it is not

intended to prohibit you from running a separate business in association with your firm or mentioning your firm, or the fact that you are a lawyer, in connection with your separate business. The provision will have the following implications:

(a) You could not properly carry on your separate business under the same name as your firm, because that would create too strong a suggestion that the business, like the firm, is regulated by the Law Society. On the other hand, 21.05(2) does not prohibit you from running your separate business in association with your firm, or using a similar or related name or "brand". However, in order to comply with 21.05(2) you would need to properly differentiate the separate business from your firm and make it clear on the face of any notepaper or other publicity of the separate business using a similar or related name that the services of the separate business are not the services of practising lawyers.

(b) You could not properly market your separate business to potential customers on the basis that it is owned and run by practising solicitors and/or RELs, because that would create too strong a suggestion that the services of the separate business are provided by practising lawyers regulated by the Law Society. On the other hand, 21.05(2) does not prohibit you from marketing your separate business on the basis that it is run and owned by persons who are qualified as lawyers – provided you make it clear that no lawyer involved in the separate business is practising as such through the separate business.

(c) 21.05(2) does not prohibit the use of the word "solicitor", "lawyer" or "attorney" in connection with your separate business. However, it would be a breach of 21.05(2)(a) if such a reference suggested that lawyers regulated by the Law Society practise through the separate business – so any such reference must be appropriately qualified so as to make it clear that the services of the separate business are not the services of practising lawyers. If the reference is in a letterhead or other publicity that statement should be in the same document.

Rule 22 – Waivers

22.01

(1) In any particular case or cases the Council of the Law Society shall have power to waive in writing the provisions of these rules for a particular purpose or purposes expressed in such waiver, and to revoke such waiver.

(2) Notwithstanding (1) above, the Council of the Law Society shall not have power to waive any of the provisions of the following rules:

   (a) rule 1 (core duties);

   (b) 3.01 to 3.05 (conflict of interests, excluding provisions relating to alternative dispute resolution, conveyancing and property selling);

   (c) rule 4 (confidentiality and disclosure);

   (d) rule 6 (avoiding discrimination);

   (e) 15.01, 15.03, 15.04, 15.18, 15.22, 15.23 and 15.24 (overseas practice provisions which apply provisions that cannot be waived for practice in England and Wales);

   (f) rule 18 (property selling);

   (g) rule 22 (waivers);

   (h) rule 23 (application); and

   (i) rule 24 (interpretation).

Guidance to rule 22 – Waivers

1. If you apply for a waiver, you will need to show that your circumstances are exceptional in order for it to be granted. Advice may be obtained from the Law Society's Professional Ethics department.

2. The list in 22.01(2) should not be taken as an indication that any other rule may be waived in any circumstances. A waiver cannot be granted where to do so would run counter to the overall purpose of the rule. For example, it is difficult to foresee circumstances in which many of the provisions of rule 2 (client care) would be waived.

Rule 23 – Application of these rules

23.01

Subject to 23.03 below these rules apply to you (and "you" must be construed accordingly) if you are:

    (a)   a solicitor, in relation to practice as a solicitor from offices in England and Wales and outside England and Wales;

    (b)   an REL, in relation to practice as a lawyer of an Establishment Directive state from offices in England and Wales, Northern Ireland and Scotland;

    (c)   a recognised body incorporated in England and Wales, in relation to practice from offices in England and Wales and outside England and Wales;

    (d)   a recognised body incorporated in an Establishment Directive state but outside England and Wales:

        (i)   in relation to practice from offices in England and Wales; and

        (ii)   in relation to practice from offices outside England and Wales, but only to the following extent:

            (A)   1.10 (profession);

            (B)   12.04(4) (framework of practice);

            (C)   rule 14 (incorporated practice); and

            (D)   rule 15 (overseas practice), but only to the extent that rule 15 specifically applies any provision of these rules to a recognised body incorporated outside England and Wales;

    (e)   an RFL, in relation to practice as a foreign lawyer from offices in England and Wales, as:

        (i)   a partner in an MNP as defined in rule 24 (interpretation);

        (ii)   a director of a recognised body which is a company; or

        (iii)   a member of a recognised body which is an LLP; and

    (f)   a solicitor who was formerly an REL, in relation to practice as a lawyer of an Establishment Directive state from offices in the UK;

but see also 3.07(1) in relation to acting for seller and buyer, and 3.16(1) in relation to acting for lender and borrower.

23.02

The following apply in relation to other forms of practice, and outside practice;

    (a)   1.10;

    (b)   10.01:

        (i)   if you are a solicitor, in England and Wales and overseas; and

        (ii)   if you are an REL, within the UK;

    (c)   10.05(1)(c) and (d), (2) and (3), and 15.10(2)(a)(ii) and (iii), (b) and (c);

    (d)   12.03(2) and 12.03(3).

23.03

The provisions of rules 1 to 14 and 16 to 25 of these rules will only apply to your overseas practice if specifically applied by rule 15 (overseas practice).

Guidance to rule 23 – Application of these rules

1.   The rules apply in different ways to a solicitor, an REL, a recognised body incorporated in England and Wales, a recognised body incorporated outside England and Wales, and an RFL.

2.   The key to the application of a rule is whether a matter relates to practice from an office in England and Wales, or to practice from an office outside England and Wales. This does not mean that different rules apply at different times during a cross-jurisdictional transaction. For example, if a client gives instructions for a transaction to your London office, then that transaction will fall into the category of practice from an office in England and Wales.

3.   A solicitor's, REL's or recognised body's practice from an office in England and Wales is subject to all the rules except rule 15 (overseas practice). However, in relation to practice from an office outside England and Wales:

    (a)   a solicitor is subject to the rules as applied or modified by rule 15;

    (b)   a recognised body incorporated in England and Wales is subject to the rules as applied or modified by rule 15;

    (c)   an REL is subject to the rules as applied or modified by rule 15 in relation to practice from an office in Scotland or Northern Ireland, but is not subject to any of the rules in relation to practice from an office outside the UK, except 1.10 (profession); and

    (d)   a recognised body incorporated outside England and Wales is subject to 12.04(4) (framework of practice), rule 14 (incorporated practice), and to the rules as applied or modified by rule 15 (overseas practice). Only a few of the rules apply, and only in particular circumstances.

4.   An RFL who is a partner in an MNP, a director of a recognised body which is a
      company, or a member of a recognised body which is an LLP is subject to the
      rules in relation to practice from an office in England and Wales. An RFL is not
      subject to any of the rules in relation to practice outside an MNP or a
      recognised body, or in relation to practice from an office outside England and
      Wales, except 1.10 (profession).

5.   Certain rules also apply in relation to other forms of practice, and outside
      practice:

      (a)   Under 1.10 (profession) you must do nothing as a solicitor, REL, RFL or
             recognised body to damage the reputation of the profession.

      (b)   Under 10.01 (not taking unfair advantage) you must not take unfair
             advantage of your position as a solicitor, or (within the UK) as an REL.

      (c)   Under 10.05(1)(c) and (d), (2) and (3), and 15.10(a)(ii) and (iii), (b) and
             (c) you must fulfil an undertaking even if it is given outside the course of
             your practice as a solicitor or as an REL, if you give the undertaking as a
             solicitor or (within the UK) as a lawyer of an Establishment Directive
             state.

      (d)   Under 12.03(2) and (3), if you are an RFL you must not be held out as an
             RFL, or as regulated by or registered with the Law Society, except in the
             context of practice as a partner in an MNP, director of a recognised body
             which is a company, or member of a recognised body which is an LLP.
             Note that if you are an RFL you are not required specifically to fulfil an
             undertaking given as an RFL but outside the course of practice as an
             RFL, or prohibited from taking unfair advantage of your position as an
             RFL - but if you did either of these things you would breach 12.03(2) or
             (3) and possibly 1.10.

Rule 24 – Interpretation

24.01

In these rules, unless the context otherwise requires, all references to legislation include existing and future amendments to that legislation and:

arrangement	in relation to financial services, fee sharing and the introduction of clients, means any express or tacit agreement between you and another person, whether contractually binding or not;
associated companies	means two companies which are subsidiary companies of the same holding company;
associated firms	means two or more partnerships with at least one partner in common; two or more companies without shares with at least one member in common; two or more LLPs with at least one member in common; two or more companies with shares with at least one owner in common, or any combination of these;
CCBE Code	means the Code of Conduct for Lawyers made by the Council of the Bars and Law Societies of the European Union;
client account	in rule 15 (overseas practice), means an account at a bank or similar institution, subject to supervision by a public authority, which is used only for the purpose of holding client money and/or controlled trust money, and the title or designation of which indicates that the funds in the account belong to the client or clients of a solicitor or REL or are held subject to a trust;
	(for the definition of "client account" in relation to practice from an office in England and Wales, see the Solicitors' Accounts Rules 1998);
client money	in rule 15 (overseas practice), means money you receive or hold for or on behalf of a client;
	(for the definition of "client money" in relation to practice from an office in England and Wales, see the Solicitors' Accounts Rules 1998);
company	in rule 14 (incorporated practice), means a company registered under Part I of the Companies Act 1985, or an oversea company incorporated in an Establishment Directive state and registered under section 690A or 691 of the Companies Act 1985, or a societas Europaea;

contentious proceedings	is to be construed in accordance with the definition of "contentious business" in section 87 of the Solicitors Act 1974;
contingency fee	means any sum (whether fixed, or calculated either as a percentage of the proceeds or otherwise) payable only in the event of success;
controlled trust	in rule 15 (overseas practice), means a trust of which:

(a) you are the sole trustee; or

(b) you are co-trustee only with one of more of your, or your firm's, employees, partners; officers (in the case of a company, including a recognised body); or members (in the case of an LLP, including a recognised body); or

(c) you are co-trustee only with your firm (in the case of a partnership with a separate legal identity, a company or LLP, including a recognised body);

(for the definition of "controlled trust" in relation to practice from an office in England and Wales, see the Solicitors' Accounts Rules 1998);

controlled trust money	in rule 15 (overseas practice), means money which is subject to a controlled trust of which you are a trustee;

(for the definition of "controlled trust" in relation to practice from an office in England and Wales, see the Solicitors' Accounts Rules 1998);

corporate firm	means a body corporate which carries on the practice of a solicitor or an REL but is not an in-house practice;
court	in rule 11 (litigation and advocacy) means any court, tribunal or enquiry of England and Wales, or a British court martial, or any court of another jurisdiction;
director	means a director of a company, and includes the director of a recognised body which is a company; and in relation to a societas Europaea includes:

(a) in a two-tier system, a member of the management organ and a member of the supervisory organ; and

(b) in a one-tier system, a member of the administrative organ;

documents	in rule 20 (requirements of practice) includes documents, whether written or electronic, relating to the solicitor's client and office accounts;

eligible to be a member and eligible to be a shareowner	in rule 14 (incorporated practice), mean a person who falls within one of the following categories:

    (a)   a solicitor with a practising certificate;

    (b)   a registered European lawyer;

    (c)   a registered foreign lawyer;

    (d)   a non-registered European lawyer;

    (e)   a recognised body; or

    (f)   a European corporate practice;

and "ineligible" must be construed accordingly;

employee   except in rule 6 (avoiding discrimination) includes, in the case of a solicitor or an REL:

    (a)   a solicitor or REL who is a director of a company;

    b)   a solicitor or REL who is engaged under a contract of service (for example, an assistant solicitor); or

    (c)   a solicitor or REL who is engaged under a contract for services (for example, a consultant or a locum);

and "employer" and "employment" must be construed accordingly;

Establishment Directive	means the Establishment of Lawyers Directive 98/5/EC;
Establishment Directive Regulations	means the European Communities (Lawyer's Practice) Regulations 2000 (SI 2000 No. 1119);

Establishment Directive state	means a state to which the Establishment of Lawyers Directive 98/5/EC applies – currently all the states of the EU plus Iceland, Liechtenstein, Norway and Switzerland;
EU	means the European Union;
European corporate practice	means a lawyers' practice incorporated in or formed under the law of an Establishment Directive state other than the United Kingdom, which does not have an office in England and Wales, and is either:

(a)   a body corporate wholly owned (whether directly or indirectly) and directed by RELs and/or non-registered European lawyers, or by such persons together with solicitors with practising certificates, RFLs and/or barristers of England and Wales; or

(b)   a lawyers' partnership with separate legal identity whose partners are all RELs and/or non-registered European lawyers, or such persons together with solicitors with practising certificates, RFLs and/or barristers of England and Wales.

European cross-border practice	has the meaning assigned by 16.01(1);
firm	means any business which carries on the practice of a solicitor or an REL, except in-house practice;
foreign lawyer	means a person who is not a solicitor or barrister of England and Wales, but who is a member, and entitled to practise as such, of a legal profession regulated within a jurisdiction outside England and Wales;
holding company	has the meaning assigned by the Companies Act 1985;
in-house practice	means:

(a)   a solicitor's employment in England and Wales as a solicitor, or an REL's employment in England and Wales as a lawyer of an Establishment Directive state, by any business which is not:

(i)   the business of a solicitor or an REL practising as a sole principal;

(ii)   a recognised body; or

(iii)   a partnership with at least one partner who is

(A)   a practising solicitor;

(B)   an REL practising as such; or

(C)   a recognised body; and

(b)   a solicitor's employment outside England and Wales as a solicitor, or an REL's employment in Scotland or Northern Ireland as a lawyer of an Establishment Directive state, by any business which is not:

(i)   the business of a lawyer practising as a sole principal;

(ii)   a partnership of lawyers, or of lawyers together with other persons, within rule 12; or

(iii)   a body corporate wholly owned, for the purpose of practising law, by lawyers, or by lawyers together with other persons, within rule 12;

lawyer   except in rule 12 (framework of practice), means a member of one of the following professions, entitled to practise as such:

(a)   the profession of solicitor, barrister or advocate of the UK;

(b)   a legal profession of an Establishment Directive state other than the UK;

(c)   a legal profession which has been approved by the Law Society for the purpose of multi-national partnerships in England and Wales; or

(d)   any other regulated legal profession which is recognised as such by the Law Society;

(for the definition of "lawyer" for the purpose of rule 12 (Framework of practice) see 12.05);

lawyer of an Establishment Directive state   means a member, and entitled to practise as such, of a legal profession which is covered by the Establishment of Lawyers Directive 98/5/EC, and includes a solicitor or a barrister of England and Wales;

legal profession   means a profession whose members are lawyers as defined in this rule;

LLP	means a limited liability partnership formed by being incorporated under the Limited Liability Partnerships Act 2000;
member	in relation to a recognised body, means:

(a) a person who has agreed to be a member of a company and whose name is entered in the company's register of members; or

(b) a member of an LLP;

MNP	means a multi-national partnership as defined in section 89(9) of the Courts and Legal Services Act 1990;
non-lawyer	means:

(a) an individual who is not a lawyer as defined in this rule; or

(b) a body corporate which includes an individual who is not a lawyer as defined in this rule; or

(c) a partnership which includes as a partner an individual who is not a lawyer as defined in this rule;

non-registered European
lawyer means a lawyer of an Establishment Directive state who is based at an office or offices outside England and Wales and who is not:

(a) a solicitor, REL or RFL; or

(b) a barrister of England and Wales, Northern Ireland or the Irish Republic, or a Scottish advocate;

officer	in relation to a company, means a director or the company secretary;
overseas	means in or of a jurisdiction other than England and Wales;
overseas practice	means:

(a) the practice of a solicitor or a recognised body from an office or offices outside England and Wales; and

(b) the practice of an REL from an office or offices in Scotland or Northern Ireland;

owner	in relation to a body corporate, means a person with any ownership interest in the body corporate;

partner	includes both an equity partner and a salaried partner in a partnership;
partnership	means an unincorporated body falling within the definition of partnership in section 1 of the Partnership Act 1890, and does not include an LLP;
person	includes an individual, a body corporate, or other legal person;
practice	means:

(a) the activities of a solicitor, in that capacity;

(b) the activities of an REL in the capacity of lawyer of an Establishment Directive state, from an office or offices within the UK;

(c) the activities of an RFL from an office or offices in England and Wales as:

    (i) a partner in an MNP;

    (ii) a director of a recognised body which is a company; or

    (iii) a member of a recognised body which is an LLP; and

(d) the activities of a recognised body;

and "practise" and "practising" should be construed accordingly;

practice from an office	includes practice carried on:

(a) from an office at which you are based; or

(b) from an office of a firm in which you are a principal, director, member or owner, even if you are not based there;

and "practising from an office in England and Wales", etc., should be construed accordingly;

practice through a body corporate	includes having an ownership interest in a body corporate or being a director of a company, even if you yourself undertake no work for clients of the body corporate;

and "practising through a body corporate" should be construed accordingly;

principal	means a sole practitioner or a partner in a partnership;
principal in a firm	means:

(a)   a solicitor or recognised body practising either as a sole principal or as a partner;

(b)   an REL practising in the UK either as a sole principal or as a partner; or

(c)   an RFL practising from an office in England and Wales as a partner in an MNP;

providing a service through a separate business   means having any active involvement in a separate business which provides that service, and includes:

(a)   any substantial ownership in the business;

(b)   any direct control over the business, and any indirect control through another person such as a spouse; and

(c)   any active participation in the business or the provision of its services to customers;

(being a non-executive director or providing services under rule 13 (in-house practice) does not, *on its own*, constitute active involvement);

publicity   includes all promotional material and activity, including the name or description of your firm, stationery, advertisements, brochures, websites, directory entries, media appearances, promotional press releases, and direct approaches to potential clients and other persons, whether conducted in person, in writing, or in electronic form, but does not include press releases prepared on behalf of a client;

recognised body   means a body corporate (which can be a company or an LLP) for the time being recognised by the Law Society under section 9 of the Administration of Justice Act 1985 and the Recognised Bodies Regulations;

The Recognised Bodies Regulations   means the Recognised Bodies Regulations [2004]

REL (registered European lawyer)   means an individual registered with the Law Society under regulation 17 of the Establishment Directive Regulations;

register of European lawyers	means the register of European lawyers maintained by the Law Society under the Establishment Directive Regulations;
RFL (registered foreign lawyer)	means an individual registered with the Law Society under section 89 of the Courts and Legal Services Act 1990;
register of foreign lawyers	means the register of foreign lawyers maintained by the Law Society under the Courts and Legal Services Act 1990;
right of audience and right to conduct litigation	are to be construed in accordance with Part II and section 119 of the Courts and Legal Services Act 1990;
separate business	means a business which does not carry on the practice of a solicitor, REL or recognised body but which offers a service or services that could properly be offered by a solicitor, REL or recognised body in the course of practice;
shareowner	means:

(a) a member of a recognised body which is a company with a share capital, who owns a share in the body, or

(b) a person who is not a member of a company with a share capital, but owns a share in the body, which is held by a member as nominee;

societas Europaea	means a European public limited liability company within the meaning of article 1 of Council Regulation 2157/2001/EC;
subsidiary company	has the meaning assigned by the Companies Act 1985;
UK	means United Kingdom; and
undertaking	in 10.05 and 15.10, means a statement made by you or your firm to someone who reasonably relies upon it, that you or your firm will do something or cause something to be done, or refrain from doing something. The undertaking can be given orally or in writing and need not include the words "undertake" or "undertaking".

Rule 25 – Commencement and repeals

25.01

(1)   These rules, together with the Recognised Bodies Regulations [2004], shall come into force on [the first day of the fourth month commencing after notification of the Lord Chancellor's approval under Schedule 4 to the Courts and Legal Services Act 1990].

(2)   The following provisions are repealed by these rules:

    (a)   the Solicitors' Practice Rules 1990;

    (b)   the Solicitors' Publicity Code 2001;

    (c)   the Solicitors' Introduction and Referral Code 1990;

    (d)   the Employed Solicitors Code 1990;

    (e)   the Solicitors' Separate Business Code 1994;

    (f)   the Solicitors' Costs Information and Client Care Code 1999;

    (g)   the Law Society's Code for Advocacy;

    (h)   the Solicitors' Anti-Discrimination Rules 2004;

    (i)   the Solicitors' Overseas Practice Rules 1990; and

    (j)   the Solicitors' Incorporated Practice Rules 2004.

(3)   These rules also replace the conduct obligations imposed by virtue of *The Guide to the Professional Conduct of Solicitors (1999)* and *Guide Online*.

(4)   For the avoidance of doubt, the following will remain in force after the coming into force of these rules:

    (a)   the Solicitors' Accounts Rules;

    (b)   the Solicitors' Indemnity Insurance Rules;

    (c)   the Solicitors' Indemnity (Enactment) Rules;

    (d)   the Solicitors' Financial Services (Scope) Rules;

    (e)   the Solicitors' Financial Services (Conduct of Business) Rules;

    (f)   the Solicitors' Compensation Fund Rules; and

    (g)   the Solicitors' Compensation Fund (Foreign Lawyers' Contributions) Rules.

Recognised Bodies Regulations [2004]

Rules dated [date of commencement] *made by the Council of the Law Society with the concurrence of the Master of the Rolls under section 9(2) of the Administration of Justice Act 1985, making provision as to the form and manner of applications relating to recognition of a recognised body, and as to the list of recognised bodies, the duration of recognition and revocation of recognition.*

Regulation 1 - Applications for recognition and for renewal of recognition

1.1   Applications for initial recognition and for renewal of recognition must be made on the prescribed form, and accompanied by the prescribed fee and such information and documentation as the Law Society may require.

1.2   A recognised body wishing to continue in practice after the renewal date must send its application for renewal of recognition so as to be received by the Law Society on or before the renewal date.

1.3   A recognised body not wishing to renew its recognition must notify the Law Society on or before the renewal date that it does not seek renewal of recognition.

Regulation 2 - Discretion to grant or refuse applications

2.1   The Law Society may grant an application for initial recognition or renewal of recognition, if satisfied that the applicant body corporate:

(a)   is registered under the Companies Act 1985 or the Limited Liability Partnerships Act 2000 either in England and Wales or in Scotland, or registered outside England, Wales and Scotland as a societas Europaea;

(b)   complies with rule 14 of the Law Society's Code of Conduct in relation to its internal structure, direction and ownership;

(c)   has a name that complies with rule 7 of the Law Society's Code of Conduct; and

(d)   complies with or is exempt from the Solicitors' Indemnity Insurance Rules as to qualifying insurance and top-up insurance.

2.2   The Law Society may refuse an application for initial recognition or renewal of recognition if:

(a)   the Law Society is satisfied that a director, member or shareowner is not a suitable person to be engaged in the direction or ownership of a recognised body, by reason of that person's character, conduct or associations; or

(b)   for any other reason the Law Society thinks it proper in the public interest not to recognise the body.

Regulation 3 - Appeals

3.1 If the Law Society refuses an application for initial recognition or renewal of recognition, the applicant is entitled to receive notice in writing of the grounds for refusal, and may appeal to the Master of the Rolls under paragraph 2 of Schedule 2 to the Administration of Justice Act 1985.

3.2 If the Law Society neither grants nor refuses recognition within three months of the date an application was received, the applicant may appeal to the Master of the Rolls under paragraph 2 of Schedule 2 to the Administration of Justice Act 1985 as if the application had been refused.

Regulation 4 - Duration of recognition and renewal date

4.1 Recognition lasts for three years and continues in force until it is revoked.

4.2 Renewal of recognition commences on the day following the renewal date.

4.3 The renewal date following initial recognition is the last day of the last calendar month of the three year period; and thereafter, the day before the end of each subsequent three year period of recognition.

Regulation 5 - The list of recognised bodies

5.1 The Law Society shall keep a list of recognised bodies.

5.2 The list of recognised bodies may be kept in electronic form and must contain, for each recognised body:

  (a)   the recognised body's name;

  (b)   the recognised body's registered office;

  (c)   all the recognised body's practising addresses; and

  (d)   whether it is a company limited by shares, a company limited by guarantee, an unlimited company, an oversea company registered in England and Wales, an oversea company registered in Scotland, a societas Europaea, or an LLP.

5.3 The Law Society must make a copy of any entry in the list available for inspection on request by any member of the public.

Regulation 6 - Certificates of recognition

6.1 Once a body is granted initial recognition or its recognition is renewed, the Law Society shall issue a certificate of recognition.

6.2 Each certificate of recognition shall state, in respect of the recognised body:

  (a)   its name;

  (b)   its registered office (or its principal practising address in England and Wales, if it is a company or LLP incorporated in Scotland, an oversea company, or a societas Europaea registered outside England and Wales);

(c)   whether it is a company limited by shares, a company limited by guarantee, an unlimited company, an oversea company registered in England and Wales, an oversea company registered in Scotland, a societas Europaea, or an LLP;

(d)   that it is recognised by the Council of the Law Society as suitable to provide legal services;

(e)   the date from which recognition is granted or renewed; and

(f)   the next renewal date.

Regulation 7 - Revocation of recognition

7.1   Recognition may be revoked after the renewal date stated on the last certificate of recognition has passed, if the Law Society has not received an application for renewal of recognition and all required fees, information and documentation.

7.2   Recognition may be revoked at any time, if:

(a)   the Law Society is satisfied that recognition was granted as a result of error or fraud; or

(b)   the Law Society is satisfied that the body would not be eligible to be recognised if it were at that time applying for initial recognition.

Regulation 8 - Automatic expiry of recognition

8.1   Recognition will automatically expire if a recognised body ceases to be registered, either:

(a)   under Part I of the Companies Act 1985 as an unlimited company, a company limited by shares or a company limited by guarantee;

(b)   under section 690A or 691 of the Companies Act 1985 as an oversea company incorporated in an Establishment Directive state;

(c)   under the Limited Liability Partnerships Act 2000 as an LLP; or

(d)   as a societas Europaea.

8.2   Recognition will automatically expire if a winding-up order or administration order is granted under Part II of the Insolvency Act 1986, or a resolution is passed for voluntary winding-up, or an administrative receiver is appointed, in respect of a recognised body.

Regulation 9 - Interpretation

9.1   All terms in these regulations are to be interpreted in accordance with rule 24 of the Law Society's Code of Conduct.

Regulation 10 - Waivers

10.1 In any particular case or cases the Council of the Law Society shall have power to waive in writing the provisions of these regulations for a particular purpose or purposes expressed in such waiver, and to revoke such waiver.